IMPRESSIONISM
AND THE NORTH

Nationalmuseum, Stockholm

IMPRESSIONISM

Late 19th Century French Avant-Garde Art and the Art in the Nordic Countries 1870–1920

AND THE NORTH

Torsten Gunnarsson · Per Hedström · Flemming Friborg · Peter Nørgaard Larsen · Nils Messel
Karin Hellandsjø · Bengt von Bonsdorff · Foreword by Hans Henrik Brummer

Lenders

Swedish lenders

Eskilstuna, Eskilstuna Konstmuseum
Gävle, Länsmuseet Gävleborg
Göteborg, Göteborgs konstmuseum
Karlstad, Värmlands museum
Lund, Lunds universitets konstsamling
Malmö, Malmö Konstmuseum
Mora, Zornsamlingarna
Mörbylånga, Per Ekströmmuseet
Norrköping, Norrköpings Konstmuseum
Sala, Sala konstförening – Aguélimuseet
Saltsjöbaden, Vår Gård Kursgården AB
Stockholm, Handelsbanken
Stockholm, Moderna Museet
Stockholm, Prins Eugens Waldemarsudde
Stockholm, Stockholms stad

Foreign lenders

Amsterdam, Stedelijk Museum
Amsterdam, Van Gogh Museum (Vincent van Gogh Foundation)
Bergen, Bergen Art Museum, Bergen Billedgalleri
Birmingham, The Trustees of the Barber Institute of Fine Arts,
    the University of Birmingham
Cardiff, National Museums & Galleries of Wales
Chicago, The Art Institute of Chicago
Cleveland, The Cleveland Museum of Art
Dallas, Dallas Museum of Art
Haag, Gemeentemuseum Den Haag
Fort Worth, Kimbell Art Museum
Frederikssund, J.F. Willumsens Museum
Helsingfors, Amos Andersons konstmuseum, Sigurd Frosterus samling
Helsingfors, Konstmuseet Ateneum, Statens konstmuseum i Finland
Helsingfors, Sigrid Jusélius Stiftelse
Köln, Wallraf-Richartz-Museum – Fondation Corboud
Köpenhamn, Den Hirschsprungske Samling
Köpenhamn, Det Danske Kunstindustrimuseum
Köpenhamn, John J. A. Hunovs Samlinger
Köpenhamn, Ny Carlsberg Glyptotek
Köpenhamn, Statens Museum for Kunst
Lillehammer, Lillehammer Kunstmuseum
London, Courtauld Gallery, Courtauld Institute of Art
London, The National Gallery
München, Bayerische Staatsgemäldesammlungen
New York, The Metropolitan Museum of Art
Nordea-Merita, Nordea Konstsamlingen i Finland
Oslo, Munch-museet
Oslo, Nasjonalgalleriet
Oslo, Næringslivets Hovedorganisasjon
Paris, Musée d'Orsay
Paris, Musée Marmottan Monet
Philadelphia, Philadelphia Museum of Art
Skagen, Skagens Museum
Washington, D.C., The Phillips Collection
Åbo, Åbo Konstmuseum
Aalborg, Nordjyllands Kunstmuseum

And private lenders

Contents

Foreword

AN EXHIBITION ENTITLED *Impressionism and the North* hints at a major artistic event. Indeed, there is no doubt that the selection of exhibited works and the underlying research more than meets the highest expectations.

The project co-ordinator Torsten Gunnarsson and the curator Per Hedström have succeeded in securing a series of notable loans of French Impressionist paintings— all the great masters are represented. This would not have been possible were it not for the great generosity towards the Nationalmuseum of a number of institutions and private individuals. The aim of the project has been to document acquisitions of Impressionist works by Scandinavian art collectors. At the same time, the scenographer Henrik Widenheim's austerely designed presentation is worthy of reflection, admiration, and remembrance in its own right.

Scandinavian interest in French Impressionism, however, went well beyond far-sighted art collecting activities. A commitment certainly existed that left its mark on the emerging art literature in the Scandinavian languages. When called for, impressions and experiences were exchanged by artists and like-minded people in conversations in artists' studios, in correspondence, during travels, and at art exhibitions.

Any description of the Scandinavian reception of Impressionism is complicated by the fact that the course of events lacks clear continuity. There are multiple stories, each markedly different in significance and import. The undoubtedly most brilliant and internationally interesting aspect involves the circumstances surrounding the emergence, reception, and final triumph of Impressionism. The development extends from a complex historical situation, through the different phases of heroization, to today's commercial exploitation, made possible by a demand so great that it seems ideally suited to masscommunication—indeed, Claude Monet's water lilies arouse unmatched public interest without ever becoming banale.

The following narratives take place on the periphery. Events in Parisian artistic life of the mid-1880s involving the Impressionists could not possibly have qualified as a pressing Nordic concern strictly from the point of view of artistic policy. The participation of visiting Northeners only occurred in the preserve of the attentive spectator, where Impressionism only arrived after a certain delay. Herein resides the difficulty, insofar as the concept of Impressionism, for the purposes of the present project, has been extended to include an additional phase, namely that which Roger Fry, in the early 1900s, termed Post-Impressionism.

The delay involved a displacement of perspectives resulting in a powerful sanction—the Impressionist images would become incorporated with the emerging Modernism's system of norms. Here one is able to discern the outlines of two separate stories. One deals with Impressionism in its more open and contradictory "original state," the other with the ambition of posterity to make interpretations of its own. These difficult to define developments are illuminated from different angles. Torsten Gunnarsson provides a general overview of the project, while Per Hedström discusses the Swedish reception of Impressionism. It is especially gratifying that writers from our neighboring countries have been able to participate in the present publication—Bengt von Bonsdorff describes the situation in Finland, from Denmark we have the participation of Peter Nørgaard Larssen and Flemming Friborg, while Nils Messel and Karin Hellandsjø discuss the Norwegian reception.

I am convinced that this major exhibition will open up new critical perspectives. It provides different interpretations and, above all, stimulates renewed discussion about center vs. periphery. That the halls of the museum have been filled with images capable of greatly stimulating our powers of visual perception can hardly be considered a disadvantage.

HANS HENRIK BRUMMER
Director of the Nationalmuseum

Impressionism and the North

Torsten Gunnarsson

THE EXHIBITION *IMPRESSIONISM AND THE NORTH* examines the relationship between French avant-garde art and Scandinavian art during the particularly dynamic period 1870–1920. It does not limit itself to the influence of Impressionism, but, just as importantly, describes Franco-Nordic relations during the following phase of Symbolism, Synthetism, and Neo-Impressionism—often collectively referred to as Post-Impressionism.

The aim of the exhibition is not to illustrate the history of Impressionism and Post-Impressionism itself, a subject which, over the past few decades, has given rise to an extensive body of literature, and been presented in important exhibitions in both Europe and North America. The Nationalmuseum has instead chosen to examine the influence of Impressionism and Post-Impressionism on the whole spectrum of Scandinavian art. As a basis for the investigation, an inventory was taken of the first collections of French Impressionist and Post-Impressionist art ever assembled in the Nordic countries. These were a result of growing interest, both before and after the turn of the century 1900—initially of progressive artists and art critics, later of a number of devoted and wealthy collectors, especially in the 1910s and '20s. Because this Scandinavian collecting culminated at a relatively late date, the picture of these artistic movements had by then also become clearer and, consequently, acquisitions largely focused on the leading figures.

In examining Franco-Nordic relations, we have not considered the greater or lesser degree of receptiveness to French influence with a view to evaluating it, but have only sought to map existing contacts and their potential significance. Equally as important, however, has been to determine the limits of the French influence, and define how Scandinavian art of this period may be said to diverge from French paradigms and express a distinctive character. In these areas the need for a clearer, more complete picture was perceived as being greater. Our impression is confirmed by the fact that even such—from a modern perspective—sensational Franco-Nordic contacts as Paul Gauguin's stay in Copenhagen in 1884–85, Claude Monet's journey to Norway in 1895, or the spectacular 1893 exhibition of Van Gogh and Gauguin in Copenhagen, remain relatively unknown to a wider audience.

The exhibition comprises about 120 French works and about 100 Scandinavian

works, presented according to two main themes and a few subsections. The first major theme concerns the significance of documented personal contacts from the point of view of the history of artistic development, while the second describes the early private and institutional collecting of French art in Scandinavia. In the latter case, the issues involve the impetus for, and conditions of, collecting in the Nordic countries, and the significance of the presence of French avant-garde art for the development of contemporary Scandinavian art. The presentation shows that, in just a few decades, Scandinavian private collections and museums were supplied with a surprising number of first-rate works, although many privately owned works later, once more, found their way out of Scandinavia. As an example may be mentioned Paul Gauguin's spiritual testament, the monumental painting, *Where do we come from? What are we? Where are we going?* then owned by the major Norwegian collector Jörgen Breder Stang, and now in the Museum of Fine Arts in Boston (ill. p. 239). Or, Edgar Degas' *Woman Ironing*, which once belonged to the Norwegian industrialist Christian Mustad. Last but not least, the Danish insurance director Wilhelm Hansen's two specially important collections of French art, one of which is still part of the Ordrupgaard Collection near Copenhagen.

The section of the exhibition dealing with the history of collecting also demonstrates that the Scandinavian national galleries, beginning in the 1890s, in several instances conducted an active and far-sighted acquisitions policy when it comes to contemporary French art. As early as 1890, the Nasjonalgalleriet in Oslo purchased Monet's coastal landscape *Rain, Etretat* (ill. p. 222, cat.no. 144), the first Impressionist painting to become part of a state-owned Scandinavian collection. Thus, an expansionist phase was initiated that would culminate in a series of important acquisitions during, and immediately following, World War I. The Nordic countries, preserved from the war, suddenly acquired an unexpectedly strong position as buyers, and the museums' friends' associations and various consortia did not hesitate to exploit the opportunity to acquire outstanding examples of French art, which had by then won wider acceptance.

Impressionism
The historical significance of Impressionism rests primarily on the fact that the movement took a decisive initial step towards a free and subjective visual representation of the world. To simplify, one could say that the important thing now was not what was represented, but how it was represented. The brushwork itself acquired a new importance, becoming an essential part of the expression of Impressionist painting. An expression that seemed to reflect a rapid and spontaneous creative process, and a truer, more direct relationship with reality. The painter seemed to have captured and communicated a swift overall impression of the motif represented on the canvas, almost in the instant he perceived it, even if that was not always the case.

With Édouard Manet's large painting *Concert in the Tuileries Gardens* of 1862, a new type of painting, depicting life in the modern city, made its appearance in art. Like Charles Baudelaire, Manet was fascinated by Parisian life of the 1860s, and emphasized the importance of keeping pace with the times—"être de son temps."

38. **Edgar Degas** (1834–1917): **The Ironer**. Oil on canvas, 92.5 x 74. Bayerische Staatsgemäldesammlungen, München, 14310.

Édouard Manet (1832–1883): **Music in the Tuileri Gardens**, 1862. Oil on canvas, 76.2 x 118.1. The National Gallery, London.

The idea of mutability as an expression of modernity presumably also felt natural in a city that was being rapidly transformed through the extensive demolitions ordered by the town planner Haussmann, in combination with the construction of new boulevards, parks, and open public spaces. Manet used a relatively large canvas to depict this momentary image of Parisian daily life. In addition, he employed a broad and free painting technique with few details, most of the crowd being merely indicated as a swarming movement. In both respects, Manet departed from the norm of what was then considered acceptable. If not a study for the artist's own use, an insignificant subject such as this should, in the eyes of his contemporaries, only be used as a basis for a decorative vignette, or an illustration in a journal. For a serious work of art, however, it was much too inane and, furthermore, executed in a technique more suitable for a sketch.

A little over ten years later, a still nameless group of artists would, for the first time, introduces a similar type of painting. They had formed a partnership with the principal aim of organizing exhibitions, without either jury or prizes, as an alternative to the official Salon. The first exhibition was held in April of 1874, in the former studio of the photographer Nadar in the Boulevard des Capucines in Paris, and would later become known as the First Impressionist Exhibition. Another seven exhibitions would follow up until 1886. The initial reaction to the new painting was, in part, very negative, even though appreciative voices were not entirely lacking. However, neither the general public, nor the critics or the participating artists, could reasonably have suspected the enormous impact this, still relatively heterogeneous, group would have on the continued development of the Western painting. Today its influence can best be gauged by precisely the fact that we are no longer able to interpret the aesthetic codes which were self-evident in 19th-century art before Impressionism, and around which the French debate of the 1860s and '70s principally revolved. Nowhere else was the line of demarcation between an emerging avant-garde and established art circles as clearly drawn as in France. The latter held to principles firmly rooted in an idealistic belief in the higher purpose of art which, since the 17th century, had guided European art academies. Academic art was not supposed to reproduce reality, but lend it a higher dignity through a meaningful content and an ideal form. The subject and content of a work of art was, therefore, at least as important as its execution.

That the new art of the Impressionists, completely lacking in significant content and barely differing in its execution from a sketch, awakened resistance in many quarters is, thus, not especially surprising. In fact, Impressionist painting accentuated what artists of all ages have tried to conceal, namely, the painting technique itself and the brushwork. One also did not seek a harmonious, unified colour scheme, but allowed pure, unmixed colours to simply co-exist, unmediated by other colours. The motif was split into a kind of colour modules, frequently so loosely tied together that they were basically transformed into signs. This rejection of the illusionistic representation of reality associated with Classical tradition, in favour of an art built on visual signs and symbols, was also an important prerequisite for the following phase of Symbolism and Synthetism and, ultimately, also for the Modernist breakthrough after the turn of the century 1900.

Despite its radicalism, Impressionism was not based on a unified aesthetic theory, but more on a common orientation embraced by a number of, in part, fairly dissimilar painters. Of the little over fifty artists who participated in the eight Impressionist exhibitions during the period 1874–1886, the historically significant contribution was made by a radical core group which included Monet, Renoir, Sisley, Pissarro, Degas, and Morisot. Having their starting-point in Realism's depictions of contemporary life, and being seized by a feeling for *modernity*, they oriented painting towards a new type of representation of the subjective impression of an object, rather than a knowledge-based representation of its essential nature. The term *Impressionism* itself is derived from the French "impression," or *impression*. It had previously been used by, among others, Édouard Manet, and it reappeared in the title of Claude Monet's later so celebrated painting *Impression, soleil levant* of 1872, shown as part of the First Impressionist Exhibition in 1874. Monet's painting, depicting a hazy sunrise over the harbour of Le Havre, together with his two views of the *Boulevard des Capucines*, offered the most complete picture of what Impressionist art represented. The exhibition was otherwise a fairly complex affair, comprising extremely radical works by Berthe Morisot and Paul Cézanne, for example, *The House of the Hanged Man* (ill. p. 56, cat.no. 28), as well as more traditional paintings by artists who no longer count as Impressionists. The influential art critics Jules Antoine Castagnary and Louis Leroy both employed the term "Impressionists" in their reviews of the 1874 exhibition. Castagnary concluded that these painters were satisfied with capturing the impression and were not tempted to enter more deeply into details. Their aim was different: "They are Impressionists in the sense that they do not represent the landscape itself, but, rather, the impression of the landscape."[1]

Also the young August Strindberg who, in the 1870s, wrote art criticism, used a similar definition of the Impressionist method a few decades later. He observed that

the aim was to free oneself from one's knowledge about the world and represent only the subjective experience of its visible surface: "one should paint the impression, not Nature herself."[2] As demonstrated by Nils Messel's essay in the present volume, perhaps the most perceptive of Nordic observers was the Norwegian Professor of Art History Lorentz Dietrichson. In polemics against the painter Erik Werenskiold who, in an enthusiastic article of 1882, had defined Impressionist painting as a development of Naturalism, Dietrichson claimed that it was in fact the other way around. The Impressionists did not represent nature as they perceived it, but, rather, rendered it abstractly, using their special technique of colour dots. Impressionism, thus, was not an outgrowth of Realism, as suggested by certain contemporary notions. Nor did the Impressionists paint what they actually perceived, but offered a personal interpretation of their impressions.

Indeed, the loose painting technique and broad brushwork used, to varying degrees, by the Impressionists was not new, but had been fairly frequently employed for the independent oil sketches used in landscape painting since the end of the 18th century. Even academic and classically oriented French painters going back to Jacques Louis David used *l'ébauche*, a loose, broadly conceived monochromatic sketching technique, as an underpainting for their studio works. Rather, the novelty resided in the fact that the Impressionists now introduced this loose sketching technique even into their finished works, while taking the colour scheme to new and unsuspected heights. For a contemporary audience this was very controversial and was regarded more as a form of swindle than a valid artistic standpoint.

The Birth of Impressionism: Monet and Renoir at La Grenouillère

Claude Monet and Auguste Renoir would, towards the end of the 1860s, follow in Manet's footsteps. They came even closer to defining and solidifying the orientation of the new painting that, a few years later, would be referred to as Impressionism.

For a painter like Monet, who, in this respect, was the leader of the two, the impossibility of gaining recognition at the official Salon had become increasingly apparent. Instead of trying to adapt to the demands of academic art, he and others among the future Impressionists would, after circa 1870, go their own way and, with Paul Durand-Ruel's gallery in Paris as their first venue, gradually develop an alternative painting parallel to the Salon painting.[3]

In the late summer of 1869, Claude Monet and Auguste Renoir painted some epoch-making works at La Grenouillère in Bougival, west of Paris. This was a leisure spot by the Seine typical for the period, with boat rentals and a floating restaurant, frequented by the same bourgeois city audience which had increasingly come to dominate artistic life. La Grenouillère represented a new type of subject to which the Impressionists would frequently return, and the five preserved paintings that Monet and Renoir executed here, working side by side, in an amazingly loose technique, appear like object lessons in the orientation of the new painting.[4] Indeed, several researchers have interpreted these pictures, three of which are shown in the present exhibition, as representing a decisive moment in the history of Impressionism. This despite the fact that we cannot determine with certainty whether the preserved pictures should be considered as finished paintings or merely as sketches for larger, never executed, versions. However, Monet exhibited one of his versions in 1876, and another one in 1889, indicating that these were finished paintings. Renoir, on the other hand, never exhibited any of his versions and, simultaneously, executed paintings of a considerably more traditional character.[5] All three La Grenouillère versions exhibited here have, through their—for the period—extremely loose painting technique, abandoned the traditionally representational for a strongly subjective interpretation of visual impressions. The marked stylization acts like a form of visual shorthand, in which all parts of the painting appear to have an equal value. Gone is the demand for a story or message; here there is no story to be told, no feeling to communicate, and no three-dimensional volume to delineate. The subjective visual impression alone is of central importance, distilled as shimmering colours and water reflections, largely rendered in pure, unmixed colours.

The use of unmixed colours is a reaction to new discoveries showing that the optical mixing of pigments achieved by placing pure colours side by side using individual brush strokes significantly increased the intensity of both colour and light. All mixing of colours on the palette, on the other hand, resulted in a darker tonality than that of the original colours by themselves.[6]

While clearly distancing itself from Realism's demands for an objective representation of reality, Impressionism adhered to demands that art should depict contemporary life. This is illustrated, for example, by the absolute presence Edgar Degas conferred on the model of his *Woman Ironing* of 1869—executed in the same year as the paintings from La Grenouillère (ill. p. 10, cat.no. 38). As in his later depictions of women, however, Degas here reveals a different, and chillier, aspect of the obser-

139. **Claude Monet** (1840–1926): **La Grenouillère**, 1869. Oil on canvas, 74.6 x 99.7. The Metropolitan Museum of Art, New York, H. O. Havemeyer Collection, Bequest of Mrs. H. O. Havemeyer, 1929, 29.100.112

188. **Auguste Renoir** (1841–1919): **La Grenoullière**. Oil on canvas, 66.5 x 81. Nationalmuseum,
NM 2425. Gift from an unknown donor through Nationalmusei Vänner 1924.

vation of reality considered as fundamental to the Impressionist method. The difference, compared to Realist representations, is that for Degas and the Impressionists the depiction of contemporary life was unconnected to any social commitment, but was based on a more distanced documenting of fragments from the flow of life.

Impressionism and Scandinavian Art

As mentioned earlier, from a long-term perspective French Impressionism had a substantial impact on the development of European painting. In the Nordic countries, however, the immediate effect of the Impressionist breakthrough was not revolutionary. During the 1870s and '80s, Realism played much the same pioneering role here, as did Impressionism in France. In Scandinavia the debate in the fields of both literature and art still involved the issue of Idealism vs. Realism. Did art properly belong to a higher sphere, or should it, as asserted by the advocates of Realism, draw its material directly from everyday life, and not shy away from its darker aspects? The latter point of view gained broad acceptance in the first half of the 1880s, although Idealism would, in less than a decade, have its renaissance in the guise of Symbolism.

Scandinavian artists discovered Impressionism at a surprisingly early date. Already in the winter of 1870, long before the new painting had received a name and several years before the first exhibition was organized, the future Impressionism was identified by the Finnish painter Berndt Lindholm, one of the period's many visitors to Paris. This occurred in a letter published in the *Helsingfors Dagblad*, in which a new radical group referred to as "the tonal painting group" is mentioned. The group's main objective is said to be the exclusively study of the proper relationships of colours, while the subject matter and the details are considered unimportant. Lindholm also describes the orientation of the new group, concluding that.

This painting depicts Krohg's
artist colleague Gerhard Munthe
at the Grand Café in Oslo.
Krohg had stayed in Paris in the
early 1880s, and had been influenced by French Realism, as
well as Impressionism. The
painting is related to Impressionism–and perhaps, above all, to
Manet–both in terms of painting
technique and motif. Using
broad brush strokes, Krohg has
created an image which suggests, rather than clearly
defines, the milieu and figures.
Like the Impressionists, Krohg
has created something that may
be viewed as a momentary
image of contemporary life in the
big city.

"[…] it seeks to discover what is beautiful in Nature through careful study of the local colours of objects through all the transformations they undergo, as perceived by the eye, as a result of the varying influences of air and light, in other words, the tonal values."[7]

Although Lindholm observed that such an aim was not altogether novel in French painting, the same year he himself experimented with a loose technique in a small-scale view from his studio, looking towards the Boulevard Clichy, an experi-ment that was, however, not repeated.

During the 1870s, Scandinavian visitors to Paris mostly adopted a cautious atti-tude towards Impressionism and, in some cases, rejected it outright. The exception was Carl Fredrik Hill, who spoke of Impressionism in positive terms as the most "realistic" artistic current. Hill's choice of words, and the fact that he would himself

develop a painting whose emotional intensity was foreign to both Realism and Impressionism, also offer insights into the ideological uncertainty vis-à-vis the new that, during the 1880s, came to dominate the Nordic debate on Impressionism.

Norway

Generally, it may be said that Impressionism, and French art as a whole, played more of a role as a source of inspiration and a catalyst for the development of Scandinavian art during the 1870s and '80s, than as a slavishly imitated model. This was especially true for Norway, where Impressionism, during the 1880s, was mostly perceived as being synonymous with a radical modern representation of contemporary life, or with *plein-air* painting. To be an Impressionist in this sense was more a matter of seeking the truth, and not shying away from the darker aspects of existence, than to paint like Monet or Sisley. This is demonstrated, not least, by the art journal *Impressionisten* (*The Impressionist*), which was published by the painter Christian Krohg and the anarchist and author Hans Jæger and functioned as a mouthpiece for radical Christiania bohemians in the years 1886–1890.[8] Thus, it is not surprising that Norwegian, as well as other Scandinavian artists, who, during the 1880s, were busy renewing the art of their native countries, found their French models primarily in the work of Jules Bastien-Lepage, a competent, though not radical, Realist, without a strong tendency towards social commitment.

Generally, in Norway, as in the neighboring countries, a Scandinavian artist scarcely stood a chance of being accepted by the general public and the critics if he practiced a purely Impressionist style of painting. Painters of the middle course, such as Bastien-Lepage, would, therefore, have appeared as a reasonable choice, making possible one's own potential artistic development, as well as economic survival.

This, however, did not mean that Impressionism did not receive any attention or was not a hotly debated subject among artists, critics and art historians in Norway. Both Christian Krohg and Erik Werenskiold visited the Impressionist exhibitions of 1881 and 1882, in which Gauguin, Monet, Morisot, Pissarro, Renoir, and Sisley were richly represented, particularly in the latter exhibition. The painter Frits Thaulow was Gauguin's brother-in-law and supplied his works to the Artists' Autumn Exhibition in Oslo as early as 1884. And, as mentioned earlier, the art historian Lorentz Dietrichson engineered the first acquisition of an Impressionist painting by a public collection outside of France, with the purchase of Monet's *Rain, Etretat* (ill. p. 214, cat.no. 144) by the Nasjonalgalleriet in 1890. Both Krohg and his young pupil Edvard Munch also experimented with Impressionism.

Denmark

In Denmark interest in French art manifested itself, not least, through the great 1888 exhibition at Copenhagen, initiated by Carl Jacobsen, owner of the Ny Carlsberg brewery and founder of the Glyptotek. The selection of exhibited artworks, however, was primarily concentrated on Realist and Academic French art, though a few Impressionist works by Monet were also included. Indeed, knowledge about Impressionism was, with few exceptions, slight in Denmark before 1890.

The initial contacts between Danish art circles and French Impressionism reveal

157. **Edvard Munch** (1863–1944): **Rue Lafayette**, 1891. Oil on canvas, 92 x 73. Nasjonalgalleriet, Oslo, NG.M.01725.

quite clearly how a lack of public preparedness and acceptance led to a delayed and limited dissemination of Impressionism. Although there was no lack of initiatives, principally through Gauguin exhibiting his work in Copenhagen in 1885 and 1889 together with French and Danish painters, it came and went without leaving a trace, apart from a few insightful essays by the art critic Karl Madsen. Consequently, the Danish development was characterized by a reversed chronology, so that Impressionist painting achieved a broader impact only after Symbolism, around 1900, with the group of artists known as the *Fynboerne.*

One of the few Danish painters for whom Impressionism played a more significant role was Theodor Philipsen, the only artist with whom Gauguin became more closely acquainted during his six-month stay in Copenhagen in 1884–85. Indeed, he emerged as the first Danish Impressionist with the shimmering, carefully executed *Late Autumn at Dyrehaven. Sunlight* of 1886 (ill. p. 164, cat.no. 173). Gauguin's gift to Philipsen, *The Road to Rouen,* presumably played a role as a model (ill. p. 140, cat.no. 60) for this painting. Later on, Philipsen also developed more radical visual forms as, for example, in *Long Shadows. Cattle on Saltholm* of circa 1890, distinguished by its original composition, precise study of movement, and coloured shadows.

Sweden

Of Swedish painters, Karl Nordström, Anders Zorn, Per Ekström, and Carl Trädgårdh, among others, were strongly influenced by Impressionism. In works such as *The Forest Glade* of 1884 (ill. p. 61, cat.no. 162), or *View of Stockholm from Skansen* of 1889, Nordström not only went further than most Swedish artists, but also reveals a more spontaneous use of Impressionism's means of expression. In the

166. **Karl Nordström** (1855–1923): **View of Stockholm from Skansen,** 1889. Oil on canvas, 62 x 121. National-museum, NM 1891. Gift from Friends of Art through the Director Richard Bergh 1915.

pastel drawing *My Wife*, he even related directly to a type of motif frequently used by Renoir and other French painters.

For Nordström, Impressionism was a significant, albeit brief, phase before, as a leading member of the Konstnärsförbundet (Artists' Union), he adopted a national-ly oriented Symbolism characterized by broad, summary forms. In this respect, he is a typical representative of the majority of Scandinavian artists, for whom Im-pressionism was something of an isolated episode on the road leading directly from Realism to Symbolism.

A strongly individualistic and, in many respects, radical painter was Per Ekström. He came closest to a kind of subjective Impressionism in a series of *contre-jour* images of trees on inundated lands. These images are built entirely on painterly qualities, and are distinguished by quite a loose painting technique, using short brush strokes and colour dots. At the same time, as demonstrated by his *Landscape, Carolles*, Ekström's painting, through an absence of bright daylight and a somber palette, also exhibits a strong connection with the earlier Barbizon school.

Anders Zorn was the only major Swedish painter on whom Impressionism, to a varying degree, had a lasting influence. Already in his watercolours from the early 1880s, Zorn appeared as a master of suggestion, with a pronounced ability to per-ceive a motif as a whole, somewhat related to that of Impressionism. However, the transition to an Impressionist style of painting does not occur until circa 1888, when he had progressed beyond his early phase as a watercolourist. During the peri-od 1888–1896, Zorn resided mostly in Paris, where, like few others, he seems to have understood and adopted the aims of Impressionism. Significant proof is the gouache *Impressions de Londres* of 1890 (ill. p. 67, cat.no. 221), and the oil paint-

13. **Richard Bergh** (1858–1919): **Tank Engine by a Harbour,** 1881. Oil on canvas, 29.5 x 42. Private collection.

222. **Anders Zorn** (1860–1920): **View From the Skeppsholmen Quay,** 1890. Oil on canvas, 69 x 100. Handelsbanken, Stockholm

Opposite page: 223. **Anders Zorn** (1860–1920): **Omnibus I,** 1895 (92?). Oil on canvas, 99.5 x 66. Nationalmuseum, NM 6810. Purchased with contribution from the Kjell and Märta Beijer Foundation 1985.

163. **Karl Nordström** (1855–1923): **Oat Field, Grez,** 1885.
Oil on canvas, 117 x 147.5. Malmö Konstmuseum, MMK 1131.

165. **Karl Nordström** (1855–1923): **Oat Field, Lyrön,** 1887.
Oil on canvas, 33.5 x 50. Prins Eugens Waldemarsudde, Stockholm, W566.

44. **Per Ekström** (1844–1935):
Landscape, Carolles. Oil on
canvas, 77 x 46.5. Prins Eugens
Waldemarsudde, Stockholm,
W140.

43. **Per Ekström** (1844–1935):
**French Landscape with Water-
Lillies**. Oil on canvas, 84 x 38.
Private collection.

Opposite page: 164. **Karl
Nordström** (1855–1923): **My
Wife**, 1885. Pastell, 100 x 73.
Göteborgs konstmuseum, GKM
F111.

ings *Omnibus* of 1895 and *View from Skeppsholmskajen* of 1890, all of which, in motif as well as technique, are congenial with the momentary images of city life in French art.

Also in his brewery pictures and numerous *plein-air* nude studies, Zorn would, to a greater or lesser degree, adopt an Impressionist attitude. In most of his works, however, this occurred without sacrificing three-dimensional volume and, like the radical Impressionists, divest the objects of their physical presence. Rather, Zorn's painting after 1890 involved a cautious return to a stronger emphasis on three-dimensional volume, at the expense of a looser style of painting. During his entire career he would, however, continue to employ an Impressionist technique in isolated areas, in order to suggest the forms using swift, suggestive brush strokes.

Above: 202. **Robert Thegerström** (1857–1919):
On the Outskirts of the City. Olja på pannå,
37 x 46. Nationalmuseum, NM 6969.

7. **Gustave Albert** (1866–1905): **Moret-sur-Loing**,
1893. Oil on canvas, 54.5 x 65.5. Eskilstuna
Konstmuseum, EK 7.

95. **Anton Genberg** (1862–1939): **Kungsträdgården,** 1896.
Oil on canvas, 55 x 71. Handelsbanken, Stockholm.

213. **Victor Westerholm** (1860–1919): **The Birch Grove,** 1888. Oil on canvas, 80 x 145. Turku Art Museum, Collection Niilo Wilhelm Jokipohja, 4263.

Opposite page: 115. **Nils Kreuger** (1858–1930): **Autumn, Varberg,** 1888. Oil on panel, 32 x 41. Nationalmuseum, NM 4120. Gift according to the will of John och Ellen Josephson 1945.

Finland

In Finland Impressionism had less of an impact during the 1880s than in the rest of Scandinavia, Victor Westerholm being nearly its only representative. This may seem paradoxical in view of the fact that Westerholm was the last Finnish painter to study at Düsseldorf in 1878–86, where he was trained in a completely different tradition. However, during visits to Paris in 1888–90 he became influenced by Impressionism and executed some paintings that are undoubtedly among the most pronounced examples of Impressionism in Scandinavian painting, such as, for example, *From Paris* (ill. p. 272, cat.no. 215) and *Suresnes.* In 1888 Westerholm made an attempt to introduce the Impressionist approach in Finland by contributing his large *Birch Forest* to a state-sponsored contest in landscape painting. However, the attempt failed. Despite its fairly moderate Impressionism, the painting received scathing criticism, and the whole contest was postponed until the following year. This time Westerholm, who had returned to Realism, won the contest. Westerholm's path from Düsseldorf to French Impressionism, during the course of a few years, demonstrates that, like many other Scandinavian painters, he was ready for Impressionism by the time he came across it. The reason why it still did not achieve a broader impact is clearly illustrated by the public response to Westerholm's *Birch Forest.* The negative public reception made it practically impossible for an artist to continue down this road, unless financially independent and indifferent to public recognition. As late as 1904, when a representative Franco-Belgian exhibition of works by Impressionists such as Degas, Monet, Pissarro, Renoir, Sisley, and Symbolists and Neo-Impressionists such as Maurice Denis and Paul Signac, was held at the Finnish National Gallery, the Ateneum, at the initiative of the Belgian immigrant painter A.W. Finch, it attracted only about 3 000 visitors—considerably fewer than the annual exhibition of contemporary Finnish art.

Perhaps Impressionism's mode of aloof observation did not suit the Nordic temperament, for which, in the words of the Swedish painter Richard Bergh, art was not "a product of happiness, but of yearning." Bergh also attempted to define the

216. **Victor Westerholm** (1860–1919): **Suresnes,** 1890. Oil on canvas, 31.5 x 45.5. Turku Art Museum, 361.

difference between the French and the Nordic artistic temperament, and found that it resided primarily in a Nordic emphasis on feeling: "Only feeling can teach the painter to discover the accord, the style, through which his representation of Nature will achieve harmony, become art. In France a landscape painter might conceivably become an artist with the aid of his eye alone, like Sisley. In Scandinavia the landscape painter must also be a poet."[9]

Symbolism and Synthetism
During the second half of the 1880s, Scandinavian art again moved away from the concentration on external reality of Realism and Impressionism. Once again, this was due to French influences based on new insights about the significance of individual experience and variety. A Symbolist manifesto had been published in the *Figaro Littéraire* in the autumn of 1886 by Jean Moréas. This stated that the artist's task was to interpret reality and to express his thoughts and feelings through symbols. The motif itself was only interesting as the expression of an idea. The same year Vincent Van Gogh arrived in Paris, where he became acquainted with, among others, Paul Gauguin and Émile Bernard. Gauguin then left for Pont Aven in Brittany, where he became a leader of a group of young artists, later known as the Nabis, a spiritually oriented brotherhood whose members regarded themselves as prophets

of a new kind of spiritualized art. The young Dane Mogens Ballin (cat.nos. 9–12) joined the group a few years later.

Symbolism may be defined as a revolt of the imagination against Realism's confinement to a reality now perceived as tyranny and an impediment to artistic freedom. External reality also did not suffice to be able to visually represent the new interest in emotional life and the deeper semi-conscious layers of a personality. Dreams, visions, and hypnosis, as well as different forms of spirituality now caught the interest of artists in their search for a pure and spiritualized art, often comprising elements of Catholicism. At the same time, the temporal dimension of the images changed from the specific moment to eternal being and, especially in Scandinavian art, daylight was replaced by the melancholy atmosphere of twilight.

It was felt that the visual representation of a spiritual dimension could be achieved by a stylization of the motif, whereby the objects did not primarily depict physical reality, but were elevated to a symbolic level. In 1896 Richard Bergh, one of the most prominent figures in contemporary Swedish artistic life, who had himself undergone a typical development from Realism to Symbolism during the 1880s and '90s, wrote about the correspondence between internal and external reality, inspired by the ideas of Symbolism. He believed he had discovered it in the fact that each viewer finds his own landscape based on his own innermost feelings:

"Instinctively, the evocative painter seeks out a light, an atmosphere, a landscape which he may invest with a spirit possessing the sufferings and joys of his own soul, its light and dark dreams."[10]

In France Symbolism and Synthetism were initially combined into a new entity by Paul Gauguin and Émile Bernard around 1886–88. While Symbolism focused on thematic content, Synthetism sought a simplified surface-oriented visual language as an expression of the new spiritualized art. Parallel to this a taste also developed for what was primitive and original. Artists sought out ancient or foreign cultures, such as those of Brittany, Tahiti, and Finnish Carelia, or found inspiration in the simple visual language of medieval or folk art. In Scandinavia, Pierre Puvis de Chavannes' archaizing new simplicity became perhaps the most important source of inspiration for a new purity of form and content.

Symbolism in Scandinavia

Symbolism and Synthetism achieved a completely different, and broader, artistic impact in the Nordic countries than Impressionism. Consequently, the Realist phase was of brief duration; the final breakthrough of *plein-air* painting and depictions of everyday life, in the work of the young oppositional artists in the first half of the 1880s, had scarcely occurred before signs of something new appeared around the middle of the decade. The explanation for this rapid turn-around, culminating in the first half of the 1890s, is that it occurred mostly within the young Realists' own circle. Contrary to Impressionism, this happened more or less parallel to the emergence of Symbolism in France, where most of the Northerners still resided or had good contacts. Also important was the fact that Symbolism's emphasis on the importance of feeling was easily combined with the national currents that, around this time, were beginning to seek new artistic expressions for a national Nordic identity.

6. **Ivan Aguéli** (1869–1917):
The Plain. Oil on canvas, 23 x
39.5. Moderna Museet, Stockholm, NM 3280.

Most deeply influenced were a group of slightly younger artists who arrived in Paris in the early 1890s, including the Swedes Ivan Aguéli and Olof Sager-Nelson, and the Finn Magnus Enckell. Older Scandinavian artists, however, who had recently moved beyond Realism, only adopted the formal language of Symbolism to a limited degree. Indeed, the spiritual dimension of French Symbolism never had a similar impact in Scandinavia, and there was no equivalent of Joséphin Péladans' group of Catholic artists, the *Rose-Croix*, founded in 1888, though it strongly influenced the circle of Johannes Jørgensen and the journal *Taarnet*.

Contrary to French Symbolism, Scandinavian art of the 1890s and around the turn-of-the-century 1900 instead maintained a strongly subjective attitude towards nature, which had a definitive influence on painting. Indeed, most artists did not take the stylization of natural forms as far as Gauguin, though the exhibition does include a series of important and orthodox examples of this. The most striking exception was Edvard Munch, who consistently developed in the direction of anti-Naturalism. Nordic Symbolism developed, with few exceptions, into a romantically evocative painting, in which the landscape played an especially important role. Instead of, as earlier, being inhabited by embodied natural spirits from popular mythology, the Nordic landscape was now depicted as a projection of human emotions, alternating between wistfulness and melancholy. It was felt that one had discovered, in the twilight and the night, an apt expression for the spirit of the age, as well as the Nordic temperament, while, at the same time, the temporal dimension shifted from the momentary to a condition of timeless being.

This shift in mood occurred first in Norway in 1884–85, in some landscapes by Christian Skredsvig and Kitty Kielland. The phenomenon received a broader impact

2. **Ivan Aguéli** (1869–1917): **Motif from Stockholm** (from the area of the church of St John) 1891 ca. Oil on canvas, 46 x 55. Moderna Museet, Stockholm, NM 1913.

about a year later with the so-called Fleskum artists' colony, a loosely organized group of painters that also included Erik Werenskiold, Harriet Backer, Gerhard Munthe, and Eilif Petersen, and which, in the summer of 1886, met at the Fleskum farm not far from Oslo. In the same year, the theoretically aware and eloquent Richard Bergh wrote an essay with the telling title *Om överdrifternas nödvändighet i konsten* (*On the Necessity of Exaggeration in Art*). Here he strongly rejected Realism, asserting that: "The life of all art, of all poetry, lies hidden in the subjective perception [...] Objective representation is the complete opposite of art ..."[11]

As mentioned earlier, Bergh had turned towards Symbolism in 1888–89. A few years later he purchased Gauguin's *Landscape from Brittany* from the artist's wife in Copenhagen (ill. p. 78, cat.no. 72). With Gauguin's painting in his possession, he then joined the small artists' colony at Varberg, the future cradle of Swedish Synthetism. Typically for a Northerner, Karl Nordström, Bergh's colleague and friend in the small colony, found Gauguin's landscapes "cold and empty of feeling," while admiring their strictly decorative arrangement of forms.[12] Indeed, the latter quality would find a

first, immediate expression in Nordström's own *Storm Clouds* of 1893. Perhaps the
most original contribution in terms of the development of a new visual language was
that of the Swede Nils Kreuger. Next to Richard Bergh and Karl Nordström, Kreuger
was the third member of the small Varberg colony. His art exhibits neither the national undertones of Nordström's, nor Bergh's more Symbolist orientation. Beginning in
1893, Kreuger instead developed a completely novel way of painting, in which the
painted surface is covered by a system of dots and short lines in ink, forming a kind
of fine-meshed web. The idea was probably to thus unify the picture, but also, using
the varying density of the pattern, to emphasize, and rhythmically reinforce, the visual language. Whether or not Kreuger's ink pattern might be derived from impressions
of Van Gogh's drawings has long been a subject of debate. A conclusive answer to the
question has, however, not been found.[13] It seems probable that Kreuger never visited the 1893 exhibition of Van Gogh and Gauguin in Copenhagen.

The fairly unified Scandinavian view of the nature of Symbolism was perhaps
most clearly articulated in the Danish journal *Taarnet*, which, through great sacri-
fice, was published for only a year by the author Johannes Jørgensen. Already in
the first issue the new orientation was indicated, in a presentation of the young
Symbolist Ludvig Find, with the following statement: "Naturalism was a slave to
Nature, Symbolism is too fond of Nature to simply mimic her."[14] In his essay
"Symbolisme," published in the December 1893 issue of *Taarnet*, Johannes Jør-

gensen defined the foundation of Symbolism as belief in the existence of a hereafter.
This belief also forms the basis of its aesthetic, according to which the spiritual
dimension must not be neglected, since the eye merely sees, while the soul inter-
prets, the impressions.[15] Jørgensen also established that the true artist is therefore,
by necessity, a Symbolist, all true art being Symbolist.

If in Norwegian and Swedish art Symbolism mostly assumed the form of a mod-
erately stylized, often grandly evocative art, in Denmark and Finland it developed in
a purer form. In Danish art there are many points of contact with French Post-
Impressionism, both through personal encounters and public opinion-building initiatives as, for example, through exhibitions and acquisitions of art.

As early as 1889, the art critic Julius Lange had espoused the idea that the artist
should turn away from base reality towards a more creative introspection.[16]

In 1891, at the initiative of the painter Johan Rohde, The Free Exhibition was
founded, a principal venue for the new art. The following year, Rohde undertook a
European journey in order to study the art of Van Gogh, whose *Landscape from
Saint-Rémy*, now in the Ny Carlsberg Glyptotek, he brought back home. In 1893
Rohde and Theodor Philipsen offered the Danish public a sensational glimpse of
French Symbolism and Synthetism with the exhibition of circa fifty paintings by
Gauguin, including ten never previously exhibited works directly from Tahiti, and
close to thirty works by Van Gogh. This exhibition, rightly referred to as "the mir-
acle on the Rådhuspladsen," was made possible by the two painters' personal con-
tacts, on the one hand, with Gauguin's Danish wife Mette and, on the other, with

Cover for the journal *Taarnet*. The cover of the first issue— October 1893—was designed by Mogens Ballin. This cover was later replaced by a cover designed by Jan Verkade (numbers 1–2, April–May 1894.

Van Gogh's heirs. The present exhibition includes thirteen works shown in the 1893 exhibition (cat.nos. 58, 59, 64, 69, 71, 72, 78, 82, 96, 97, 99, 100, and 101).[17] The exhibition was displayed by itself in a separate hall, and was described by Rohde as "a mighty birch rod for our own behinds."[18] Not unexpectedly, the exhibition received a lot of attention and was vehemently criticized in the conservative press, while liberal-minded critics were somewhat more appreciative.

Kleis' art dealership in Copenhagen organized a parallel exhibition of works by Emile Bernard and the Nabis, succeeded by one devoted to the Dutch Symbolist Jan Verkade the following year. Added to J.F. Willumsen's and Mogens Ballin's already well-established contacts with Gauguin's circle, this meant that Symbolism received greater exposure and achieved a greater impact in Denmark than in the rest of Scandinavia.

Also in Finland, where Impressionism had left few traces, Symbolism became firmly rooted after its initial appearance in 1891. This was due to some of the paintings sent directly from Paris by Magnus Enckell and shown as part of the exhibition of Finnish artists in Helsingfors.[19] The reason was, not least, that Symbolism here became associated with the strong national sentiment that characterized artistic life in this period. This, in turn, was a consequence of the country's position as a Russian Grand Duchy, and was largely due to a Russification campaign that, culminating through a series of measures outlined in the so-called February Manifesto of 1899, sought to tie Finland closer to Russia. As the national messages could only be communicated in disguised form, grand wilderness landscapes became one of the most frequent national symbols in contemporary Finnish art. Also in Finland Synthetism became the signature of the new national art. This was true, not least, of Gallen-Kallela's innovative new painting, which, from the mid-1890s on, appeared as the foremost example of a new Finnish style (cf. *Autumn* of 1902, ill. p. 268, cat.no. 54). The group of Finnish artists who, in 1894, adopted Symbolism, included, in addition to Gallen-Kallela, Väinö Blomstedt who, like Pekka Halonen, had studied with Gauguin in Paris during a short period in early 1894. He had returned to Paris from Haiti in September of 1893, and had opened an art school, also frequented by the Swede Helmer Osslund and others.[20]

Blomstedt's Synthetism reveals a clear relationship with Gauguin's, but an orthodox Synthetist style like this was still relatively rare (see *The Cemetary at Bourg-la-Reine* of 1894, ill. p. 266, cat.no. 16). More revolutionary and, at the same time, more genuinely Finnish was the transformation Akseli Gallen-Kallela's painting underwent under the influence of decorative Carelian folk art. It basically transformed his art into a Synthetist surface-oriented style with a national subject matter derived primarily from the Finnish national epic, the *Kalevala*. However, Synthetism was not Gallen-Kallela's only source of inspiration. Like Ellen Thesleff, Richard Bergh, Carl Larsson, and others, he would later, during the 1890s, seek inspiration also from Early Renaissance Italian fresco painting, by many considered the primal source of all art and a counter-weight to the decadence one felt was beginning to affect contemporary French art. As mentioned above, Puvis de Chavannes was also an important model for many Scandinavian artists.

In conclusion it may be said that Impressionism, as well as Symbolism, influenced the development of Nordic art in many different ways during the period 1870–1910.

Cover of The Free Exhibition catalogue of 1893. The exhibition included 51 works by Gauguin and 29 by Van Gogh. The catalogue belongs to the Library of the Academy of Fine Arts, Copenhagen.

Building housing The Free Exhibition on the Halmtorvet (the present Rådhuspladsen). The building was designed by Thorvald Bindesbøll. Photograph from 1896 in the collections of the Municipal Museum of Copenhagen.

The following pages: 166. **Karl Nordström (1855–1923): View of Stockholm from Skansen** (detail), 1889. Oil on canvas, 62 x 121. Nationalmuseum, NM 1891. Gift from Friends of Art through the Director Richard Bergh 1915.

While the noticeable influence of Impressionism was, on the whole, lesser and somewhat belated, Symbolism and Synthetism achieved a considerably more rapid breakthrough in all Scandinavian countries.

In the hands of Scandinavian artists, however, the impressions were transformed and, not least, the special Nordic feeling for nature gave the art of this period a distinctive character that has come to be considered as genuinely national. The evocative landscape was the principal, and most distinctive, result of this fusion of the Nordic and the French. Above all, it became a vehicle for a new emotional content, for which Realism lacked a means of expression.

The new art mirrored an external, as well as an internal, reality, though Scandinavian painting characteristically retained a stronger connection with physical reality than did Continental art. Thus, it is also possible, to a certain degree, to speak of a distinctively Nordic art, despite the obvious dependency on foreign influences. A distinctiveness that, in terms of the modified Nordic Symbolism of the late 19th century, was defined by stillness, seriousness, and yearning—epithets which still appear as reflections of a way of life typical of these sparsely populated countries on the periphery of Europe.

The Swedish Reception of Late Nineteenth-Century French Avant-Garde Art
Per Hedström

72. **Paul Gauguin** (1848–1903): **Landscape from Brittany** (detail), 1889. Oil on canvas, 72.5 x 91. National-museum, NM 2156. Gift of the Director Hjalmar Granhult 1919.

ONE MIGHT THINK that the collection of late 19th-century French art in the Na-tionalmuseum would reflect aesthetic values prevalent in Sweden at the end of the 19th century. If so, the collection would primarily include works by artists such as Jules Bastien-Lepage, Albert Besnard, Jean-Charles Cazin, and Pierre Puvis de Chavannes, who were much admired by their Swedish colleagues during the last three decades of the 19th century, but more or less forgotten in the 20th century. However, the Nationalmuseum acquired scarcely any foreign art before 1900. The present collection of late 19th-century French art was primarily assembled during the 1910s. The collection mainly includes artists such as Paul Cézanne, Edgar Degas, Paul Gauguin, and Auguste Renoir, in other words, major artists associated with the art movements traditionally referred to as Impressionism and Post-Impressionism.

This essay deals with the process which led to the acceptance of French Im-pressionism and Post-Impressionism in Sweden. The process begins with the initial Swedish reactions to Impressionism around the mid-1870s, and ends with the eleva-tion of French Impressionist and Post-Impressionist art works to the status of the most desirable collector's items in the eyes of Swedish curators and art collectors.

The Dependency of Swedish Art on French Prototypes
Since the beginning of the 1980s there have been many attempts to study late 19th-century Scandinavian art from a new perspective. Earlier writers often viewed Scandinavian art as being, more or less, derivative of French art. Art historical research was rooted in Modernist ideas about artistic development, and French art was considered more progressive. The idea was that the French avant-garde was at the forefront of artistic development, from Realism through Impressionism and Post-Impressionism, a development that reached its final goal in purely Abstract art. The closer Scandinavian art was to French avant-garde art, the more highly valued it was.

The problem with this way of seeing things is, of course, that one risks overlook-ing qualities in Scandinavian art that have no obvious equivalents in late 19th-century French avant-garde art. Consequently, art historical research of the past two decades has examined the relationship of Scandinavian art with cultures other than that of the French avant-garde. The impact of French Realism and Symbolism on Scandinavian art, as well as the relationship between the Scandinavian and German artistic traditions, has been examined. Furthermore, the originality of Scandinavian art has been more strongly emphasized than previously. The advantages with these new perspectives are, of course, numerous and, indeed, late 19th-century Scandinavian art has received increasingly greater attention also internationally—precisely because of its unique qualities.

Notwithstanding the advantages with many of these new perspectives, one cannot escape the fact that French art played an important role for Swedish and other Scandinavian artists. There were few Swedish artists, active in the last three decades of the 19th century, who did not go to France. It is true that many also traveled to Germany, Holland, Italy, and Spain, but they almost always traveled to France as well.

Swedish art of the last three decades of the 19th century was, of course, strongly influenced by these travels. Swedish art education was long considered insufficient. Consequently, it was self-evident that young and ambitious Swedish artists should complete their education by studying at schools, exhibitions, and museums abroad. It would certainly be strange, therefore, if Swedish art had not developed in response to impressions and lessons from France, as well as Swedish traditions and culture. A more difficult question to answer is to what degree Swedish art was actually influenced by the French avant-garde.

To Paris

The younger generation of Swedish artists who studied abroad during the 1870s chose France over Germany, a country that had played an important role for Swedish art during previous decades. This shift of focus in the 1870s, from France to Germany, was accompanied by a change in the views on art. The Romantic, or Idealist, genre painting that had been predominant at Düsseldorf, the most important centre for Swedish artists during previous decades, would be replaced by a more realistic painting in the French mould.

Paris was the most important centre of the art world in this period. This was where the official, state-organized Salon was held, the annual high point of artistic life. Even foreigners had an opportunity to exhibit their work at the Salon, if accepted by the jury. Paris had experienced rapid growth for a number of years and had undergone major changes, not least through Baron Haussmann's transformation of the city plan in the 1850s and '60s. The population of the city had also changed. A large number of people were drawn to Paris and the opportunities for work created there through industrialization and the great building projects. Many people also visited Paris on a more or less temporary basis, as tourists or workers. It has been said that Paris was a city of strangers in the latter part of the 19th century. Among these strangers were the Swedish artists, who, beginning in the 1870s, stayed in the city.

One of the most successful Swedish artists in the Parisian art market of the 1870s

was Hugo Salmson. His career provides a perfect example of how a Swedish painter might relate to the wide spectrum of artistic styles and currents in the French capital. He had arrived in Paris in the late 1870s. During the first half of the 1870s, Salmson tried his hand at Classicizing nude painting, anecdotal genre painting in the Düsseldorf tradition, and historicizing costume painting. His teacher in Paris was Charles Comte, known mainly for paintings of the latter type.

However, in the summer of 1877 Salmson discovered a true recipe for success. Inspired primarily by Jules Breton, he executed a large painting representing farm workers in the French countryside. This painting—*Hoeing White-Beets in Picardy*—was exhibited at the Salon of 1878 with great success. By the way, Bastien-Lepage's celebrated *Les foins* (*Hay-Making*, Paris, Musée d'Orsay)—a painting of the same type, was also exhibited at the Salon. Salmson's image of farm workers harvesting beets combines the period's great interest in realism and the everyday life of working people with traditional compositional principles. Typical of this category of paintings is the ambition to represent heavy manual labor in monumental form.

Swedish Art Critics Encounter Impressionism
When Salmson painted his farm workers harvesting beets, the Impressionists had already held their third exhibition. The first exhibition was held in 1874, and the movement had begun to take shape by as early as the late 1860s. The earliest sign of Swedish awareness of Impressionism was the annual report of the Secretary of the Academy, Fredrik Wilhelm Scholander, read aloud during celebrations at the Swedish Royal Academy of Fine Arts on March 25th, 1876.[1] This account of European art in the year 1875 includes a passage quoting an anonymous French art critic, apparently referring to the Impressionists. The quotation, which deals with the "new French school of landscape painting" and its "sloppy improvisations," is sharply negative in tone.

Scholander's annual report of the following year makes it apparent that he has by now actually viewed works by the Impressionists, at the Second Impressionist Exhibition in Paris in the spring of 1876. Scholander's view of Impressionism is sharply negative, but, at the same time, he suggests that Impressionist theory might be successfully adapted to landscape painting. In other areas, however, Impressionism would be less useful.

The Second Impressionist Exhibition received considerably more attention than the first, held two years earlier. By the time of the 1876 exhibition, it was evident that Impressionism was a movement, a current to be reckoned with in French artistic life. Indeed, the exhibition was a much discussed topic in the foreign press, reported on by, among others, Henry James and Émile Zola.[2] Furthermore, a number of Swedes came into contact with the art of the Impressionists in 1876. We know that Scholander, Geskel Saloman, and Gottfrid Renholm viewed the Second Impressionist Exhibition, and that August Strindberg saw Impressionist paintings at Durand-Ruel's gallery in the autumn of 1876.

In the summer of 1876, Gottfrid Renholm published an article about that year's Parisian Salon.[3] Although the Impressionists were barely represented at the Salon, Renholm felt that the movement was not to be ignored. Apparently, he had also understood the movement's fundamental ambition—to capture the immediate impression. Even if Renholm considered the idea justifiable, he had difficulties discovering any real qualities in the practical results of the Impressionists' work. Renholm viewed the movement as basically "untrue and, therefore, unsound." He also worried about the possible consequences of the Impressionists' work: "In this manner, the public's feeling for art and natural good taste are poisoned."

Also Geskel Saloman, who, in December of 1876, described his impressions of the Second Impressionist Exhibition in Paris, had a negative view of the new movement, even if not condemning it outright.[4] Saloman felt that there were talented painters among the Impressionists, and stated he was aware that, many times, "a bold break with prevailing tastes had moved art forward." He also seemed to understand something of the Impressionists' aims. Concerning a painting by Degas of two women ironing, he noted, among other things, Degas' interest in the problem of how to represent movement.[5] "The artist simply solves the problem by not painting any hands at all, but rather painting a colour corresponding to the local colour of the hands in the place where one can imagine the back-and-forth movement of hands." Saloman's conclusion, however, is that this type of painting could not possibly result in a "true work of art." For such a work was not allowed to disregard the laws of perspective.

Having viewed a number of Impressionist paintings at Durand-Ruel's gallery, August Strindberg discussed these in an article written as a fictitious dialogue between himself and a Swedish painter familiar with Impressionist theory and practice. As with Geskel Saloman's article, his interest focused on the problem of how to represent movement. Strindberg wrote about Monet that he had wanted to paint "the swarming of a crowd on a steamship landing, not a swarming crowd; yet, swarming constitutes a movement; is it possible to represent movement?" Strindberg seems to have understood the Impressionists' ideas, but it is doubtful that he actually appreciated their work. *Likt och olikt* (*Similar and Dissimilar*) of 1884 includes a passage in which Strindberg is being highly critical of Manet's art. According to Strindberg, Manet is a bad painter—who must also have problems with his eyesight—since he employed colours that do not correspond to Nature.[6]

Impressionism in Swedish Painting

Little is known about Swedish artists' views about Impressionism in the 1870s. Only a few contemporary commentaries survive. One of the few artists known to have discussed Impressionism was Oscar Törnå, who, in a letter written in the late 1870s, mentions Impressionism as an interesting art movement. Törnå wrote that Impressionism had much to teach—"how to paint, and how not to paint."[7] However, Törnå had mixed emotions about the new movement. In his paintings from the 1870s he comes across as a faithful follower of the Barbizon school, and the distance to the Impressionists' light-filled, sketchy painting is great. Yet, an exception exists in Törnå's oeuvre—a painting in which both subject and technique come close to the essence of Impressionism. This painting was, however, conceived as a parody of Impressionist painting.

Around the mid-20th century numerous texts were published about Swedish art of the second half of the 19th century. These include artists' monographs, as well as surveys such as Viggo Loos' *Friluftsmåleriets genombrott i svensk konst 1860–1885* (*The Emergence of Plein-Air Painting in Sweden, 1860–1885*) and the first volume of Sixten Strömbom's *Konstnärsförbundets historia* (*History of the Artists' Union*), both published in 1945.[8] Shorter overviews of late 19th-century art were also included in two Swedish art historical surveys by Henrik Cornell and Andreas Lindblom (both published in 1944–46).

Oscar Törnå (1842–1894): **"Un Empressioniste"**, 1870-talet. Oil on panel. Okänd ägare.

Most of these publications from the 1940s and '50s discuss the impact of Impressionism on Swedish art of the 1870s and '80s. The authors generally come to the conclusion that, during these decades, hardly any Swedish painters became pronounced and orthodox Impressionists. However, the fact that a fairly large number of artists were, at least to some degree, influenced by Impressionism is also readily emphasized. The most frequently mentioned artists of the 1870s are Per Ekström, Carl Skånberg, Wilhelm von Gegerfelt, and Carl Fredrik Hill.

A whole chapter of Viggo Loos' *Friluftsmåleriets genombrott i svensk konst 1865–1885* (*The Emergence of Plein-Air Painting in Sweden, 1865–1885*) is devoted to the subject of "Friluftsmålarna och impressionismen" ("The *Plein-Air* Painters and Impressionism"), a chapter dealing primarily with the period of the 1870s, with Skånberg and Gegerfelt. On close examination of the author's use of the term "Impressionism" with regard to these painters, it becomes apparent that he makes no claim that any of them were strongly influenced by the leading Impressionists. Loos suggests that it was, above all, "early Impressionism" that influenced Skånberg, among others. He points to similarities between Skånberg's painting of the 1870s and that of, among others, Eugène Boudin and the Dutch Realists Jacobus Hendricus Maris and Hendrik Willem Mesdag.[9]

In the conclusion to his book about the emergence of *plein-air* painting, Viggo Loos claims that he has attributed greater significance to the impact of Impressionism on Swedish painting than had previously been done.[10] Indeed, there are undoubtedly a number of passages in which one feels that Loos has exaggerated the Impressionist tendencies in the work of Swedish artists. For example, he writes about Alfred Wahlberg's painting of the 1880s: "If one wishes to make comparisons, painters such as Pissarro, Monet, and Cézanne mainly come to mind."[11] It is true that Wahlberg had, during the 1880s, begun employing a looser brush technique, and compositions that give the impression of being randomly chosen segments of a landscape. Basically, however, his is still a form of Realist tonal painting. Nevertheless, Wahlberg surely appears more interesting when compared to Cézanne than to an older artist like Corot, or a little-known French contemporary such as Antoine Guillemet.

A tendency to exaggerate the Impressionist traits in Swedish painting can be recognized in many texts from the mid-20th century. These texts are characterized by a will to discover similarities between the work of Swedish painters and what is viewed as radical and progressive French art. Similarities with the Impressionists' work are readily emphasized, and are viewed as a sign of quality and a positive development. The reason is, of course, an underlying notion about the evolutionary history of art, a belief in a continuous development in which every new stage represents progress, also in a qualitative sense. It would seem that this tendency to compare Swedish painting of the 1870s and '80s with the work of leading Impressionists first became noticeable in the 1910s, when early Modernist art history writing had proclaimed Impressionism the most important art historical development of the 1870s. One example is August Brunius, who, in a 1916 review of an exhibition of Skånberg's works, compared Skånberg's technique to that of Renoir.[12]

Something of this tendency to exaggerate the Impressionist traits in Swedish painting of the 1870s, can still be found in some later literature, for example, in

Henri Usselmann's doctoral thesis *Complexité et importance des contacts des peintres nordiques avec l'impressionisme*, in which Skånberg's Impressionist tendencies are, once again, emphasized.[13] Usselmann, however, reaches the conclusion that Scandinavian artists never completely absorbed Impressionism.

Carl Fredrik Hill

There are two documents that describe how Hill was supposedly invited to exhibit his works together with the Impressionists in Paris. One is a letter from Hill to his parents in Lund, written in Paris on March 22nd, 1877.[14] The other is an undated letter from Oscar Törnå, in which Hill is described as the only Scandinavian artist "deemed worthy of belonging to" the Impressionist group and of exhibiting his work next to theirs.[15] It is, of course, impossible to know whether Hill actually received such an invitation. As far as we know, he was personally acquainted with only one of the artists who, periodically, were members of the Impressionist group—Albert Lebourg.

Hill became acquainted with Lebourg towards the end of 1876.[16] Earlier that year, Hill's painting had undergone a marked change. During his early days in Paris—Hill arrived in the autumn of 1873—he worked in the tradition of the Barbizon school, and was greatly influenced by the Hungarian painters László Paál and Mihály Munkácsy. Like, above all, Paál's landscapes, Hill's were characterized by chiaroscuro effects and frequent use of pigments mixed with bitumen. In 1876, however, his palette grew lighter. Possibly, this change was a result of Hill having viewed works by the Impressionists.[17] We know he had seen the exhibition Manet organized in his own studio that year, and that he has described Manet as the leader of the Impressionists. We also know that, in 1876, Hill exhibited a painting rejected by the Salon at the art dealer Durand-Ruel's. Durand-Ruel simultaneously showed the Impressionists' Second Exhibition.

In a letter to his parents dated June 4th, 1876, Hill wrote about Impressionism, which he considered the most "realistic" of contemporary artistic currents: "I like it. The aim is to execute just a small area of a painting and blur the rest. If such a thing were to be shown in Sweden, there would be a public outcry. But it is correct, because when one observes a large motif in nature, one's eyes can only focus on a small area at a time."[18] Thus, Hill viewed Impressionism as a form of Realism, its painting technique developed on the basis of knowledge about the problems of visual perception. The technique of blurring, thus, mimics the eye's perception of reality.

Hill's painting is related to Impressionism in several ways. The free and sketchy brush technique in some of his works is, at times, close to that of leading Impressionists in the mid- to late 1870s. Furthermore, beginning in the summer of 1876, Hill's palette turned fairly light, though he scarcely employed the bright, unmixed local colours of the Impressionists. A group of paintings from 1876–1877— the two series *River Landscape, Champagne* and *The Tree and the River (The Seine at Bois-le-Roi)*, among others—show great similarities with Pissarro's and, to some degree, Sisley's painting of the late 1860s. There are great similarities in the use of simplification in the representation of landscape forms. Fields and lawns are rendered as monochromatic planes without gradations of tone, buildings as simple geometric shapes.

178. **Camille Pissarro** (1830–1903): **Orchard with Flowering Trees, Spring, Pontoise,** 1877.
Oil on canvas, 65.5 x 81. Musée d'Orsay, Paris, legs Gustave Caillebotte, RF 2733.

109. **Carl Fredrik Hill** (1849–1911): **Apple Tree in Blossom,** 1877. Oil on canvas, 50 x 61.
Nationalmuseum, NM 1864. Gift from Friends of Art through the Director Richard Bergh 1915.

28. **Paul Cézanne** (1839–1906): **The Hanged Man's House**. Oil on canvas, 55 x 66. Musée d'Orsay, Paris; legs du comte Isaac de Camondo, 1911, RF 1970.

In a few instances a direct comparison between Hill's painting and that of Cézanne and Pissarro may be interesting. Several researchers have earlier pointed to similarities between Hill's *Farm, Champagne* of 1876 and Cézanne's *House of the Hanged Man* of 1873.[19] The motifs are conceived in a strikingly similar manner, and the compositions are reminiscent of each other. Both paintings show a farm, with only parts of the buildings being clearly visible. The distance between the viewer and the buildings is approximately the same in both works. A peculiar correspondence can be found in the two slender tree trunks growing close together in both pictures. As Sten Åke Nilsson has suggested, Hill's painting may be viewed as the mirror image of Cézanne's. However, these similarities are in all likelihood simple coincidences, and the differences in painting technique are striking. Hill employed much sharper contrasts of light and colour than Cézanne, who has enveloped his landscape in a hazy, unifying atmosphere.

Hill's relationship with the Impressionists remains unclear. He is the only Swede known to have made unreservedly positive statements about the movement in the

108. **Carl Fredrik Hill** (1849–1911): **Farm Yard, Champagne,** 1876. Oil on canvas, 58 x 69.5. Private collection.

1870s. Nevertheless, in later writings he never mentioned any of the Impressionists among the artists he confessed to admiring.[20] As previously noted by other writers, Hill's production from the years 1876–77 may be viewed as a parallel to Impressionism.[21] It may perhaps be said that, like the Impressionists, Hill chose French Realism as his starting-point, developing his technique towards a greater painterly freedom. Hill alternated between a formally severe painting very similar to Pissarro's work of the late 1860s, and a free and expressive style of painting without any readily apparent prototypes.

The 1880s: Realism and Impressionist Tendencies

The major breakthrough for a French-oriented Realist plein-air painting in Sweden occurred in the 1880s. A steadily growing number of Swedish artists were working and studying in France, and the public back home was able to view the new art at a few highly publicized exhibitions in Stockholm in 1885. By this time, Swedish painting was greatly influenced by French Realism.

During the warm part of the year, most of the Swedish painters lived in the French countryside, and in several places artists' colonies that included Swedish painters were formed. Best known is that in the small village of Grez-sur-Loing, a few miles southeast of Paris. The village was located in the forest of Fontainebleau, in the same area in which the first generation of realistically oriented French *plein-air* painters had been active a few decades earlier.

The Realist landscape painting practiced at Grez-sur-Loing is characterized by a pale palette, frequently dominated by light ochres, greys, pale blues and greens. The landscape painters were attracted by the tendency of the hazy French atmosphere to unify the colours of the landscape into an even, light tonality, without strong contrasts or clashes of colour. The motifs might seem randomly selected, the compositions often contain heavily cropped objects, and the foreground is frequently dominated by large monochromatic surfaces.

The most important prototypes for the Grez painters were, naturally, French. During the 1880s, the Scandinavian painters reserved their greatest admiration for Bastien-Lepage. He was regarded as the leading Naturalist, and his ability to combine light and pure colours with a faithful representation of reality was viewed as an ideal. Bastien-Lepage represented a middle ground between the Impressionist avant-garde and the Academists.

Several of the Swedish artists active in Grez occasionally employed a technique close to that of Impressionism. Karl Nordström is usually regarded as the artist who came closest to pure Impressionism. Richard Bergh has described how he ran into Nordström at the Impressionist Exhibition of 1882, and Nordström's great enthusiasm about what he saw there. Nordström supposedly pointed out that the Impressionists had confirmed his own view that, on a sunny day, shadows appear blue, rather than brown. According to Bergh, when Nordström moved to Grez later that spring, he seemed suddenly certain of the right path to follow. "He studied the effects of light, discovered the laws governing colour contrasts, and found that different objects in nature never acted independently of each other when enveloped by the same atmosphere, but join together to create the impression of a unified landscape." [...] "Being true to nature no longer depended on the careful rendering of details, but on the internal logic of their interrelationships. This was precisely what the Impressionists asserted. Like them, he mainly paid attention to external truth, to 'nature's moods'."[22]

In comments accompanying an inventory of his paintings from 1881–1890, Nordström himself described the importance of Impressionism for his work. The Impressionist Exhibition of 1882 supposedly offered him "more insights into the art of studying and representing Nature than any Salon." He also observed that the impact of Impressionism first became noticeable in his own work in some paintings from Tjörn, executed about a year after his visit to the 1882 exhibition.[23]

Despite this statement and Bergh's claim that Nordström began applying Impressionist ideas immediately after viewing the Impressionist Exhibition of 1882, it was not until 1884 that Nordström's colour treatment and conception of the motif really came close to Impressionism. In his painting *Garden in Grez,* he studied a motif bathed in strong sunlight, using blue shadows of the kind mentioned by

Bergh. Apart from that, however, his technique is only partly related to Impressionism. The vegetation is painted in a broad, impressionistic brush technique, but the thin metallic threads holding up the vines climbing the wall are rendered with extreme precision. In his painting *The Forest Glade*, the whole is rendered in a looser, more painterly manner, the image being constructed from innumerable light green and ochre colour dots, creating the impression of a play of light in the foliage. When the painting was shown as part of the Stockholm exhibition *From the Banks of the Seine* in the spring of 1885, Carl Rupert Nyblom criticized precisely the loose painting technique, which he felt represented Nature inaccurately. "Look at this path through the forest that resembles a poorly represented piece of lit firework, a light green 'Svärmare'—weakly coloured, in only grayish white, light green, pale mauve, and a whiff of blue, though powerful and lively in spreading its sparks, here consisting of fresh foliage encircling the core of the 'Svärmaren,' a funnel-like depth represented by the perspective rendering of the path, in youthful jubilation. That should give you an idea of this painting—but who has ever seen Nature, in the blessed spring, which poets of all ages have celebrated, appear as represented here?"[24] In a few paintings executed in Sweden towards the end of the 1880s, Nordström has reinforced the Impressionist traits. Especially his painting *View of Stockholm from Skansen* of 1889 is close to Pissarro's work from a technical point of view.

Beginning in 1882, Nils Kreuger lived periodically in Grez. His specialty was paintings of horses, executed during the 1880s in Paris, as well as in the French, and Swedish, countryside. In his paintings *Landscape from Öland. Riding Gipsy* of 1885 and *The Road to Orléans* of 1886, the artist was primarily interested in representing the horses' swift movement towards the viewer. Both pictures create a violently dynamic impression, though, in the French painting, the movement is counter-balanced by a row of trees lining the road. Fresh knowledge about the way horses move had spread during the 1880s due to Eadweard Muybridge's photographic experiments. Muybridge had managed to produce serial images of horses in rapid motion, in which each image freezes part of the movement. It is well known that Muybridge's work was important for Degas, who, at the beginning of the 1880s, changed his way of representing horses in motion to conform to the new photographs.[25] Whether Kreuger was familiar with Muybridge's photographs is not known, but his way of rendering the movement of the two horses in his *Landscape from Öland. Riding Gipsy* suggests that he had actually studied them.

Ernst Josephson was less influenced than most Swedes in the 1880s by the light-filled, gray-toned landscapes of the French *plein-air* Realists. Rather, Josephson was drawn to 17th-century Dutch and Spanish painting. In a general sense, these schools provided an important historical basis for contemporary Realism, but in Josephson's case the point of departure in 17th-century painting is especially evident. Velázquez' broad painterly technique would become especially important for the Swedish artist. Manet shared Josephson's interest in Velázquez, and this common basis might explain certain correspondences between their works.

Josephson was one of the Swedish artists whom contemporary critics associated with the Impressionists, especially with Manet.[26] However, it remains unclear to

112. **Nils Kreuger** (1858–1930): **The Road to Orléans, 1886.** Oil on canvas,
52.5 x 81. Lunds universitets konstsamling, LUK 283.

111. **Nils Kreuger** (1858–1930): **Landscape from Öland. Riding Gipsy,** 1885.
Oil on panel, 31 x 41.5. Malmö Konstmuseum, MM 28.800.

Édouard Manet, Émile Zola,
1868. Oil on canvas, 146 x 114.
Musée d'Orsay, gåva av fru
Émile Zola 1918, RF 2205.

**Ernst Josephson. Portrait of
August Hagborg,** 1882. Oil on
canvas, 82 x 100. Folkhems
Konstsamling.

Opposite page: 110. **Ernst
Josephson (1851–1906): Miss
Louise Breslau, the Artist,**
1883–84. Oil on panel, 54.5 x
44.5. Nationalmuseum, NM
2155. Gift of the Director
Hjalmar Granhult 1919 through
Nationalmusei Vänner.

what extent Josephson had studied Manet's work. In several instances one is able to discover in Josephson's work a certain kind of unconventional visual ideas and a painting technique reminiscent of Manet's. Perhaps the most obvious example is a portrait of August Hagborg, which is strikingly close to Manet's well-known portrait of Émile Zola of 1868. In both pictures, the sitter is shown in profile, holding a book, or a newspaper. These paintings typify the conception of the modern portrait, in which the sitter is depicted in his everyday environment—Hagborg is surrounded by his paintings, Zola is seated at his writing desk. One of the prerequisites for this type of portrait of a specific milieu was, of course, Zola's theory of Naturalism. It is worth noting that, from a technical point of view, Josephson's portrait is more sketchily impressionistic than Manet's.

Per Ekström developed a painting technique with definite Impressionist characteristics. His paintings are seldom dated and, consequently, it is difficult to pinpoint exactly when he began using his characteristically loose, painterly *contre-jour* technique. However, it would seem that, beginning in the mid-1880s, he developed a light-flickering technique through which the forms of nature become extremely simplified, rendered without any details.

During the 1880s Swedish art critics adopted a more positive attitude towards Impressionism than during the previous decade. In the spring of 1883 the art critic Georg Nordensvan, foremost defender of the Opponents' generation, wrote about Impressionism in the *Ny Illustrerad Tidning*.[27] He believed Swedish art had scarcely been influenced by French Impressionism at all. According to Nordensvan, Carl Skånberg and Ernst Josephson were more closely associated with the movement than other painters, but not even they employed the Impressionist technique. Nordensvan oscillated between appreciation and condemnation in his view of Im-

pressionism. He was fairly positive towards Monet's landscape painting, while being extremely critical of Renoir's figure painting. According to Nordensvan, the Impressionist technique was not at all suited to figure painting. Nordensvan concludes his article by observing that Impressionism "is a false art movement"—if taken to an extreme. On the other hand, he felt that a moderate form of Impresionism provided a good counter-weight to contemporary photographically realistic painting.

Anders Zorn

Anders Zorn is probably the Swedish painter with the largest number of works that can be described as Impressionist. After circa 1888 he developed a painting technique distinguished by a flowing painterly breadth. The feeling of being confronted with a fleeting image, a rapidly, but expertly, executed representation of a person or milieu, is especially strong with Zorn's work. An important reason why Zorn's pictures often seem like sure renderings of a moment in time is that he readily used photographs as his starting-point.[28]

Contrary to the leading Impressionists, Zorn used a subdued palette, frequently dominated by grays. He also did not usually employ colour shading. Zorn normally limited passages of brighter colour to a few simple accents, frequently in red. As a colourist he was closer to the Realists than the Impressionists.

Contemporary city life—one of the most important motifs of French Impressionism—was seldom represented by Scandinavian painters. Next to Zorn, Hugo

15. **Hugo Birger** (1854–1887): **Outside a Restaurant in the Bois de Boulogne. Study**. Oil on canvas, 33 x 52. National-museum, NM 4232.

Opposite page: 221. Anders **Zorn** (1860–1920): **Impressions de Londres**, 1890. Watercolour, 71 x 54. Göteborgs konstmuseum, GKM 2514.

220. **Anders Zorn** (1860–1920): **The Small Brewery**, 1890. Oil on canvas, 47.5x78. Nationalmuseum, NM 6875. Purchased with contribution from the Pripps Breweries.

Opposite page: 137. **Édouard Manet** (1832–1883): **Young Boy Peeling a Pear.** Oil on canvas, 85 x 71. Nationalmuseum, NM 1498. Gift from the artist Anders Zorn 1896.

Birger was the only Swedish painter who treated contemporary life in the streets and cafés of Paris more than once or twice. In Birger's version of life in the modern city, one primarily encounters elegantly dressed ladies out for a stroll, or seated at café tables. His painting technique and conception of the motif was, however, not at all Impressionist, and to find something that generally resembles Impressionism one must look at his sketches. Another artist who, to some degree, adopted the motifs of Impressionism was Georg Arsenius, whose specialty was paintings of horses. Like Degas and Manet, he frequently depicted high society life at the racetrack, but his painting technique, like Birger's, has hardly anything to do with Impressionism.

In his watercolour *Impressions de Londres*, Zorn has captured a fleeting moment in the city's traffic. A woman wearing a long, black skirt is crossing a street where a green carriage is just passing. To the right are a horse and a building, both seemingly cropped at random. The impression of a fleeting image is created by the composition, with its boldly cropped objects, as well as by the sketchy, loose painting style. Zorn creates a strong impression of movement by using two equally emphasized directions of movement. One runs parallel to the street, indicated by the carriage moving out of the picture space at the left. The other runs perpendicular to the street, set up by the woman walking into the picture space and by the darkly clad figure walking towards the viewer from the other side of the street. At the same time, Zorn provides a counter-balance for these movements in the strongly emphasized vertical and horizontal lines of the building façade, the sidewalk, and the lamppost. From the same year, 1890, we have Zorn's *View from the Skeppsholmen*

quay—one of the few Impressionist pictures of life in the streets of Stockholm (ill.
p. 27, cat.no. 222).

Like Degas, Zorn depicted working women on several occasions. Paintings
depicting heavy manual labour were, of course, also common with the Naturalists,
but Zorn's images of brewery interiors from 1890 undeniably have a strong Impressionist character. For Zorn, whose mother had worked in a brewery, the brewery milieu had strong personal associations. His representations, however, can
scarcely be understood as being critical of the dangerous working milieu and the
hard labour. Rather, his interest seems directed towards the movements of the
women and the play of light in the dimly lit interiors.[29]

Hans Henrik Brummer has compared Degas' images of women bathing with a
Zorn watercolour of his wife Emma in the bathtub, and discovered marked differences in attitude between the two painters.[30] Such differences can also be found in
a comparison between Degas' images of working women and Zorn's brewery workers. Degas' female workers are frequently represented in ugly poses. Several times he
has, for example, depicted a yawning laundress. Degas does not shy away from ugli-
ness, studying his motifs by trying out unconventional poses and movements. The
models in Zorn's pictures of working people are perhaps not beautified, but, at the
same time, nothing about them challenges traditional ideas of how women must be
depicted.

Zorn was one of the few Swedish artists who were personally acquainted with
leading figures in French art circles. He has not himself provided any detailed information about his contacts with French artists, but we know that he had contact
with, among others, Renoir and Degas.[31] Zorn also knew several other leading cultural personalities such as the actor Coquelin Cadet and the opera singer Jean-
Baptiste Faure. The latter gave Zorn Manet's painting *Young Boy Peeling a Pear*,
which Zorn subsequently donated to the Nationalmuseum in 1896.

Thus, it is only towards the end of the 1880s—at a time when Zorn is experi-
menting with an Impressionist technique—that Impressionism achieves a broader
impact on Swedish painting. Anshelm Schultzberg, Carl Johansson, Carl Trägårdh,
and Justus Lundegård were all staying in France around 1890, developing a moder-

172. **Hanna Pauli** (1864–1940): **Breakfast-Time,** 1887.
Oil on canvas, 87 x 91. Nationalmuseum, NM 1705.

120. **Carl Larsson** (1853–1919): **Girl by a Flowering Hawthorn Bush.** Watercolour och gouache, 36 x 45,5. Göteborgs konstmuseum, GKM 1259.

Opposite page: 119. **Carl Larsson** (1853–1919): **Woman Reading,** 1888. Pastel, 98.5 x 72.2. Zornsamlingarna, Mora, ZKA92.

The shimmering, loosely painted quality of this pastel painting recalls the painting of the French Impressionists, as does the motif, which is reminiscent of Renoir's many images of women reading or sewing.

ate Impressionist landscape painting, important aspects of which are a sketchy brush technique and colour shading. In the late 1880s, several artists who had previously adhered to Realism occasionally experimented with Impressionist methods. Margareta Gynning has described Hanna Pauli's *Breakfast-Time* as a painting combining a basically Realist style of painting with certain Impressionist characteristics.[32] The treatment of form and the spatial conception are rooted in a Realist tradition, while the choice of subject, the treatment of colour, and the representation of light were clearly inspired by Impressionism. It may be noted that *Breakfast-Time* received its fair share of criticism in the press. One critic believed Hanna Pauli was making fun of the audience, that it looked as if the tablecloth in the painting had been smeared with lingonberry jam and cream. Georg Nordensvan, on the other hand, came to the painting's defense: "It is a bold study, a painting filled with air and sunlight. I cannot be the judge of whether or not the play of colours is as thoroughly untrue as it has been said. It may seem exaggerated. Yet, it is certain that whoever painted this outdoors, after Nature, studied the colour effect more carefully than those who, having viewed the painting only briefly in the exhibition, declare

with certainty that a white tablecloth is white and to paint it blue and full of spots is a mistake."[33]

One may wonder why Impressionism had such limited impact on Swedish art before the late 1880s, when the movement had been in existence for about two decades and was about to be abandoned by the French avant-garde. We must first point out that the Swedish situation was in no way unique. Impressionism scarcely achieved its international breakthrough until precisely the late 1880s. It is true that, already during an early phase, a few non-French painters were working in the Impressionist style in France, but these were individual artists directly associated with members of the French Impressionist group. Among these painters were the Italians Giuseppe de Nittis and Federico Zandomeneghi, and the American Mary Cassatt. These artists were personally acquainted with one or more of the French Impressionists, and participated in the Impressionist Exhibitions.[34]

One of the most important reasons why Impressionism had such little influence on Swedish painters was undoubtedly French social conditions. A majority of Swedish painters who lived in France during the 1870s and '80s socialized primarily with their compatriots. Only a few moved in French art circles and hardly any Swedes came into contact with the Impressionists before the late 1880s. Practically all the Swedish painters tried to further their careers by receiving favourable notice at the Salon. Anyone could submit a work to the Salon, and hope for it to be accepted. For a work to be accepted, however, a certain degree of adaptability was required. Impressionism was a hotly debated movement, and whoever tried to submit an Impressionist work to the Salon ran the risk of having it rejected. The only venue for an artist who wished to work in the Impressionist style and still have the opportunity to exhibit his work was the Impressionist Exhibitions. And at the Impressionist Exhibitions only invited artists were allowed to exhibit.

Another circumstance that deserves mention is the fact that in the 1880s Impressionism was beginning to be questioned even in French avant-garde circles. At the same time, it was still an extremely radical art in the eyes of many. Consequently, there were two reasons for the Swedes to assume a cautious attitude towards the movement—a pronounced Impressionist work risked going unappreciated by both the general public and radical art circles. The avant-garde was now moving towards Synthetist forms and a stronger emphasis on content. Imagination and subjectivity were becoming increasingly important.

The Impact of French Post-Impressionism on Swedish Art of the 1890s

Swedish painting of the 1890s is generally regarded as a National Romantic reaction against the Realism of the previous decade. The so-called Varberg school is usually identified as being most typical of Swedish painting of the 1890s. The Varberg school is the name given to a group of artists, including Richard Bergh, Nils Kreuger, and Karl Nordström, who were active at Varberg during the years 1893–95. In the 1880s all three painters had adopted a basically Realist tonal painting in the French tradition, but after returning home in the late 1880s they attempted to move away from French Realism.

Two main theories are used to explain the artistic development of the Varberg school. According to one theory this development resulted from the three artists' ambition to create a national Swedish art. There was an attempt to find an appropriate visual expression for the Swedish landscape, and to represent the spirit of the Swedish artist. This theory is based on the notion that every country possesses a unique landscape and its people a unique spirit. A majority of the leading Swedish artists had lived in France for extended periods during the 1880s, where they had been taught a method suitable for representing the French landscape. It was argued that this method—Realism—could not possibly work in Sweden. According to a second theory, the art of the Varberg school is explained as the result of the three artists' encounter with the art of Gauguin and Van Gogh.[35]

The text that contributed most to the idea of Gauguin's major influence on Swedish art of the 1890s is Richard Bergh's "Karl Nordström och det moderna stämningslandskapet" ("Karl Nordström and the Modern Evocative Landscape") of 1896. Not only was Bergh's article about Nordström significant for the notion of Gauguin's important role, but it has also been interpreted as a manifesto of Swedish art of the 1890s. In Bergh's text Nordström's artistic development is described in terms of a search for an adequate visual expression for, on the one hand, his own "spirit," and, on the other, the "spirit" of the coastal landscape of Bohuslän, Nordström's native soil. According to Bergh, Nordström achieved this goal in 1893, the year in which the artists' colony at Varberg was formed.

In his article about Nordström and the evocative landscape, Bergh wrote that Nordström had first become acquainted with Gauguin's art at Copenhagen in the autumn of 1892. However, Bergh described Nordström's attitude towards Gauguin's painting as divided: "No matter how little attracted he felt to the mostly cold and empty spirit of his paintings, he still found a quality in them that appealed to him all the more as he had himself been moving in the same direction for some years. He discovered in the pictures a perfectly conscious, strictly ornamental arrangement of volumes, which gave them a highly decorative value."[36]

Thus, the weakness of Gauguin's painting was an absence of "mood," while its strength lay in its decorative qualities. According to Bergh, Gauguin's Synthetism confirmed for Nordström that his own search for a decorative art was right. However, while Gauguin, according to Bergh, employed ornamental forms solely for a decorative purpose, Nordström used decorative elements to underline what was central to his art, namely, the "mood."

Still, Gauguin was certainly not the only artist who, around 1890, was attempt-

Opposite page, above: 167. **Karl Nordström** (1855–1923): **The Varberg Fortress,** 1893. Oil on canvas, 62 x 88.5. Prins Eugens Waldemarsudde, Stockholm, W573.

Opposite page: 72. **Paul Gauguin** (1848–1903): **Landscape from Brittany,** 1889. Oil on canvas, 72.5 x 91. Nationalmuseum, NM 2156. Gift of the Director Hjalmar Granhult 1919.

171. **Georg Pauli** (1855–1935): **Sunrise, Visby,** 1894. Oil on canvas, 110 x 66. Private collection.

55. Paul Gauguin (1848–1903). **Portrait of Ingel Fallstedt**, 1877. Black chalk, 20 x 25. Göteborgs konstmuseum.

The Swedish sculptor Ingel Fallstedt was one of Paul Gauguin's many Scandinavian contacts. This drawing was executed at an early date, before Gauguin had begun his artistic career. In 1888 Gauguin contacted Fallstedt and asked for his help in organizing an Impressionist exhibition in Sweden. The exhibition was never realised.

ing to create an art with decorative qualities. Outlines emphasized for a decorative purpose, and entire planes of colour without gradations of tone, were common stylistic features of the art of the early 1890s. The artist most often cited as a precursor of this decoratively stylized painting was Pierre Puvis de Chavannes, who, in turn, was mainly inspired by 15th-century Italian painting. Even Richard Bergh admired Puvis de Chavannes. In an 1893 essay titled "Treenighet" ("Trinity"), which must also be considered representative of the theories adopted by the Varberg school, Bergh discussed three principles he considered essential to painting: the decorative, the subjective, and the objective principles. The essay is, above all, an exhortation to artists to pay more attention to the decorative principle than they had done during the period of Realism. As Björn Fredlund has observed, Bergh never mentions Gauguin or Van Gogh in this text. Rather, he points to Puvis de Chavannes as the foremost example of an artist who paid attention to the decorative principle.[37]

Yet, in examining Karl Nordström's paintings from the years 1893–95, Puvis de Chavannes' art scarcely seems the most immediate point of reference. An interest in Puvis de Chavannes' art is more evident in the paintings of Richard Bergh, Prince Eugen, and Georg Pauli. Nordström employed a more severe formal language, and did not use the pale colour scheme typical of Puvis de Chavannes. On the other hand, certain characteristics of Gauguin's painting of the late 1880s undoubtedly recur in Nordström's landscapes. The work most often held up as the starting-point for Nordström is Gauguin's *Landscape from Brittany*, which Richard Bergh purchased in Copenhagen in 1892. The painting was subsequently kept in Bergh's home in Varberg, and was, thus, accessible to members of the local artists' colony.

In some of Nordström's paintings from 1893 one becomes aware of the artist's attempt to focus on the outlines of the landscape, following Gauguin's example. The rhythmically billowing horizon line in *Storm Clouds*, and the formal reduction of a work such as *The Varberg Fortress*, might easily be derived from Gauguin's Breton landscapes. Like Gauguin, Nordström also used a coarse and abbreviated technique in order to emphasize the unity of the landscape, rather than its details. However, Nordström's goal was obviously quite different from Gauguin's. Nordström's pictures are defined by a sense of drama, monumentality, and an atmosphere most accurately described as threatening. Nordström really seems to have searched for a visual expression that corresponded to the spirit of the harsh landscape of the

Swedish west coast and perhaps—if we are to believe Bergh—an expression in tune with his own spirit.

Richard Bergh and Karl Nordström were clearly interested in Gauguin's Synthetism. But only in the decoratively stylized forms of Gauguin's work from the late 1880s, not the Primitivist, exotic painting from Tahiti. In Gauguin's work, Bergh and Nordström sought suitable visual forms for the nationally oriented evocative painting they were both striving to create. Instead of the Primitivism, critical of western civilization, represented by Gauguin's paintings from Tahiti, the Swedes were searching for a specifically Nordic visual expression, and forms capable of reflecting the artist's personality in his native landscape. One might possibly claim that Gauguin and the Varberg painters were similar in that they all sought to leave the life of the modern city behind.[38]

For Swedish artists, Gauguin was undoubtedly the most familiar of the Impressionists. The reason for this was, of course, the Scandinavian contacts Gauguin had established during his long marriage to the Dane Mette Gad, whose sister was, in turn, married to the Norwegian painter Frits Thaulow. During the 1890s, when he was associated with the circle of William Molard and Ida Ericson-Molard in Paris, Gauguin had many Swedish acquaintances.[39] The composer William Molard was raised in France, but had a Norwegian mother and spoke fluent Norwegian. The Swedish sculptress Ida Ericson had moved to Paris in the late 1880s and during the 1890s the couple's home in the rue Vercingétorix functioned as a meeting place for a wide circle of artists, musicians, and writers. In addition to Gauguin, Edvard Munch, the composer Frederick Delius, the painter and poster artist Alfons Mucha, and August Strindberg, periodically formed part of the circle.

The friendship between Gauguin and Strindberg led to an interesting collaboration, with Strindberg writing the introduction to a catalogue of Gauguin's works to be sold at auction at the Hôtel Drouot in Paris at the beginning of February 1895. Strindberg's introduction is written as an imaginary response to a request by Gauguin to write this very introduction. Initially, Strindberg wants to decline Gauguin's invitation—since he claims he does not understand Gauguin's art. Soon, however, Strindberg changes his mind. He becomes aware of something truly interesting and novel about Gauguin's art, and likens the painter to "the savage, who hates a troublesome civilization, […], who, unlike the masses, prefers to see the sky as red, rather than blue."[40]

For about six weeks at the beginning of 1894, Paul Gauguin was also the teacher of the young Helmer Osslund. Gauguin ran his small art school for a brief period, also teaching the Finnish painter Pekka Halonen. In the late 1890s, Osslund produced a few works that come very close to Gauguin's Synthetism.[41] However, Osslund later developed a personal, more expressive style, while painting the grand wilderness of Norrland.

Next to Osslund, Ivan Aguéli was the Swedish painter most closely associated with the French Synthetism of Gauguin and the Pont-Aven school. Aguéli had traveled to Paris in the spring of 1890 and, in the autumn of that year, he had become acquainted with Émile Bernard, who introduced him to Symbolist ideas and taught him Synthetist painting. The theoretically inclined young Swede seems to have

Above: 168. **Helmer Osslund** (1866–1938): **Autumn Day, Fränsta,** 1898–99. Oil on canvas, 63 x 82. Private collection.

169. **Helmer Osslund** (1866–1938): **The Son Fjeld,** 1904. Oil on canvas, 69 x 107. Göteborgs konstmuseum, GKM 2347.

Above: 192. **Olof Sager-Nelson**
(1868–1896): **The Anarchist
(The Artist Ivan Aguéli)**, 1895.
Oil on canvas, 38.5 x 61.
Värmlands museum, Karlstad,
VM.17.928.

3. Ivan Aguéli (1869–1917):
Landscape from Gotland,
1892. Oil on canvas, 55 x 34.
Sala konstförening – Aguélimuseet.

quickly become well oriented about the esoteric teachings preached by the Symbolists. From the paintings produced by Aguéli after his return to Sweden in 1891, it becomes apparent that he attempted to apply the lessons he had learnt in France. His paintings—frequently of small dimensions—are characterized by an extremely simplified formal language. The process of formal reduction in these works is based on French Synthetism's treatment of forms, but the aim does not seem to be to create a decorative effect. Rather, it would seem that Aguéli was searching for some basic constructive principles for his painting. An instructive example is *Motif from Visby*. The forms in the lower half of the picture are perceived as land, the pale yellowish area over the horizon is probably a hazy sky, while the area at the top, shaped like a wave, must be perceived as clouds. The grayish-blue area at the extreme right might also be interpreted as the surface of the sea, with a sharply drawn horizon line. The anti-naturalist colours and the absence of any gradations of tone, however, make it difficult to interpret the remaining forms in the lower half of the picture. Aguéli probably based his representation on the shapes of small trees, shrubs, and cliffs, but all forms are simplified and located in the surface plane so that it becomes impossible to interpret them clearly as a landscape. The vol-

4. **Ivan Aguéli** (1869–1917): **Motif from Visby**, 1892. Oil on canvas,
50 x 90.5. Moderna Museet, Stockholm, NM 2381.

1. **Ivan Aguéli** (1869–1917):
Egyptian Woman, early 1890s.
Oil on canvas, 41 x 33. Moderna
Museet, Stockholm, MOM 839.

umes of natural forms are transformed into planes that together form a pattern on
the surface of the painting. As opposed to a majority of Swedish landscape painters
during the 1890s, Aguéli was completely uninterested in discovering a specific visual expression for national, or regional, characteristics.

Aguéli eventually became both an anarchist and a practicing Muslim. In 1893 he
traveled to Egypt, where he also painted some remarkable and radically simplified
pictures. One of the most peculiar of these represents an Egyptian woman with a
rough-hewn face and black eye-sockets. Years later, Aguéli would formulate his
views on art in an essay titled "L'Art pure," published in the journal *La Gnose. L'art
pure* signified for Aguéli an absolute emphasis on form, based on notions of har-

Above: 5. **Ivan Aguéli** (1869–1917): **Summer Evening (Landscape)**, 1892. Oil on canvas, 45 x 65. Stockholms stad, 103–0834.

193. **Olof Sager-Nelson** (1868–1896): **La Porte St. Croix, Bruges.** Oil on panel, 24.5 x 32.5. Göteborgs konstmuseum, GKM 543.

In the autumn of 1894 Olof Sager-Nelson went to Paris where he got in contact with symbolist circles. In some landscapes from Bruges 1894 he developed a style which obviously was influenced by Gauguin's Synthetism.

monious proportions and the ability of colour and light to create planes and volumes in a picture. All literary or narrative aspects were repudiated.

Aguéli was presumably the only Swedish artist to take a certain interest in Cézanne's painting before 1900. Through his acquaintance with Émile Bernard he would have been aware of Cézanne's views on art at an early date, as Bernard was a great admirer of Cézanne. Cézanne was otherwise little known in Sweden prior to the great commemorative exhibition of his work at the Autumn Salon in Paris in 1907. One of the Swedes who visited the 1907 exhibition was Gösta Sandels.[42] However, one scarcely finds any Swedish art directly inspired by Cézanne until after 1910, in the work of Karl Isakson and Leander Engström, among others.

That Gauguin and the Synthetism of the Pont-Aven school had a significant influence on a number of Swedish artists is, thus, well documented. Traces of Van Gogh's influence are considerably less evident in the 1890s. The extent of Van Gogh's influence on Nils Kreuger is a frequently discussed topic. In Kjell Boström's 1948 monograph about Kreuger, the artist's change of styles around 1893 is explained by his having viewed works by Van Gogh.[43] Kreuger's potential interest in Van Gogh is, however, not confirmed by letters or other documents from the 1890s. Furthermore, it is uncertain whether Kreuger actually viewed the great exhibition of Van Gogh and Gauguin organized in connection with The Free Exhibition at Copenhagen in the spring of 1893. Proof of Van Gogh's influence on Kreuger has, instead, been sought in Kreuger's paintings and drawings.

Possibly, Van Gogh's *Landscape from Saint-Rémy (ill. p. 191)*, exhibited in Copenhagen in 1893, influenced Kreuger's treatment of clouds in his painting *Hailstorm, Apelvik* of 1893. The differences between the two paintings are otherwise quite striking. Unlike Van Gogh, Kreuger did not use impasto, or extremely bright colours. However, the similarities between Van Gogh and Kreuger become more evident when one compares Van Gogh's late style of draughtmanship with some of Kreuger's painting from 1893 and 1894. At that time, Kreuger was developing a unique technique, which consisted of drawing a pattern of lines and dots in ink on top of the painted surface. This drawing technique greatly resembles Van Gogh's way of using lines and dots to build up his landscape drawings.

It is, however, difficult to know whether Kreuger had actually seen drawings by Van Gogh by the time he started to develop this new technique. In addition to the Copenhagen exhibition of 1893—as mentioned earlier, we do not know whether Kreuger actually saw it—one has referred to a series of photographs of works by Van Gogh and Cézanne supposedly available in Sweden at an early date. These photographs were supposedly brought back from France by Ivan Aguéli in the spring of 1891, and were probably shown to several Swedish artists. In all likelihood, none of the photographs showed any drawings by Van Gogh—only paintings.[44] The significance of these photographs has been discussed in several different contexts. Still, one might wonder just how inspiring a series of black-and-white photographs of Van Gogh's paintings could possibly be.

Not until a few years after 1900 do we find clear evidence of Van Gogh's influence on Swedish art. Axel Törneman had studied with Carl Wilhelmson at the Valand Art School in Gothenburg, and in 1910 he traveled to Munich to continue

Above: 114. **Nils Kreuger**
(1858–1930): **Evening
before the Storm,
September.** Oil on canvas,
62,5 x 93. Per Ekström-
museet, Mörbylånga.

113. **Nils Kreuger** (1858–
1930): **After the Hail Storm,
Halland,** 1892. Oil on canvas,
48 x 67. Länsmuseet Gävleborg. Gift from Lars Matton,
Gävle, 1941, GM 8502.

207. **Axel Törneman** (1880–1925): **The Farmer from Brittany,** 1905. Oil on canvas, 90 x 83. Vår Gård Kursgården AB, Saltsjöbaden.

206. **Axel Törneman** (1880–1925): **Self-Portait with Still Life,** 1904. Oil on canvas, 61.5 x 50.5. Moderna Museet, Stockholm, NM 6160.

his studies there. During the period 1902–1905 he resided mainly in France. Six drawings by Törneman were exhibited at the Independents' Salon in the spring of 1905, and the exhibition also included an extensive commemorative exhibit of Van Gogh's oeuvre. Judging by Törneman's work from the summer of 1905, he had thoroughly examined Van Gogh's painting technique. During that summer Törneman was staying in the Breton village of St. Jean de Doight. Here he executed his painting *The Farmer from Brittany*, a work reminiscent of both Gauguin and Van Gogh. In the manner of Van Gogh, Törneman has applied his colours in marked rhythmical parallel loops. Like Van Gogh, he also used bright local colours.

Interest in Neo-Impressionism, and the Divisionist technique developed by George Seurat in the mid-1880s, was very limited in Scandinavia. Only in Finland, where Alfred William Finch introduced Neo-Impressionism in the late 1890s, was the Divisionist technique actually practiced. Swedish interest in Neo-Impressionism was insignificant.

One of the few Swedish examples of the use of the Divisionist technique is Prince Eugen's *The Temple of Happiness* of 1892. At the beginning of the 1890s, Eugen had also begun to search for alternatives to Realism, showing an interest in Puvis de Chavannes and Arnold Böcklin, and creating images imbued with an atmosphere of loneliness and melancholy. Like Bergh, Kreuger, and Nordström, Eugen often depicted the dim light at dusk. In a letter to Helena Nyblom, Prince Eugen has described his work with *The Temple of Happiness*: "I join together all the colours of life, unmixed and side by side, but in such a way that they form a shimmering, harmonious whole, a gleaming golden temple dreaming on a quiet, quivering evening, sheltered by some mighty pines."[45] The work was painted at the Palace of Ulriksdal, and the temple itself was intended for the Prince's close friends Ellen Nyblom and Theodor Lundberg, who had just celebrated their engagement. Hans Henrik Brummer has suggested that the ideas on which Eugen based his Divisionist colour experiments may have been derived from Goethe's colour theory. However that may be, Eugen's ideas recall Symbolist notions about the correspondences between different colours and emotional states.[46]

It must be observed that Eugen's painting technique is closer to that of Henri Martin than to Seurat and Signac. Martin depicted a twilight atmosphere more frequently than did the pioneers of Neo-Impressionism and, furthermore, his colour accents were not as strong. Like Eugen, Henri Martin combined a painting technique influenced by Neo-Impressionism with influences clearly derived from Puvis de Chavannes' images, predominantly balanced Classicizing compositions based on 15th-century Italian frescoes. Prince Eugen might possibly have conceived the idea for his experiments with a Divisionist technique during a visit to Paris in the spring of 1892. At that time, Henri Martin was showing his Divisionist paintings at the Salon. When Georg Pauli mentioned Martin's Divisionism in an essay about the Paris Salon of 1892 in the journal of art and literature *Ord och Bild*, he especially noted that Martin had abandoned the academic style of his teacher J.P. Laurens for a Pointillist technique.[47]

In the same year that Prince Eugen painted *The Temple of Happiness*, Richard Bergh published his essay "Intensitet och harmoni" ("Intensity and Harmony"), based on observations made at an exhibition of Erik Werenskiold's paintings at Stockholm. The essay, however, deals primarily with Divisionist colour theory and the optical mixing of pigments. For example, Bergh refers to Michel Eugène Chevreul's colour experiments, but also mentions a new art movement based on the Impressionist technique of placing pure, unmixed colours side by side. Rather than capturing a fleeting impression, the new movement was, according to Bergh, primarily concerned with achieving a balance between the various components of a painting in order to create a harmonious whole. Bergh speaks of "the calculated impression," which replaces "the direct, unanalyzed impression." Although the text does not specifically state which artists were the representatives of the new artistic current, Bergh evidently feels that Werenskiold's art is closely related to it. However, he is clearly referring either to the Neo-Impressionists, headed by Seurat, or their followers.

In the same way that the influence of Impressionism on Swedish painting has often been exaggerated in earlier Swedish art historical writings, the major Post-

47. **Prins Eugen** (1865–1947): **The Tempel of Happiness**, 1892. Oil and tempera
on canvas, 71 x 72. Prins Eugens Waldemarsudde, Stockholm, WE64.

Impressionist artists have also been assigned greater importance for Swedish painting than is warranted. For example, it may be mentioned that Sixten Strömbom explained the comparatively intense colour scheme of Prince Eugen's *The Old Castle* as the result of Van Gogh's influence.[48]

Exhibitions

It was not until the late 1890s that works of French Impressionism and Post-Impressionism were publicly exhibited in Sweden. The greatest event was the General Exhibition of Arts and Industry at Stockholm in 1897. The art section comprised more than 1800 works from approximately fifteen countries and the contents were highly varied. The Swedish section was naturally the largest, followed by the Norwegian and Danish sections. The French section included works by 22 artists representing quite different artistic currents. Impressionism was represented by Monet and Pissarro, showing, respectively, six and three paintings. Four of Monet's paintings had been executed during his stay in Norway in 1895. Post-Impressionism was represented by Paul Gauguin. However, his two paintings, both from Tahiti, were finally not exhibited, possibly due to the protests of Georg von Rosen, a member of the exhibition committee.[49]

In the year following the great Exhibition of Arts and Industry, the poet and art critic Julien Leclercq organized an exhibition of contemporary French art, which

103. **Vincent van Gogh** (1853–1890): **The Road Menders.** Oil on canvas, 73.6 x 92.7. The Phillips Collection, Washington, D.C., 0799.

This painting—or a work with an almost identical subject, now in The Cleveland Museum of Art—was exhibited at the exhibition of French art which was shown in Stockholm, Gothenburg, Copenhagen and Christiania (Oslo) in 1898.

traveled to Christiania, Copenhagen, Stockholm, and Gothenburg. The exhibition included 116 items, and among the exhibited works were paintings by Denis, Gauguin, Guillaumin, Raffaëlli, Ranson, Van Gogh, and Vuillard, and prints by Cross, Cézanne, Redon, and Sisley.

The exhibition was apparently a financial disaster for the organizer Leclercq. It did, however, receive a fair amount of attention in the press, not all of it negative. Most admired was Aman-Jean's fashionably elegant portrait of his wife. Most hotly debated were undoubtedly the works submitted by Gauguin and Van Gogh. Above all, Gauguin's paintings from Tahiti and two paintings by Van Gogh, a male portrait and a street scene, gave rise to protest.[50] One of the most agitated critics was Herman Anakreon Ring, who, in the daily *Nya Dagligt Allehanda*, described Gauguin's and Van Gogh's paintings as "sickly, bizarre pictures poking fun at the public."[51] As had already happened at the great Exhibition of Arts and Industry the previous year, one of Gauguin's paintings was considered so offensive that it was never included in the exhibition. This was the so-called *Apparition* (Tahiti 1892), a work no doubt identical with *Manao Tupapau* (The Spirit of the Dead Watches W 457), now in the Albright Knox Art Gallery in Buffalo. As opposed to most critics,

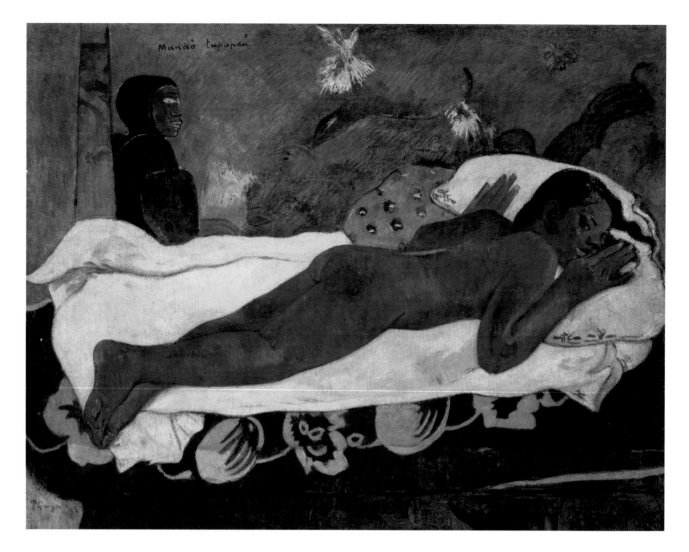

Above: **Paul Gauguin** (1848–1903): **Manao Tupapau (The Spirit of the Dead Watching),** 1892. Oil on canvas, 73 x 92. Albright Knox Art Gallery, Buffalo, New York, A. Conger Goodyear Collection, 1965.

Paul Gauguin (1848–1903): **Te tamari no atua (The Birth of Christ),** 1896. Oil on canvas, 96 x 128. Bayerische Staatsgemäldesammlungen, München.

The painting is included in the catalogue of the major Exhibition of Art and Industry at Stockholm in 1897, but was never actually shown in the exhibition. Probably, Georg von Rosen, a member of the exhibition committee, had objected to Gauguin's contribution, whereupon the painting was rejected. However, the following year the painting was included in the major ambulating exhibition of French art organized by Julien Leclercq, which traveled to Stockholm, Gothenburg, Copenhagen, and Christiania.

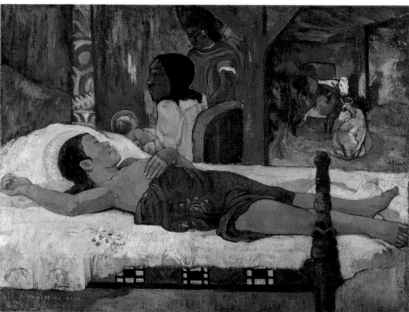

John Kruse and Gustaf Uddgren wrote highly appreciatively of Gauguin's paintings from Tahiti. Kruse lamented the fact that *Apparition* was never shown to the public, since, in his opinion, the painting was the best work submitted by Gauguin. What Kruse most appreciated about the Tahiti paintings was their luminous colours and decorative qualities.[52]

Impressionism and Post-Impressionism in the Collections of Swedish Art Museums

Like a majority of European national art museums, the Nationalmuseum in Stockholm generally did not acquire any French avant-garde art before 1900.[53] The first acquisition of an Impressionist painting by the French state occurred in 1888, but it was not until Gustave Caillebotte's donation to the French state was put on display at the Musée du Luxembourg in 1897 that a collection of Impressionist paintings was permanently exhibited in Paris. Those interested in viewing Impressionist painting had previously had to rely on temporary exhibitions and those art dealers—principally Durand-Ruel—who sold Impressionist art. In Europe outside of France, German museums were the first to purchase more than the occasional French avant-garde work. Leading the way was the Nationalgalerie in Berlin, which in 1896, under the directorship of Hugo Von Tschudi, began investing ambitiously in Impressionist painting.[54]

Apart from Manet's *Young Boy Peeling a Pear*, which Anders Zorn had received as a gift from the opera singer Jean-Baptiste Faure, and had subsequently donated to the Nationalmuseum, there were no Impressionist paintings in the Museum's collections. On the whole, few foreign works were acquired before the 1910s. However, in connection with the major Exhibition of Arts and Industry at Stockholm in 1897, a modest campaign was launched. In retrospect, the selection of works from the foreign section of the exhibition may seem peculiar. Although Impressionism had, by the late 1890s, gained fairly wide acceptance, none of the French Impressionist works in the exhibition were purchased. Instead of works by Monet and Pissarro, the Museum purchased a Realist painting by Raffaëlli and a landscape by Émile René Ménard. Perhaps it was the high prices fetched by Monet's paintings that discouraged any acquisitions. Monet's paintings were among the most expensive in the French section.

It is worth noting that the few French paintings acquired by the Nationalmuseum during this period display qualities reminiscent of contemporary Scandinavian art. Raffaëlli's *Sailors from the North* closely resembles Scandinavian Realist paintings, while Ménard's *Solitude* recalls a type of Symbolist "evocative landscapes" with figures produced in the 1890s by, among others, Richard Bergh and Georg Pauli. Lucien Simon's *Conversation at Twilight*, purchased by the Museum in 1902, has the same Nordic appeal.

A combination of different factors led to the expansion of the collection of contemporary French art during the 1910s and '20s. Richard Bergh, and the rapid transformation of the Museum that he carried out, played a major role in this. Bergh was well oriented about the latest international developments in the field of curatorial work. He had studied the museology and exhibition methods that had emerged around 1900, and had primarily been inspired by the pedagogical ideas and lighting technology developed by Alfred Lichtwark at the Hamburger Kunsthalle. In his essay "Konstmuseet som skönhetsvärld" ("The Art Museum as a Universe of Beauty") published in the journal of art and literature *Ord och Bild* in 1915, Bergh formulated his ideas. Bergh wanted to emphasize aesthetic values more than he felt had been done previously. Art to be exhibited at the Museum should be selected based on aesthetic quality, and art of a lesser quality should be put into storage. This would result in a less dense and more distinguished display.

As regards new acquisitions, Bergh primarily worked towards expanding the collection of works by his own generation of Swedish artists, but he also attempted to build up the collection of contemporary French art. In March of 1913 Bergh was hired by the Museum as an Adjunct Director, and on April 1st, 1915, he was appointed Director. However, even before Bergh assumed his position, the Assistant Curator Axel Gauffin had taken the initiative to acquire several Impressionist works. The founding of the Association of Friends of the Nationalmuseum in 1911 was, of course, highly significant in this context. The Association was founded at the initiative of Thorsten Laurin and the Crown Prince Gustaf Adolf, and for Laurin, a great francophile, it was only natural to search for new acquisitions among the French works offered for sale.

The new acquisitions policy, however, also depended on new attitudes in Swedish art circles generally. The attitudes towards art of the younger generation of artists and art critics were completely different from those that had prevailed at the Nationalmuseum in previous years. At the end of 1910 Birger Simonsson launched a verbal attack on the Museum. Simonsson claimed that acquisitions of Swedish, as

Lucien Simon (1861–1945): **Talking in the Twilight.** Oil on canvas, 140 x 190. Nationalmuseum, NM 1601.

Opposite page: 39. **Edgar Degas** (1834–1917): **Lady in Black.** Oil on canvas, 60 x 51. Nationalmuseum, NM 1759. Gift from Nationalmusei Vänner 1913.

69. **Paul Gauguin** (1848–
1903): **Landscape from Arles,**
1888. Oil on canvas, 72.5 x 92.
Nationalmuseum, NM 1735.

Gauguin's *Landscape from
Arles* was the first work by an
Impressionist artist purchased
by the Nationalmuseum. The
painting was acquired by the
Museum in 1911, but had been
in Sweden since 1893, when it
was purchased by the newspaper editor Fredrik Vult von
Steijern in connection with being
shown at the major exhibition of
works by Gauguin and Van
Gogh in Copenhagen.

well as foreign, art had been seriously neglected during the previous decades. As
regards foreign art, he primarily wished to see Gauguin, Van Gogh, and Cézanne
represented in the Museum collection. The criticism intensified following the return
of the Director of the Nationalmuseum, Ludvig Looström, from an acquisitions trip
to Germany in the autumn of 1911. On this trip Looström had purchased Max
Liebermann's *Rider on the Beach* and Mihály Munkácsys *Self-Contempt*. Simonsson wrote: "Michael de Munkacsy was never anything but an empty decorative painter and, consequently, he has been reduced to his true worth everywhere
else in Europe: now he is ready for the Swedish Nationalmuseum. Max Liebermann
is, and will always remain, a third-rate Manet, despite his efforts to avoid bitumen."[55]

However, in 1911 the Museum purchased its first work by an artist from the
Impressionist group. This was Gauguin's *Landscape from Arles*, a painting owned
by the newspaper editor Fredrik Vult von Steijern.[56] The painting had been exhibited at The Free Exhibition in Copenhagen in 1893, and Vult von Steijern had presumably purchased it in connection with the exhibition.

It is interesting to note that precisely the three artists championed by Birger
Simonsson—Cézanne, Gauguin, and Van Gogh—were now beginning to be re-

199. **Alfred Sisley** (1839–1899): **On the Shores of Loing,** 1896. Oil on canvas, 54 x 65. Nationalmuseum, NM 1770. Gift from Nationalmusei Vänner 1913.

garded as the three major precursors of modern art. Generally held notions about the starting-point and artistic roots of Modernism basically assume their final shape around 1910. These notions were cemented in John Rewald's volumes about mid-19th-century Impressionism and Post-Impressionism.

Above all, Julius Meier-Graefe's writings about modern art, and the exhibition of Manet and the Post-Impressionists organized in London by Roger Fry, had a decisive influence on the ideas and terminology formulated around 1910. Meier-Graefe introduced a formal-aesthetic history of artistic development, in which all narrative and literary-oriented art was viewed as reactionary. His violent critical assault on Arnold Böcklin is well known, and presumably exerted a major influence on the negative evaluation of late 19th-century literary-oriented Symbolism that was predominant during the 20th century. The term Post-Impressionism was coined by Roger Fry's exhibition title. The exhibition was shown at the Grafton Galleries from November of 1910 until January of 1911, and Swedish critics used the term Post-Impressionism by as early as February of 1911.[57]

In 1913 the Nationalmuseum acquired no less than four works by French Impressionists. Three of these—Alfred Sisley's *On the Shores of Loing*, and Degas' two paintings *Lady in Black* and *Two Dancers*—were gifts from the Association of Friends. The fourth work was Renoir's *Young Parisian Woman*, which, like the two paintings by Degas, came from the Wagram Collection in Paris.

The Association of Friends donated yet another foreign work in 1914. This was a painting titled *The Cornshocks*, which Axel Gauffin had discovered at the Parisian

Above: 40. **Edgar Degas** (1834–1917): **Three Russian Dancers.** Pastel, 62 x 67.
Nationalmuseum, NMB 380.

Opposite page: 41. **Edgar Degas** (1834–1917): **Two Dancers.** Pastel, 63 x 54.
Nationalmuseum, NMB 345. Gift from Nationalmusei Vänner 1913.

art dealer Paul Rosenberg's. The painting was attributed to Van Gogh, but its authenticity has been questioned on several occasions. After a technical examination of the painting by the Conservation Department of the French Art Museums in 1999, it is now evident that this is not an authentic work by Van Gogh.[58]

Under the directorship of Richard Bergh, the Nationalmuseum continued to expand its collection of foreign art during the 1910s, in the midst of World War I. Bergh made his own contribution by donating a series of eight woodcuts from Gauguin's so-called *Noa Noa* series in 1915. Degas' *Three Russian Dancers* and Cézanne's *Landscape* were acquired in Berlin in 1916, and later that year the Norwegian artist and collector Walther Halvorsen offered to buy Renoir's *Conversation*. The painting was added to the Museum collection in 1918, after Conrad Pineus and G.A. Kyhlberger had contributed funds for its purchase.[59]

As a result of the ongoing war the Swedish economy grew stronger in relation to

185. **Auguste Renoir** (1841–1919): **Girl in a Spanish Jacket,** 1900 ca. Oil on canvas, 56 x 46. Göteborgs konstmuseum, GKM 585.

Opposite page: 131. **Édouard Manet** (1832–1883): **A Parisian Lady.** Oil on canvas, 192 x 125. Nationalmuseum, NM 2068. Gift from a consortium 1917.

those of the warring countries. The wholesale merchant Axel Beskow felt the situation should be exploited, and he made a proposal to Bergh capable of greatly increasing the Nationalmuseum's holdings of foreign art. A consortium was formed for the purpose of financing a large number of acquisitions in the countries at war. Richard Bergh and Axel Gauffin selected the works in consultation with Beskow. The Museum reserved the right to select art for the equivalent of 10% of the total value of all acquisitions. The remainder of the purchased works would go to those who had financed the project.[60] Three acquisitions trips were financed by similar consortiums in 1917 and 1918, resulting in the acquisition of three new Impressionist works for the Museum collection: Manet's *A Parisian Lady*, Monet's *View over the Sea*, and Pissarro's *Landscape from Pontoise*. These journeys did not otherwise center on the acquisition of 19th-century French art. A large number of the acquisitions were older Italian, Dutch, and English works.

83. **Paul Gauguin** (1848–1903): **Composition with Figures and a Horse ("Changement de résidence")**, 1902. Oil on canvas, 28 x 45.5. Nationalmuseum, NM 2322. Gift in accordance with to the will of Miss Esther Lindahl 1921.

The Nationalmuseum's collection of 19th-century French art thus acquired its present make-up during the 1910s. One could say that Richard Bergh's efforts were founded on deep insights and an acute feeling for aesthetic quality when it comes to French painting of the late 19th century, and that, contrary to his predecessors, he was capable of making the right choices. However, Bergh was active at a time when French Impressionism and Post-Impressionism were already part of the past. Modernist art history writing, which had emerged after circa 1900, had proclaimed the leading Impressionists, together with Cézanne, Gauguin, and Van Gogh, the most important artists of the late 19th century. By the 1910s Bergh already possessed a key to history that facilitated his work. Had he been appointed Director of the Nationalmuseum as early as 1893, he would surely have chosen works by Cazin and Puvis de Chavannes rather than—or possibly, in addition to—paintings by Degas, Van Gogh, and Renoir.

The Art Museum of Gothenburg acquired its first French Impressionist works when Pontus Fürstenberg's art collection came into the Museum's possession following his death in 1902. Axel Romdahl later directed the Museum for an extended period, for 40 years beginning in 1906. Through his efforts, a top quality collection of international art was assembled, in which French Impressionism and Post-Impressionism played an important role. The first of these acquisitions made during Romdahl's directorship occurred in 1917, when three paintings were purchased from Bernheim-Jeune in Paris.[61] These were Van Gogh's *Olive Grove, Saint-Rémy*, Renoir's *Girl in a Spanish Jacket*, and Bonnard's *The Hunt*.

90. **Paul Gauguin** (1848–1903): **Noa Noa (Fragrance).** Woodcut, 35.5 x 20.5. National-museum, NMG 614/1915. Gift from the Director Richard Bergh 1915.

17. **Pierre Bonnard** (1867–1947): **The Hunt**, 1908 ca. Oil on canvas, 110 x 127. Göteborgs konstmuseum, GKM 586.

Opposite page: 18. **Pierre Bonnard** (1867–1947): **Interior with a Woman in a Wicker Chair**, 1920. Oil on canvas, 72 x 51. Nationalmuseum, NM 2733. Gift 1929 from Föreningen för inköp av svensk och fransk konst.

Several private art collectors in Gothenburg contributed to the expansion of the collection through gifts of a number of important works. Among these collectors should be mentioned, first and foremost, the shipping magnate Werner Lundqvist and the industrialist Gustaf Werner. Gustaf Werner's contribution to the collection of French Impressionism and Post-Impressionism consisted of Monet's *Village Street, Vétheuil*, and Cézanne's *The Avenue*, previously part of Gauguin's art collection at Copenhagen.

Werner Lundqvist's contribution was unusual. At the time of his donation, in 1918, of works previously acquired from Ole Kruse and Ivar Arosenius, Lundqvist also entered into an agreement with the Museum. According to this agreement, Lundqvist would continue to build up a collection at the Art Museum of Gothenburg. Lundqvist's acquisitions were to be made in consultation with the Museum. Acquisitions of primarily Scandinavian art continued, but as early as 1918

180. **Camille Pissarro** (1830–1903): **Landscape, Bazincourt**, 1881.
Oil on canvas, 65 x 81.5. Göteborgs konstmuseum, GKM WL34.

98. Vincent van Gogh (1853–1890): **Olive Grove, Saint-Rémy,** 1889.
Oil on canvas, 74 x 93. Göteborgs konstmuseum, GKM 590.

198. **Alfed Sisley** (1839–1899): **Seine by Saint-Cloud,** 1877. Oil on canvas,
38.5 x 46. Göteborgs konstmuseum, GKM WL35.

63. **Paul Gauguin** (1848–1903): **Marine**, 1886. Oil on canvas, 71 x 92.
Göteborgs konstmuseum, GKM WL19.

30. **Paul Cézanne** (1839–1906): **Landscape**. Oil on canvas, 73 x 92.
Nationalmuseum, NM 1999. Gift from Nationalmusei Vänner 1916.

143. **Claude Monet** (1840–1926): **View over the Sea**, 1882. Oil on canvas,
64 x 82. Nationalmuseum, NM 2122. Gift from a consortium 1919.

several French works were added to the Museum's Lundqvist Collection—Bonnard's *Artist's Model*, Gauguin's *Marine*, Pissarro's *Landscape, Bazincourt*, and Sisley's *Seine by Saint-Cloud*.[62]

Private Collections

None of the Swedish collections of French Impressionism and Post-Impressionism assembled during the years 1880–1930 were nearly as extensive as the largest Danish and Norwegian collections. Most Swedish art collectors concentrated on Swedish painting. However, some of them made the occasional French acquisition.

Pontus Fürstenberg assembled the first really major collection of late 19th—century Swedish art at Gothenburg. Having bought some paintings by Swedish "Düsseldorfers" in the 1870s, in the 1880s Fürstenberg instead began collecting primarily Swedish painting by artists working in the French Realist tradition. He patronized the younger Opponents' generation both through the acquisition of artworks and through direct financial support. During the 1880s he assembled the most representative collection in the country of works by artists who were members of the Konstnärsförbundet (Artists' Union). His collection included key works by, among others, Carl Larsson, Anders Zorn, Bruno Liljefors, Ernst Josephson, Richard Bergh, and Karl Nordström.

However, Fürstenberg also purchased some non-Scandinavian art. Principally French artists came to be represented in the collection. His acquisitions from the 1880s and '90s give the impression of a fairly wide focus, ranging from the principal

work of the French collection, Raphaël Collin's painting *Summer*—truly a prime example of academic nude painting—to a winter landscape by Paul Gauguin. Four acquisitions from around 1890 may be described as Impressionist or Post-Impressionist works. These included two Impressionist landscapes by Albert Lebourg, purchased in Paris in 1887, Raffaëlli's *Parisian Boulevard*, acquired in 1889, and the above mentioned winter landscape by Gauguin, probably acquired in Copenhagen in 1892 from Mette Gauguin. Through these acquisitions Fürstenberg actually becomes the first collector in the country to purchase French Impressionist paintings, though neither Lebourg nor Raffaëlli today count among the major Impressionists. Both had, however, participated in the Impressionist Exhibitions.

The second major Swedish private collector can be found in Stockholm. The banker Ernest Thiel began collecting art in the late 1890s, partly with the same focus as Fürstenberg's. Ernst Josephson, Bruno Liljefors, Carl Larsson, and Anders Zorn were well represented also in Thiel's collection. However, this collection, eventually housed in a large villa on Djurgården designed by Ferdinand Boberg in 1904, included more of Swedish turn-of-the-century evocative painting than Für-stenberg's. Furthermore, his foreign acquisitions were of an entirely different nature. Most remarkable was, of course, Thiel's extraordinary collection of works by Edvard Munch. He did, however, purchase an additional few works by French artists. A painting by Van Gogh, purchased in Berlin in 1905, was the first Swedish-owned work by this artist.[63] Thiel lost his entire fortune at the time of the great stock market crash following World War I, and in 1924 the Swedish state purchased the building which housed his art gallery and collection. The collection has been accessible to the general public since 1926.

Slightly younger than Thiel was Klas Fåhræus, who would, similarly, house his collection in an enormous villa and adjoining art gallery. The villa, known as Villa Högberga, was designed by Carl Westman and built on Lidingö in 1911. Fåhræus was a close friend of several artists of the Opponents' generation and a number of the country's leading cultural personalities. He was also active as an art critic and

70. **Paul Gauguin** (1848–1903): **Winter Landscape,** 1888. Oil
on canvas, 72.5 x 92. Göteborgs konstmuseum, GKM F29.

Pontus Fürstenberg probably purchased this painting from Paul
Gauguin's wife Mette in Copenhagen in the autumn of 1892.

182. **J.F. Raffaëlli** (1850–1924): **Boulevard in Paris.** Tempera on cardboard,
50.5 x 67. Göteborgs konstmuseum, GKM F130.

When acquired by Pontus Fürstenberg in 1889, this Parisian motif by Raffaëlli was
one of the first French Impressionist works in Swedish possession.

Vincent van Gogh (1853–1890): **Wheat Field with Poppies**, 1889. Oil on canvas, 73.5 x 92,5. Národní galerie, Prague, O 3208.

This painting was acquired by Ernest Thiel in Berlin in 1905, becoming the first Van Gogh painting in Swedish possession.

must definitely be considered one of the most initiated of the great Swedish art collectors of this period. Indeed, there can be no doubt that his collection of French art was the most distinguished in the country.

Most of Fåhræus' acquisitions of French art were probably made during the first half of the 1910s. The collection included three paintings by Cézanne, three drawings by Van Gogh, and individual paintings by Degas, Manet, Monet, and Renoir.[64] After a period of financial problems in the mid-1920s, Fåhræus was forced to sell most of his art collection. Several of the most important works—Cézanne's *Still-Life with Statuette*, Monet's landscape, and Renoir's tavern scene—were then acquired by the Nationalmuseum with financial assistance from the Association of Friends. The remainder of the French works ended up in foreign collections.

Next to Thiel and Fåhræus, Prince Eugen was the most important collector of late 19th-century painting in Stockholm at the beginning of the 20th century. His art collection included mostly works by his Scandinavian artist friends, and one is forced to conclude, with some astonishment, that he acquired very little of French avant-garde art. The Prince had a hand in ensuring that Monet, Pissarro, and Gauguin

152. **Berthe Morisot** (1841–1895): **In the Bois de Boulogne.** Oil on canvas, 61 x 73.5. Nationalmuseum, NM 5525. Gift from C.B. Nathorst through Nationalmusei Vänner 1960.

This painting was one of the few French Impressionist works in Thorsten Laurin's extensive art collection, which was largely dominated by late 19th-century Swedish art.

were represented at the Stockholm Exhibition of 1897, but he never acquired works by these painters himself.[65]

Among the other collectors should be mentioned Thorsten Laurin in Stockholm and Conrad Pineus in Gothenburg. Both were mainly interested in Swedish art, but also purchased some French works. Laurin collected primarily 19th-century Swedish art, and his collection of works by members of the Konstnärsförbundet (Artists' Union) was among the foremost in the country. Among the foreign works in the collection were a chalk drawing by Degas, Berthe Morisot's *In the Bois de Boulogne*, and several smaller canvases by Renoir.[66]

The average adjuster Pineus became known primarily for his large collection of contemporary art, in which Gösta Sandels was prominently represented. However, in the 1910s Pineus made some spectacular acquisitions of French art. In connection with a major exhibition of French art in Copenhagen in the summer of 1914, he purchased Pissarro's splendid *Pont-Neuf* of 1901. A few years into the 1920s, Pineus was forced to sell his French art collection for financial reasons. Included in a list of works he planned to sell in 1923–24 are 17 French works.[67] Among these were paint-

To the right: **Camille Pissarro** (1830–1903): **Pont Neuf, Afternoon, Sunshine,** 1901. Oil on canvas, 73 x 92. Philadelphia Museum of Art.

Opposite page: 151. **Claude Monet** (1840–1926): **From the Mouth of the Schelde.** Oil on canvas, 34 x 74. National-museum, NM 2513. Gift from Nationalmusei Vänner 1926.

This painting was purchased by Klas Fåhræus in the 1910s, and was one of the works from Fåhræus' collection later acquired by the Nationalmuseum.

142. **Claude Monet** (1840–1926): **Village Street, Vétheuil,** 1879. Oil on canvas, 52.5 x 71.5. Göteborgs konstmuseum, GKM 736.

This painting belonged, for a period of time, to Conrad Pineus in Gothenburg, and was later acquired by the Gothenburg Museum of Art.

ings by Cézanne, Cross, Gauguin, Pissarro, Renoir, and Sisley. A painting by Renoir, referred to as a *Landscape*, is undoubtedly identical with the large *Landscape near Wargemont* of 1879, today in the Toledo Museum of Art, Ohio. Pineus had, however, already sold several important French Impressionist works, among others, Monet's *Village Street, Vétheuil*, which ended up in the Gothenburg Art Museum, and Renoir's *Les amoureux*, purchased by the National Gallery of Prague.

Here one should also mention Gösta Olson and his Svensk-Franska konstgalleriet. Having worked in Paris for a few years as a physical therapist, Gösta Olson returned to Sweden in 1918 to open an art gallery.[68] His first contribution consisted in organizing a major exhibition of French art from the early 19th-century through the 1910s. In addition to works by contemporary artists such as Matisse and Picasso, the exhibition included works by, among others, Degas, Cézanne, Delacroix, Manet, and Seurat. Swedish collectors acquired a few of the exhibited works. For example, the Nationalmuseum purchased Renoir's *Bathing Women*. The exhibition marked the beginning of Gösta Olson's career as owner of a gallery focused on Swedish and French painting—the Svensk-Franska konstgalleriet (The Franco-Swedish Art Gallery), where a first exhibition was held in November of 1918. Gösta Olson also promoted contemporary French art as publisher of the art journal *Konstrevy*.

It is not entirely unfounded to assert that Swedish art collecting reflects the relationship of Swedish art to French Impressionism and Post-Impressionism. Pontus

32. **Paul Cézanne** (1839–1906): **Still Life with Statuette**. Oil on canvas, 63 x 81. Nationalmuseum, NM 2545. Gift from Nationalmusei Vänner 1926.

This painting was purchased by Klas Fåhræus in the early 1910s, and was acquired by the Nationalmuseum about a decade later when, for reasons of financial difficulties, Fåhræus was forced to sell his art collection. As opposed to other Swedish collectors, Fåhræus published essays about several artists and works of art that interested him. In 1919 he published an essay on Cézanne in the journal *Ord och Bild*, a piece that concludes with a summary characterization of the artist: "The whole of Cézanne's art is,

thus, an extremely complex and debatable equation of coarseness and refinement, of vision and reality, of surface and depth. It has been said about him that his brush is as feverish as Goya's, that he shares the richly decorative conception of the Italians, that he recalls Poussin, and competes with Chardin. But if one wishes to summarize his lasting merit with a single term, one has to choose the word style."

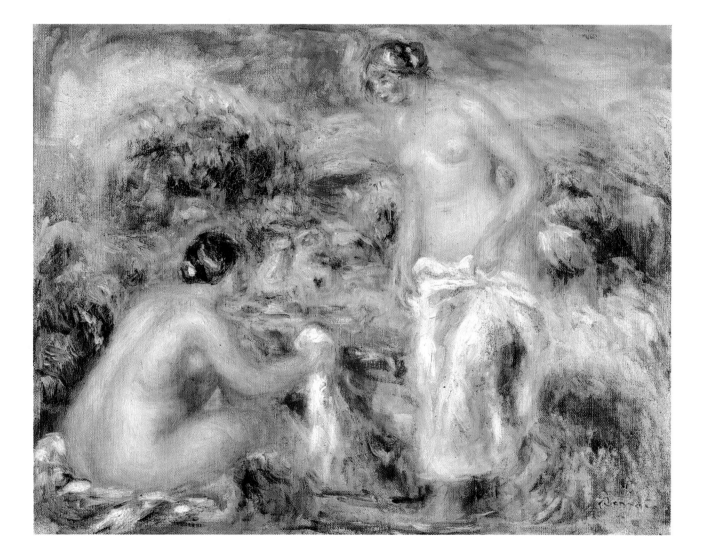

186. **Auguste Renoir** (1841–1919): **Women Bathing.**
Oil on canvas, 40.5 x 51. Nationalmuseum, NM 2103.

Fürstenberg's art collection reflects the fairly modest influence of Impressionism on Swedish painting. Impressionism was represented in the collection, by works of Lebourg and Raffaëlli. One could perhaps say that Pontus Fürstenberg's collecting largely illustrates the relationship between Swedish and French art during the 1880s and '90s. The Classicism of the Academists (Collin), Naturalism (Raffaëlli), Impressionism (Lebourg), and Synthetism (Gauguin), were appreciated. What the collection lacked, above all, was works by Bastien-Lepage and Puvis de Chavannes.

A breakthrough for the collecting of Impressionist and Post-Impressionist painting in Sweden occurs when these movements become broadly accepted in Swedish art circles. The leading Post-Impressionists are introduced to the general public, in Swedish, around 1910. The first major presentation of Gauguin in the Swedish language was published in 1908 in the first issue of Harald Brising's journal *Arktos*. In Brising's essay Gauguin, Cézanne, and Van Gogh were also presented together, for the first time in Swedish, as the leading figures of contemporary art.[69] Georg Nordensvan published the first monographic treatment of Cézanne in Nordisk Familjebok in 1906.[70] Nordensvan was also responsible for the first major Swedish-language presentation of Van Gogh in 1908, also published in Nordisk Familjebok.

It is, thus, in connection with what is usually referred to as the Modernist breakthrough that the leading Impressionists, followed by Gauguin, Van Gogh, and Cézanne, begin to be regarded as major art historical figures. It is true that Richard Bergh and Karl Nordström appreciated Gauguin already in the 1890s, but it is only around 1910 that Cézanne, Gauguin, and Van Gogh, become obvious models for Swedish artists. Birger Simonsson, Gösta Sandels, and Sigrid Hjertén, had no doubts about which artists were the major precursors of contemporary Modernist art. Interestingly enough, in letters and essays on art written by Matisse's own pupils around 1910, more attention is devoted to Cézanne than to Matisse.[71]

The process initiated by the first Swedish encounters with Impressionism in the 1870s may be said to have come to an end when late 19th-century French avant-garde art works were elevated to the status of the most desirable collector's items in the eyes of Swedish curators and art collectors. To a great extent, this process involves the filtering and refining of art history writing. The unsurpassed diversity Swedish artists seemed to experience when viewing art exhibitions in Paris in the last three decades of the 19th century, is transformed, in the eyes of posterity, into a field where what is radical and of high quality becomes easily distinguishable from what is conservative and mediocre. By the time Swedish art collectors and museums are purchasing late 19th-century French art, in the 1910s, most artists admired during the 1870s, '80s, and '90s, have been forgotten. Cézanne, Degas, and Monet have replaced Besnard, Breton, and Cazin. Most private art collections of this period have now been dispersed. However, museum collections of late 19th-century French art remain, as a memorial to the period's aesthetic and financial considerations.

Before and After: Paul Gauguin in Copenhagen 1884–85

Flemming Friborg

"Copenhagen is very picturesque, and where I am living one can find very typical and pretty things to paint. At this moment it is ten degrees below zero and horse-drawn sledges transporting wood are going through the streets."

SHORTLY AFTER HIS arrival in Copenhagen in November of 1884, Paul Gauguin painted this optimistic and idyllic image of a wintry Copenhagen. This boded well for his stay in Scandinavia, but the happiness would, in every respect, be short-lived; neither the country, the climate, nor the people lived up to Gauguin's considerable expectations and even greater ambition for a career as a painter. His stay turned out to be a short one, the painter holding out for only about seven months before leaving the country again—for France, then the South Seas.

The story of Paul Gauguin's visit to the Danish capital, and his rather unsuccessful encounter with the Danish public is, at the same time, familiar and unfamiliar. It took place in the winter of 1884–85, when the painter was living with his family in Copenhagen under difficult circumstances, wrestling with his painting and the local lack of understanding of his art. The Danish Gauguin specialist Merete Bodelsen has thoroughly described and analyzed Gauguin's formative years, his art collecting activities and his relationship with the new painting, and individual later contributions have revealed various aspects of the painter's stay in Denmark.[1] As a result of this research significant information has come to light about the Copenhagen milieu of art critics and art collectors in the period 1885–1915, of importance for understanding the development of the early reception of Impressionism outside of France. However, the events in Scandinavia have, on the whole, been dismissed as parenthetical in art history, as mere distant echoes of the truly important events occurring at the centre of the new artistic developments, in Paris. In Gauguin's case, it has been said that his short stay in Denmark was merely a brief episode in a long and successful career as an artist, the more significant events of which occurred elsewhere. Nevertheless, it is worth taking a closer look at this phase of Gauguin's creative life.

Previous pages: 182. **J.F. Raffaëlli** (1850–1924): **Boulevard in Paris** (detail). Tempera på papp, 50.5 x 67. Göteborgs konstmuseum, GKM F130.

To the left: 59. **Paul Gauguin** (1848–1903): **Self-Portrait**, 1885. **Oil on canvas**, 65.2 x 54.3. Kimbell Art Museum, Fort Worth, Texas, AP 1997.03.

106. **Armand Guillaumin** (1841–1927): **Garden Behind Old Houses, Damiette**, 1878. Oil on canvas, 58.5 x 72. Ny Carlsberg Glyptotek, Copenhagen, SMK 3569.

This painting formed part of the art collection Gauguin assembled in Paris and which was later kept in his Copenhagen home in the mid-1880s. Gauguin often used works in his collection as starting-points for his own compositions. In his painting *Snow-Covered Garden* (Wildenstein 140, private coll.), Gauguin has included a figure which strongly recalls the man raking leaves in Guillaumin's painting.

Copenhagen, The Winter of 1884–85

Paul Gauguin's stay in Denmark occurred at a decisive moment in his life as a painter. This was, at the same time, a transitional period for Impressionism. A number of the leading figures of the new artistic movement—Renoir, Degas, Pissarro—were experiencing a crisis in the years following the sixth Impressionist exhibition of 1881, despite the fact that this had been a relatively successful event in comparison with the first five Impressionist exhibitions. An economic downturn had made it more difficult for these artists to sell their paintings, but the crisis was about more than money. Their artistic goals, individual and collective, were intensively debated, and Gauguin played an important role in these events.

It was primarily for financial reasons that Gauguin decided to follow his Danish-born wife Mette and the couple's four children to Copenhagen in the autumn of 1884. Following the Franco-Prussian War there had in fact been an economic upturn, which also made itself felt in the art world; for a short period even the Im-

179. **Camille Pissarro** (1830–1903): **Woodland Scene. Spring** 1878. Oil on canvas, 73 x 54. Ny Carlsberg Glyptotek, Copenhagen, SMK 3574.

Of the Impressionists Pissarro was, for a long period of time, closest to Gauguin. The painting *Woodland Scene. Spring* was exhibited in the Fourth Impressionist Exhibition (1879), and was already in Gauguin's possession. When Gauguin moved to Copenhagen in 1884, he brought the painting with him, together with several other works from the collection of contemporary painting that he had been assembling since the late 1870s.

pressionists were able to benefit from the easy access to money, and there was reason to hope the interest would last. However, in 1882 the large newly established bank, L'Union Générale, went bankrupt, resulting in great losses for a number of businesses and private individuals—among them Gauguin. The story has traditionally been told of Gauguin as a capable young banker, who suddenly abandoned his profession to devote himself to painting, first as a "great collector," then as a working painter; however, to call him successful is somewhat of an overstatement.

130. **Édouard Manet** (1832–
1883): **Marine in Holland.** Oil
on canvas, 50.1 x 60.3. Philadelphia Museum of Art, Purchased with the W.P. Wilstach
Fund, W'1921-001-004.

This painting was one of several
works by French Impressionists
in Gauguin's art collection.

Modernism's myth-making mechanisms have taken possession of the figure of the
artist, distorting the story in such a manner that the painter who simply must paint
at all costs emerges in full force.

In purely artistic terms, Gauguin was already synthesizing his impressions and
experiences of his own (as well as other artists') work during this *Copenhagen
phase*, as it should perhaps be called—to give it an independent place among the
many phases of his oeuvre. Loneliness, the financial and artistic crises, and being a
foreigner, combined with an irresistible urge to paint, resulted in a relatively productive period for the artist, where the inspiration, and point of departure, of his
paintings came almost exclusively from earlier compositions—those of others, as
well as his own. The fairly large and representative collection of contemporary art
that Gauguin had assembled through hectic, almost feverish, buying during the
1870s and '80s, now acquired new significance for him, namely, as a means of satis-
fying his hunger for artistic development. Scenes and figures from Cézanne,

57. **Paul Gauguin** (1848–1903): **Skaters in the Frederiksberg Garden**, 1884. Oil on canvas, 65 x 54. Ny Carlsberg Glyptotek, Copenhagen, MIN 3213.

59. **Paul Gauguin** (1848–1903): **Self-Portrait**, 1885. **Oil on canvas**, 65.2 x 54.3. Kimbell Art Museum, Fort Worth, Texas, AP 1997.03.

Pissarro, Guillaumin, and Degas, were adapted in a series of compositions in different techniques, of varying sizes and character. Writers have focused on how rapidly Gauguin distances himself from early Impressionism during these years, a development that seriously took off in Denmark. Typically, this development does not occur as a direct consequence of his coming in contact with a new, unfamiliar environment, but, rather, as a result of a steadily increasing consciousness of an inner motivation for painting; this introversion being nourished by Gauguin's almost complete isolation in Copenhagen. There he was with a family he could no longer support, with a still unrealized potential as a painter, and a feeling of being persecuted, no matter which way he turned. The Danish painters he had met were uncomprehending vis-à-vis his artistic standpoint and visions. And he who, judging from his letters to his mentor Pissarro, was so dependent on the empathy of others and on a favourable spiritual and artistic exchange of important ideas, found no echo here.

Even the "picturesque frost," which he described in his letter [of 1884], turned into an average Danish winter in December of that year, and that was less exciting. Rather than venturing out into the darkness and sleet of an inhospitable Copenhagen, Gauguin now concentrated his efforts indoors, indulging in "fantasies," as Anne-Birgitte Fonsmark writes in her book about the artist in Denmark.[2] A large portion of his work from the first few months of 1885 is, more or less, directly derived from the paintings decorating the walls of his apartment at Gl. Kongevej 105, where the family had moved shortly after Christmas of 1884. Even the fairly numerous winter motifs are based on recollections, reinforced by the paintings with which he surrounded himself (ill. pp. 134–136, 139). Reverie and melancholy go hand in hand, gloom and introversion suffuse his letters, which become increasingly bitter and sad. At the same time, his high level of productivity was maintained, and now even a few Danish painters became interested in, if not sympathetic to, the avant-garde artist from France. This was, of course, flattering to Gauguin who, nevertheless, maintained his characteristic *hauteur* in front of the interested artists. But then they were completely different from Gauguin, even those who should have been able to come close to his ideals and those of the new painting.

The only artist who, as far as we know, was in closer contact with Gauguin's painting and with the artist himself, was Theodor Philipsen, who also employed Gauguin's conception of nature, and painting technique, as a corrective. Gauguin's small-scale replica of a painting from Rouen, which he had brought with him from France (ill. p. 140, cat.no 60), was admired by Philipsen and possibly also copied by him. In a famous letter to his fellow artist Schuffenecker, Gauguin writes that he has caught a Danish painter in the act of copying a painting he lent him, despite his claim of not understanding the Impressionist conception of nature: "You can imagine the result: Impressionist colours combined with Academic draughtsmanship."[3] In some ways, Theodor Philipsen was inspired by Gauguin's style of painting, and at least one of the Frenchman's compositions found its way into Philipsen's work— Gauguin's *Road to Rouen II* was the point of departure for Philipsen's large painting *A Late Autumn Day in Dyrehaven. Sunshine* of 1886 (ill. p. 164, cat.no 173).[4] The painting was exhibited fairly soon after Gauguin's departure, and his words

23. **Paul Cézanne** (1839–1906): Avenue. Oil on canvas, 73.5 x 60.5. Göteborgs konstmuseum, GKM 946.

60. **Paul Gauguin** (1848–1903): **The Road to Rouen (II)**, 1885. Oil on canvas, 57 x 40. Ny Carlsberg Glyptotek, Copenhagen, NCG M.I.N. 3231.

This painting was executed in Copenhagen in 1884, as a variant version of another picture he had painted in Rouen the previous year. This version was offered by Gauguin as a gift to Theodor Philipsen who, in his work *A Late Autumn Day at Dyrehaven. Sunshine* (cat.no. 173), had, to some degree, tried to apply Gauguin's brush technique.

about it are quite justified: despite the partially assimilated hints of a new way of painting, it is basically a traditional piece of nature lyricism—more closely related to the aims of the Barbizon painters than anything else. Indeed, Philipsen's painting is quite traditional in comparison with both the use of colour and the bold perspective of Gauguin's motif of an avenue—which, by the way, was strongly influenced by a Cézanne painting in Gauguin's own art collection (*Avenue*, now in the Göteborgs Konstmuseum, ill. 139, cat.no 23).

Gauguin's characterization of Philipsen's painting recalls his reaction to the unusually positive reviews of his large painting *Woman Sewing (Suzanne cousant)* of 1880 (ill. p. 142, now in the Ny Carlsberg Glyptotek). This painting had been shown at the Sixth Impressionist Exhibition in Paris in 1881, at a time when the critics were becoming gradually accustomed to Impressionism and were beginning to deepen their knowledge of this particular artistic universe. J.-K. Huysmans' enthusiastic review of *Woman Sewing*—though not published until 1883, two years after the exhibition—marks one of the first real instances of acceptance in print of the New Painting, and is still valid today. However, Gauguin was not happy about the sudden praise, and not because of his natural inclination towards the martyr's role; in this case he felt completely misunderstood. Gauguin was, at an early stage, attentive to the signs of a potential crisis in Impressionism, which he found in its superficial way of dealing with real life. This sceptical attitude is revealed in a letter to Pissarro, written in the late summer of 1881, in which Gauguin expresses his irritation with the many landscape paintings being produced, as if this were the only real task for an artist. He points out that Impressionism thus risks becoming a mass product focused on a false landscape ideal.[5] Nevertheless, the artist felt somewhat flattered by the well-known critic Huysmans' strong praise for his *Woman Sewing*, which corresponded perfectly to one of Courbet's definitions of realism, and was therefore regarded as "pure Realism" by Huysmans. That Gauguin's intention with the painting was not at all introverted or literary becomes clear from his reflections on the review in an 1883 letter to Pissarro: "He only considers the literary aspects, and therefore he observes them [i.e. the Impressionists] only through Degas and Raffaëlli Bartholomé & Co., *because they paint figures*; basically, he is flattered by Naturalism … I am still dismayed at the shameless flattery he is throwing my way, yet despite his flattery I realize *that he is only interested in the literary associations of my nude study, not its painterly qualities*."[6] The italics are mine, stressing how Gauguin distinguishes between a painting's painterly and literary content. According to his artistic view, *Woman Sewing* is not so much a figural painting as a painting containing a figure—Gauguin does not reject the painting's "literary" aspect, but assigns it a lower priority compared to its purely painterly elements. Gauguin resented any interpretation of art in which painting and sculpture were regarded as mere stagings of a literary content, whether in the form of Huysman's literary Naturalism, or a one-sided "moral" focus on everyday life—contemporary existence for good or bad, as a subject in its own right. The wording of the letter would suggest that Gauguin associated the figurative aspect of Degas and like-minded artists with this false conclusion. He was irritated that, in his painting of the maid sewing on the bed, the painterly aspect and the experience of the painterly in its own right, would be obscured by the figurative in the minds of the critic and the public alike. But what does he mean by the "painterly qualities"? Probably the same quality displayed by works such as the celebrated wood relief of *La Chanteuse* (the Ny Carlsberg Glyptotek) from the same year as the *Woman Sewing*—a strong emphasis on the decorative aspect of the pictorial arts, surface patterns and forms, combined to form a powerfully expressive whole. In such a whole the motif should—though still recognizable, figurative—be subordinated to a certain degree of abstrac-

Paul Gauguin (1848–1903):
Woman Sewing, 1880. Oil on
canvas. 114.5 x 79.5. Ny Carlsberg Glyptotek, Copenhagen,
SMK 3453.

tion, moving away from the purely figurative. Rather than differentiating between expression and content, figure and abstraction, Gauguin seems to be striving for a synthesis, in which the extremely extroverted (the decorative, the combination of colour and form) becomes inseparably linked with the introverted (the soul's "prim-itive," natural, or instinctual depth). An unintentional symbolism thus reveals itself in Gauguin's work.

In *Woman Sewing*, Gauguin allows his own and the viewer's glance to disinter-estedly survey a woman's external, nude form, inscribed within a decorative whole, which masks the observed as realism—and it becomes understandable why the artist was less satisfied with Huysmans' positive review, feeling that he had partly failed. Through his merciless (i.e. ugly, anti-Classical) unmasking of the female body, and all the painting's social and human connotations, as the critics saw them, Gauguin risked losing an important part of his project, namely, to make the figure a part of a something purely painterly, like actual "dead" or immobile objects. This transfor-mation was a necessary step towards Gauguin's Pont-Aven painting, and remains central to him. It is, among others, these elements which are being refined during the period Gauguin spent in Copenhagen.

In addition to this transformation of the figure, Gauguin is doing something sim-ilar in his landscape paintings. Although the real change of direction in his work, today known as Synthetism, does not actually appear until several years later, the ideas are already nascent in Denmark; during his Rouen period and up until 1886 Gauguin kept a small diary, which he had earlier titled "Notes synthetiques." The term exists only in the title, and the word "synthetique" does not acquire any real significance for him until 1888.[7] Yet, during this period Gauguin remains open to influences, and his diary entries about—finally—reaching a stage where colour and drawing fuse, becomes the basis for his future work.

Synthetism can almost be understood quite literally in the paintings from Gauguin's stay in Denmark; the numerous quotations from the works of Impres-sionist colleagues in the artist's collection are like parts of a careful and absolutely nec-essary basic research project. Gauguin *samples* his way towards a style of painting that is entirely his own—but this must not mislead us into thinking that it is a question of "influence" from the more fully-fledged Impressionists. Gauguin is about to become conscious of the possibilities of a NEW way of painting, rendering Im-pressionism obsolete—a way of painting he will be a part of creating from the very beginning. He is thus quite consciously using his art collection as a study archive, not in order to paint like Pissarro or Cézanne, but to be able to paint like Gauguin. However, it is not merely a question of getting away from the usual Modernist "anxiety of influence," of finding one's own unique style beyond plagiarism. Among his generation of painters, Gauguin probably saw it most clearly, free of all illusion: the present task was to reach beyond the level of the skillful landscape- and portrait painting lovingly created by Monet and Renoir, though the first leg of the journey might well go by way of *plein-air* painting with, precisely, landscape motifs.

In the spring of 1885, Gauguin experiences a brief period of optimism. The desire to paint is reinforced by the arrival of spring, making it possible to move about out-doors. He now tries out his lighter, "airier" palette in the parks and recreational areas

20. **Paul Cézanne** (1839–1906): **Midday L'Estaque**, 1879 ca. Oil on paper mounted on canvas, 54.2 x 74.2. National Museums & Galleries of Wales, NMW A 2439.

This painting was one of two paintings by Cézanne that Gauguin bought from the Parisian art dealer Tanguy in 1883. Gauguin brought it with him to Copenhagen in 1884, where he used it as a starting-point for a composition of his own—a study for a fan (to the right). Cézanne's landscape was later sold to the Danish collector Edvard Brandes.

62. **Paul Gauguin** (1848–1903): **French Landscape,** 1885. Gouache on canvas. 27.9 x 55.5. Ny Carlsberg Glyptotek, MIN 1950.

Several of the Impressionists—among others, Degas and Pissarro—experimented with the fan-shape. At the Fourth Impressionist Exhibition in Paris in 1879, Pissarro exhibited as many as 12 fans. Gauguin owned a pair of fans by Pissarro, and this composition of a landscape was probably inspired by one of these.

of Copenhagen, feeling carefree for the first time in a long while: "I personally feel that enormous progress has been made. I feel it, my work is more refined, brighter, more luminous, even though my method is unchanged." His large composition, *The Queen's Mill, Østervold* of 1885 shows how he has moved beyond the Rouen period's darker colours and whole way of seeing, indeed, how he has even distanced himself from the smaller *Road to Rouen,* painted immediately after his arrival in Denmark. The light in the Østervold painting has a unifying quality, all forms seem to have the same value as parts of the surface, and this unity is the painting's most characteristic aspect—almost to a monotonous degree, so that the painting does not immediately catch the viewer's attention in the Ny Carlsberg Glyptotek's rich Gauguin collection. Still, this is an interesting work, since it so clearly shows the artist in transit through Impressionism. It is "synthesizing" in the sense that everything is gathered together and made subordinate to a strong, even tonality—everything from the tightly painted Cézannesque area in the left middle ground, to the chlorophyll-green rushes in the foreground with its vibrating nuances going from pale yellow to malachite. The man walking down the path towards the viewer is directly lifted from a pastel drawing by Pissarro, but only as an hommage. Artistically, Gauguin is no longer where he was when he painted together with Pissarro at Osny in the summer of 1883.

At the same time, Gauguin is also intensively aware of the commercial aspects of his project. He has been busily occupied with becoming an artist, not least in the eyes of others. Pissarro once described Gauguin as the ultimate commercial artist. Already before his journey to Denmark, Gauguin had, fired by his dreams, tried to settle in Rouen, being drawn there for two reasons—firstly, because a few of the Impressionists had painted there just before his arrival, and, secondly, because he believed this was where wealthy patrons could be found. This assumption proved unfounded, and his stay in Rouen did not turn out to be as successful as he had hoped. Gauguin's optimism was maintained during the early days of his stay in Denmark, due to his becoming a representative, in Denmark and Scandinavia, of a French company selling tarpaulins, which, at least, guaranteed financial security for himself and his family. He was

58. **Paul Gauguin** (1848–1903): **The Queen's Mill**, 1885. Oil on canvas, 92.5 x 73.4. Ny Carlsberg Glyptotek, Copenhagen, MIN 1850.

thus able to devote his spare time to painting. However, business was less than good, whereupon Gauguin's irritation with Denmark and the Danes increased, and even his business letters become imbued with bitterness—on one occasion he describes the Norwegians as being, on the whole, a lot easier to do commerce with.

Only a few Danish art collectors seem to have taken an interest in Gauguin's painting during his stay in Denmark and the following five years until the early 1890s. French art did not otherwise lack patrons in Denmark; the founder of the Glyptotek, director of Carlsberg Breweries, Carl Jacobsen (1842–1914), thus purchased contemporary art in France, though mainly at the Salon and mainly sculpture—by, for example, Rodin and Carpeaux. Through his contacts with artistic circles Jacobsen was guaranteed advisors in such matters. For example, it was through the Skagen painter P.S. Krøyer—one of the painters we have come to regard as, to some degree, related to the Impressionists—that Jacobsen acquired Jules Bastien-Lepage's large painting *The Beggar*. Jacobsen would hardly have associated this painting with Impressionism, which he considered offensive and mannered, and *The Beggar* was purchased as much for its "edifying" content as for its artistic qualities. Bastien-Lepage set the example for a series of Danish artists (L.A. Ring, among others), to no small degree thanks to Krøyer, who praised the Frenchman in Denmark for continuing and for further developing Impressionism! This judgment upset Gauguin, who wrote to Pissarro about it—how could a fellow artist think in those terms? Yet, Krøyer's views are perhaps also a form of criticism of Impressionism's superficiality in its selection of themes and motifs, only from a different viewpoint than Gauguin's—Krøyer had trained with the Salon painter Léon Bonnat, had become initiated into French painting, and had absorbed both Academic virtuosity and Impressionism, but may have wished for a wider range of attitudes towards motifs and the artist's role than he was able to find in either camp. Krøyer himself never developed into a Realist, neither in the mercilessly moralizing nor the sentimental style, but he also stayed away from the charged Symbolism that was the immediate continuation of Bastien-Lepage's painting.

Gauguin travelled in the other direction: through his and Van Gogh's striving towards a simplified ("primitive," in the sense of original and natural) artistic expression, painting develops in the direction of a decorative force in colour and form, moving away from a narrowly figurative relationship with the surroundings.

1885: Kunstforeningen ("The Copenhagen Art Association")
Although things did not work out the way the hopeful enthusiast had dreamed, an exhibition of Gauguin's latest work was, nevertheless, organized while he was still in Denmark—an historic event, at least with the hindsight of art history.

Already in the early summer of 1885, the Board of the Copenhagen Art Association had—probably through Krøyer's mediation—invited Paul Gauguin to exhibit his work. Long almost unknown, this presentation of the young French artist's works ran only from May 1st until the 6th of that year, and, next to its short run, there are two main reasons for its disappearance from the art history books: there was no catalogue, and no reviews appeared.[8] Still, Gauguin did get something out of it: he presents his own version of the truth when, in a letter to Schuffenecker in Paris, he describes how the Royal Danish Academy ordered the exhibition closed after only five days—this is simply not true: solo exhibitions organized by the Art Association in those days were always such brief affairs. Furthermore, it is highly unlikely that the Academy, had it actually possessed that much power, would have meddled in such a way. Indifference would undoubtedly have triumphed instead, and that would surely have been worse for Gauguin than harsh criticism.

Another tall story, undoubtedly spread by the artist himself, was that the frame-makers of Copenhagen refused to work for him, the reactionary Academy supposedly being behind their absolute refusal to cooperate. Both claims must be understood as a personal advertisement, deliberately formulated in letters to Pissarro and Schuffenecker, in the full knowledge that rumours would spread. Gauguin could use anything that might substantiate his image as an avant-garde artist, and if the small Danish exhibition could be blown up to the proportions of a veritable *succès de scandale*, the circle of Parisian artists, who had not yet fully accepted him, might be impressed. Yet, that was probably not the only reason; feelings of persecution were something Gauguin carried around with him, and it was at least true that he had not been received with open arms in Copenhagen. Gauguin was, in all respects, larger than life, both in terms of his personality and his artistic ambitions, and this did not tally with the cultural climate of the Danish capital. Thus, only a few contemporary Danish artists, and even fewer art collectors, found anything of value in his art. Philipsen remained the most interested of the Danish artists. He thus purchased *Woman Sewing* from Mette in 1892—all in all to Gauguin's great satisfaction, and furthermore: Gauguin declared himself pleased to see it owned by another artist. The Danish painter wanted the painting transferred to the Louvre, but this never happened, instead Philipsen bequeathed the work to the Statens Museum for Kunst at Copenhagen. The Museum accepted the painting, but made it part of a large-scale exchange of artworks with the Ny Carlsberg Glyptotek in 1922.

Viewed against the background of this indifference towards the new painting, it is all the more remarkable that the relatively conservative Art Association should have wanted to introduce the unknown Frenchman with the wild paintings. Although this Art Association, founded in 1825 with something resembling Enlightenment ideals, was a forum for the established bourgeoisie, it was also a stage for Danish artists and intellectuals. The activities of the Art Association were, indeed, organized primarily by those artists who were members, and the selection of exhibitions varied between, on the one hand, the safe and familiar and, on the other, the experimental. Thus, in the same year—1885—it was possible to open with a presentation of the Golden Age painter Christen Købke, and then to follow up later with Paul Gauguin, bearing witness to the fact that the Association also, and notably so, favoured living artists.[9] However, the presentation of Gauguin's works was an exhibition by and for artists, initiated by a very small—and less than homogeneous—progressive circle in Copenhagen in those years. Gauguin was right thus far in his general disappointment with Denmark, that the Danish art critics probably hardly knew what to make of him, and had therefore chosen to ignore the exhibition, and its short run had hardly been helpful. Things did not look much better in 1889, when

82. **Paul Gauguin** (1848–1903): **Parahi te Marare (Sacred Mountain)**, 1892. Oil on canvas, 66 x 88.8. Philadelphia Museum of Art, Gift of Mr. And Mrs. Rodolophe de Schauensee, 1980-001-001.

This painting belonged to a group of recently finished works which Gauguin sent from Tahiti to Copenhagen to be shown at The Free Exhibition in the spring of 1893. T. Thorup wrote a highly appreciative piece about the painting in the *Aarhus Amtstidende*. What Thorup admired most of all was the painting's combination of vivid colours, noting that it was unimportant whether or not one could identify the red plants in the foreground, "when the whole makes such a harmonious impression, so refreshing for the eye."

the Art Association organized an exhibition of contemporary French art, again with Gauguin's participation. Not much more is known about this exhibition, which, in any case, was not a great success—but neither did it cause a scandal. Such a scandal did, however, almost occur in 1893, in connection with the newly established Danish secessionist exhibition, Den frie Udstilling ("The Free Exhibition"), in which 51 paintings by Gauguin met an interested, but also highly skeptical, Copenhagen audience.[10]

1893: The Free Exhibition

Two years after its scandalous founding in 1891, the Danish secessionist group, The Free Exhibition chose to organize an exhibition with two of the most important, and most controversial, French artists, Gauguin and Van Gogh. As regards Gauguin, the decision rested on solid Danish grounds; Mette Gauguin was administering the affairs of her husband, then living in South Sea exile. She kept a large number of his paintings in her apartment, paintings she attempted to sell in Denmark with varying success. In addition, Mette continuously received new works, sent directly from Polynesia, or through various Parisian art dealers. There existed an elite

97. **Vincent Van Gogh** (1853–1890): **Pont de Langlois**, 1888. Oil on canvas, 49.5 x 64. Wallraf-Richartz-Museum–Fondation Corboud, Köln, WRM 1197.

This painting was shown at The Free Exhibition in Copenhagen in the spring of 1893, together with 28 other works by Van Gogh and 50 works by Gauguin. The motif is from Arles, and Van Gogh executed several similar paintings of this bridge—the Pont de Langlois. Both motif and style clearly reflect Van Gogh's interest in the art of the Japanese woodcut. Like the Japanese printmakers, Van Gogh strove to give the image a decoratively surface-oriented quality.

of art connoisseurs in Copenhagen who were able to appreciate Gauguin's work, but they were few and, for the most part, had limited financial means. On the other hand, through their connections, and in cooperation with Mette, they were able to organize this large presentation of the two modern painters—at the pavilion the equally modern, if merely Danish, group of artists', a temporary wooden structure by the Vesterport Passage at the Rådhuspladsen.

Philipsen selected the works from Mette's collection, and handled the negotiations for the exhibition to take place, while Gauguin was kept continuously informed, to the extent this was possible. The idea was for Gauguin and Van Gogh, as representatives of the new French painting, to exhibit their works alongside those of the Danish members of The Free Exhibition group. One of the artists J.F. Willumsen whose work was most closely associated with that of the French artists was also among those who had initiated the new Danish artists' association. Willumsen had, however, received such harsh reviews during previous seasons that he chose not to exhibit his work in 1893. It is thought-provoking that the daily news-

101. **Vincent Van Gogh** (1853–1890): **Poppy Field near Auvers-sur-Oise**, 1890. Oil on canvas, 73 x 91.6. Collection Gemeentemuseum Den Haag, The Hague, long term loan of the ICN, the Netherlands, SCH-1948X0003.

This painting was one of 29 works by Van Gogh shown at The Free Exhibition in Copenhagen in the spring of 1893.

paper *Berlingske Tidende*—keeping in mind its veritable persecution of Willumsen—with obvious irritation had to content itself with censuring the Dane *in absentia*, by calling Gauguin and Van Gogh "surrogates for Willumsen"![11] This shows, if nothing else, that one was able to deal with what was close and familiar, but not that which was French and foreign …

Gauguin himself looked forward to the exhibition in Denmark, but due to a lack of funds he had to abandon the thought of being present in Copenhagen for the opening on March 26th, 1893.[12] However, he succeeded in convincing an officer in the French Navy to transport to Paris a crate containing the latest paintings from Tahiti, and have them sent on to Copenhagen by train. The Danish exhibition organizers, led by Philipsen, Mette Gauguin, and the painter Johan Rohde, assembled as many as 79 paintings by Gauguin and Van Gogh. Opinions were divided, and the exhibition was the great topic of conversation in Copenhagen in the spring. Several reviews were positive, or at least adopted a cautious wait-and-see attitude,[13] while others were furious attacks on modern painting as pure nonsense.

78. **Paul Gauguin** (1848–1903): **I raro te Oviri**, 1891. Oil on canvas, 67.3 x 95.8. Dallas Museum of Art, Foundation for the Arts Collection, gift of the Adele R. Levy Fund, Inc., 1963.58.FA.

Among the fifty works by Gauguin exhibited at The Free Exhibition at Copenhagen in 1893 were ten paintings executed by Gauguin in Tahiti in 1891–92. Gauguin painted an additional version of this motif, a very similar painting, today in The Minneapolis Institute of Art.

The *Dagbladet Politiken* actually carried two reviews—the first one on the day of the opening, by the art historian Emil Hannover (when only two paintings by Van Gogh had yet arrived), the second on April 16, by the poet Johannes Jørgensen, a leading figure within the Symbolist circle in Denmark. Jørgensen's review sounds like an actual Symbolist poem or artistic manifesto. About Gauguin he wrote: "He lusts for the sun of the Capricorn, the colours of the Equator, the pale red soil and pitch black shadows of the tropical islands, Tahiti's violent and magnificent vegetation."[14] Gauguin would undoubtedly have appreciated this reception. Also outside of the daily newspapers, the two French artists caused a stir. The composer Carl Nielsen, married to the sculptress Anne Marie Carl-Nielsen, wrote in his diary on the day of the opening: "Basically, Gauguin is incoherent, like practically all modern artists. No solidity, but plenty of talent. Only experiments and not a single finished work of art."[15] A resounding yes to experiments on the altar of modernity, but this was still quite difficult material even for a sophisticated audience. A number of the paintings shown in The Free Exhibition are today in the Ny Carlsberg Glyptotek.

After Gauguin: The French Art Exhibition at the Art Association in 1911
In April of 1911 an exhibition of works by French artists represented in private Danish art collections opened at the Art Association. This was not a large-scale exhibition, and it has undoubtedly been somewhat ignored in the history of the earliest manifestations of Impressionist art outside of France. It was, however, quite important in a Danish context. Thus, Merete Bodelsen writes that the exhibition was part of a new orientation with regard to France and French art, led primarily by the youngest artists in Denmark.[16]

96. **Vincent Van Gogh** (1853–1890): **Kitchen Gardens at Montmartre,** 1887. Oil on canvas, 96 x 120. Stedelijk Museum, Amsterdam. Gift of Association for the Formation of a Public Collection of Contemporary Art (VVHK), A2234.

This painting was one of few examples of Van Gogh's Impressionist painting shown at The Free Exhibition in Copenhagen in 1893. The Impressionist traits were noted by the art critic Th. Thorup, who also felt that the painting succeeded in depicting the poverty and desolation typical of the outskirts of a big city.

As far back as 1888 and 1897, Carl Jacobsen had organized major exhibitions of French art, brought over from France. From a Modernist perspective, however, that was a long time ago, and the selection had been almost accidental; many of the more respectable French Academists had participated at the expense of more "progressive" artists, whose time had now come. Clearly, the collection of French paintings at the Glyptotek was not a source of inspiration for the youngest Modernists—Carl Jacobsen's sculptural ideals led him to Rodin and Meunier, for whom there was both interest and appreciation, but his acquisition of paintings had occurred too long ago to satisfy the avant-garde. Jacobsen's pronounced resistance to Impressionism, for example, must have appeared incomprehensible to the young French-oriented artists. Thus, the art historian Leo Swane was quite critical of the collection of French paintings at the Glyptotek, which he referred to as *slag*, accidental accretions of a—by implication—larger and more beautiful whole, shamelessly unknown in Denmark.

By this time, to be internationally oriented had assumed national importance, especially in the sense of being French-oriented. The pronouncements of the *Kunstbladet* and the Art Association offer striking proof of just how rapidly Impressionism and the new painting had achieved a breakthrough in European art. Scandinavia and, not least, Denmark, was at the cutting edge when it came to art collecting and interest in Modernist art during the following two decades—a circumstance which has so far received very little attention. A list of art collectors intent on acquiring modern art in the years 1910–1930 includes, in and around the Danish capital alone, several prominent names: Tetzen-Lund, Rump, Heilbuth, Wilhelm Hansen, and Helge Jacobsen—Carl Jacobsen's son, who, in complete contrast to his father, turned his back on the 19th-century Salon and classical Academism in favour of the Impressionists and Post-Impressionists. Although Helge Jacobsen was backed by an already quite established art museum, it was his activities as a private collector that were to have a decisive impact: the younger Jacobsen thus bequeathed his collection of French art to the Glyptotek as early as 1919, then did the same with his valuable Gauguin paintings in 1927, two years after resigning as Director of the Board of the Glyptotek. He then completely withdrew from the museum. Typically, it is the private art collectors who take the lead during the initial phase of building the great collections of contemporary art, not the government bodies. On Danish soil, the Statens Museum for Kunst did not lead the way—the Board of Directors simply was not interested enough in the latest developments, which were viewed as ephemera.

When the Impressionist exhibition of 1911 finally opened it was quite a successful event, at least judging from the reviews in the daily newspapers. Critics emphasized the importance of Gauguin, whose work was richly represented in the exhibition. Several critics remarked on the curious fact that, through this exhibition, the public finally had an opportunity to view the very same French works which Danish artists had known for years to be in the possession of Danish art collectors and fellow artists, and which they referred to in their own works. On April 9th, the day of the opening, the *Avisen København* summed up the state of contemporary art as follows: "The literate painters, of whom this country has its fair share, [previously] indulged in mystical names, swinging their censors in honour of the demigods of an unknown Olympus—Cezanne, von Gogh. It is not entirely unlikely that a couple of fumbling Danish imitators have come to quite absurd conclusions as a result of this mystique. A sounder approach to both the foreign models and our own painters' personal attitudes towards this influence must be the only true means of re-establishing a sound and secure relationship between contemporary painting and the people whose culture it should be an essential part of."[17]

And so it had finally happened. Despite the unintentional misspelling of a few of the artists' names (both "von Gogh" and "Cezanne" without the *accent aigu* recur later in the article), these words were well meant, and fairly describe the transformation that, in the course of a few years had set in among the critics of the new painting.

A lone, brave conservative voice was heard in the *Kristeligt Dagblad*, defining the term "Impressionism" as "for example, painting a cow green and the grass red, human skin becomes bluish violet, and, in short, all possible colours other than that of skin. And instead of a brush, either the hands alone or a flat wooden stick are used to paint with."[18] O tempora, o mores … Few people, however, were by now provoked by the mild-mannered Impressionism, and the situation could have been much worse considering all that was new and foreign. Internationally, the public had had a few years to get used to Modernism, and both Impressionism and Paul Gauguin, the former *enfant terrible* of Danish-French relations, were finally accepted in artistic circles all over Europe.

Painterly Perception and Images of the Soul:
Impressionism and Post-Impressionism in Denmark
Peter Nørgaard Larsen

THAT IMPRESSIONISM PRE-DATES Post-Impressionism in the development of the pictorial arts seems so self-evident that it needs no mention in an art historical context. If this article, nevertheless, opens with a superfluous statement such as this, it is because Danish Impressionism and Post-Impressionism appear to be governed by a somewhat different developmental logic. Here Impressionism is, indeed,—when viewed as a widely practiced form of pictorial expression—a phenomenon belonging to the years around 1900, its most important exponents being the group of artists called Fynboerne (the Funen Painters), while Post-Impressionism, by as early as circa 1890, emerges as an essential alternative to Naturalism.

There were, however, exceptions to this inverse development, and what follows is primarily an account of—at least as far as Impressionism is concerned—the two major exceptions, Theodor Philipsen and Anna Ancher. Above all, the former.

Theodor Philipsen's Danish Impressionism
Theodor Philipsen has been assigned the role of a great regenerator in the history of Danish painting. Philipsen, with his origins in the landscape- and animal painting of the late Golden Age, lead Danish painting out of the smoke-filled salons, throwing open the French windows onto a much more contemporary style of painting, filled with light and colour. Visits to the Impressionist exhibitions in Paris, his encounter with the southern sun during trips to Spain and Italy and, not least, his friendship with Paul Gauguin in the mid-1880s, are rightly emphasized as important for Philipsen's assimilation of Impressionism. Yet, there is no doubt that posterity's great admiration for, and worship of, anything to do with Impressionism, has also lead to a quite undifferentiated conception of the nature and extent of Philipsen's Impressionism. At least until very recently, when several exhibitions have shed new light on Philipsen and the way in which Philipsen's Impressionism developed in relation to the French avant-garde.[1] While Danish art historians, and their colleagues in countries similarly situated on the periphery of the history of Western art, have been quite preoccupied with establishing a French-oriented national art history, more recent research about Philipsen is characterized by a much greater receptivity

219. **J.F. Willumsen** (1863–1958): **Two Breton Women Parting After Having a Chat,** 1890. Oil and tempera on canvas, 100.4 x 93.2. Nordjyllands Kunstmuseum, Aalborg, NK 811.

to the value of regional distinctiveness. In other words, rather than forcing Philipsen into a one-sided Francophile context, one is now able to value and describe Philipsen's ability to adopt an Impressionist way of seeing and painting style, in his effort to develop his Naturalism towards an increasingly objective representation of reality.

Philipsen's initial encounter with the French Impressionists dates to his first stay in Paris in 1874–76, when, in all likelihood, he visited the second Impressionist exhibition of 1876. Still, the Barbizon painters Theodore Rousseau, Constant Troyon, and perhaps especially Jean-François Millet made the greatest impression on him during his stay in Paris. And we have to wait another six years or so before we find the first clear hints of Impressionist influence in Philipsen's work. This occurs during the years 1882–84 in Paris, where he viewed the seventh Impressionist exhibition at the Galerie Durand-Ruel. From Paris he continued his journey to Andalusia, then on to Tunis in North Africa, and later to Rome and, especially, to Sora. A number of paintings rightly described as pre-Impressionist date from this journey. The encounter with the strong southern light, and the somewhat pale colours, as well as the association with the Belgian semi-Impressionist painter Remy Cogghe, encouraged Philipsen to increase the light- and colour intensity of his paintings.

A painting such as *Street in Tunis* (Statens Museum for Kunst) is one of the finest examples of this pre-Impressionism. The areas of violet and pink shading in the foreground reveal Philipsen's awareness that areas of shading contain coloured reflexes. The broad, quiet, and light pale colour planes, on the other hand, bear witness to the fact that Philipsen had not yet fully understood the Impressionists' desire to achieve strong light effects through the use of pure and saturated complementary areas of colour and brush strokes. In a painting such as *Water Wheel in the Liri River, Sora*, on the other hand, one can see that Philipsen appears to be consciously moving towards an Impressionist conception of the motif, focusing on movement, reflection, and an unexpected cropping of forms. In a swift, sketchy technique, Philipsen has captured a momentary impression. An impression, not of the hectic street life and pleasures of the city, or of suburban parks and recreational activities, but, rather, as nearly always with Philipsen, of the varied richness of Nature.

In Flemming Friborg's article "Before and After. Paul Gauguin in Copenhagen 1884–85", one reads about Gauguin's problems in Copenhagen in 1884–85. A six-months' stay that was hardly particularly productive for Gauguin, but which, in return, seems to have had a decisive influence on the creation of Philipsen's principal early Impressionist work *A Late Autumn Day in Dyrehaven. Sunshine* of 1886. For Gauguin, Philipsen was not only an excellent painter sympathetic to the aims of the Impressionist movement, but also—of great importance—a French-speaking Danish artist. A conversational partner and interested listener. In return, Philipsen received a thorough introduction to the arguments about colour theory underlying Impressionism and, not least, practical instructions. Karl Madsen, Philipsen's close friend, the art historian and spokesman for Danish Naturalism, has, based on his conversations with Philipsen, described Gauguin's advice: "To achieve an impression of vibrating light and colour, he should try using different means, long and thin brushes, short and firm brush strokes, making sure the brush is loaded with pigment, so the colours of the painting become clear and well defined, rich and saturated."[2]

In *A Late Autumn Day in Dyrehaven. Sunshine*, Philipsen for the first time employs Gauguin's brush technique. The result is a, from very point of view, consistently executed Impressionist painting. The short brush strokes saturated with colour, and the finely tuned complementary colour contrasts, occur throughout the painting, which vibrates with light, colour, and atmosphere. Add to this an original composition, consisting of a perpendicular road sign, repeated, and mirroured, in the crossroads.

Philipsen cemented his connection with Impressionism in 1889, by participating in the exhibition "Scandinavian and French Impressionists." An exhibition organized at the Copenhagen Art Association at the initiative of Karl Madsen, who wished to combine examples of French Impressionism in private Danish ownership, with the works of some Scandinavian artists wishing to publicize their association with the still much decried art movement. The French paintings were mainly from Gauguin's large collection of Impressionist art, made available to the Danish public by his wife Mette, while the limited selection of Scandinavian artists—with the exception of Philipsen—consisted of Viggo Johansen, Oda and Christian Krohg and Erik Werenskiold.

Philipsen was not entirely satisfied with the exhibition. He found his own works

Above: **Theodor Philipsen** (1840–1920): **A Shower of Rain,** 1890. Oil on panel, 56.7 x 57.1. Aarhus Kunstmuseum.

Opposite page, above: 176. **Theodor Philipsen** (1840–1920): **Cattle seen against the sun on the Island of Saltholm,** 1892. Oil on canvas, 63 x 102. Statens Museum for Kunst, Copenhagen, KMS6340.

Opposite page, below: 174. **Theodor Philipsen** (1840–1920): **A Cowshed on the Island of Saltholm,** 1890. Oil on canvas, 56.5 x 82.5. Statens Museum for Kunst, Copenhagen, KMS3333.

173. **Theodor Philipsen** (1840–1920): **A Late Autumn Day in Dyrehaven. Sunshine**, 1886. Oil on canvas, 66,5 x 84.5. Statens Museum for Kunst, Copenhagen, KMS1950.

inadequate, seemingly more closely associated with the colours and climate of the Danish landscape than he would have wanted at this time. Although he would produce several Impressionist masterpieces over the next few years, works such as *Long Shadows, Cattle on the Island of Saltholm* (1890) and *Cattle seen against the sun on the Island of Saltholm* (1892), it is doubtful whether Philipsen regarded them as more in tune with the French Impressionists' works. What was considered a deficiency in Philipsen's eyes in 1889, is the same quality that would much later be mentioned as important when discussing Philipsen's characteristically Danish brand of Impressionism: his ability to apply and develop his Impressionist colour scheme, based on close studies of the Danish climate.

The frequent comparison between Philipsen and the French Impressionists is, thus, not especially fruitful. If the aim is to postulate similarities based on an expected commonality of motifs and colours, Philipsen's uniqueness is actually being disregarded. Consequently, he will necessarily seem less of a radical and revitalizing force than his French contemporaries. "Contemporary life" apparently did not interest Philipsen. Rather, in his paintings he turns his back on it, preferring instead a simple life of communion with nature. A life sometimes imbued with an Arcadian atmosphere and, at other times, assuming the shape of an almost overly sensuous celebration of the dominant power of light, pointing towards Vitalism's later worship of nature and light. On other occasions, he is able to adapt his Impressionist colour scheme, to an astonishing degree, to the gray weather of Denmark. As Terman Fredriksen points out in the context of a description of Philipsen's painting of rain and stormy weather, *A Shower of Rain* of 1890: "The French 'rainbow palette' would have gotten Philipsen nowhere in his attempt to produce a naturalistic representation of a light-poor, damp cold, and thoroughly harsh gray weather motif such as this."[3] Instead, Philipsen developed his Impressionist gray weather colour scheme of gray tonalities and brownish earth pigments, allowing him to faithfully represent the Danish climate.

Philipsen's assimilation of the Impressionist way of seeing and painting style corresponds to the requirements later formulated by the Danish author Johannes V. Jensen as a precondition for being able to speak of an actual Danish Impressionism. In his review of the Spring Salon at Charlottenborg and The Free Exhibition of 1912, both in Copenhagen, Jensen mocks "the obligatory adaptations of French Impressionism, which, in their monotony, constitute nearly the most archconservative element in the annual exhibitions."[4] The strength of the French Impressionists lies in their ability to base their representations on "their own conditions, on French people, French air." So that, "instead of falsifying French motifs in a French mode," it was, according to Jensen, of decisive importance for Danish painters, living and working in Denmark, to devote themselves to the secrets of Danish air, which cannot be imported. "[...] A Danish Impressionist is obliged to paint Danish objects in Danish air, using Danish colours."[5]

It is not known whether Johannes V. Jensen had Philipsen in mind when he listed these requirements of the ideal Danish Impressionist. That was probably not the case, however. On the other hand, Jensen greatly admired the Funen Painters, above all, Peter Hansen, Johannes Larsen, and Fritz Syberg. Artists who all acknowledged their great indebtedness to Philipsen and, in the years around the turn of the century 1900, established themselves with a figurative- and landscape painting marking the belated breakthrough of Impressionism in Danish art. Philipsen's innovative work with cropped motifs, light, colour, and atmosphere, is continued in the Impressionist *plein-air* painting of the Funen Painters.[6]

"Only as colour" — Anna Ancher

Together with Theodor Philipsen, Anna Ancher is considered the most important Impressionist painter in Danish art. As opposed to the French Impressionists' association with contemporary life in and around the big city, however, the two Danish artists' paintings were produced at the periphery of modern life, on the island of Saltholm and in Skagen. In opposition to, rather than in harmony with, the hectic, the fleeting, and the momentary, that generally characterizes Impressionism.

Through her marriage to Michael Ancher in 1880, and her friendship with several of the great masters of Scandinavian Naturalism, such as P.S. Krøyer and Christian

Krohg, Anna Ancher received a thorough knowledge of contemporary *plein-air* painting. She admired Krøyer's brilliant technique and ability to "paint with light," but it may well be that Krohg's intimate knowledge of the French Impressionists, both in terms of the cropping of motifs and saturated colours, contributed more to Anna Ancher's liberation as a painter. In any case, parallel to Michael Ancher's heroic representations of the life of local Skagen fishermen, Anna Ancher is, toward the end of the 1880s, approaching a style of painting that is much more concerned with light and colour. Just how conscious she was of her intentions is revealed in a letter of 1889 to the painter Viggo Johansen, in which Anna Ancher writes about her painting *Evening Prayer* (Skagens Museum) of 1888, "my only message is one of colour."[7]

There are many examples revealing the extent to which Anna Ancher often thought of her paintings only in terms of colour, but few show it more superbly than *Sunshine in the Blue Room* of 1891. As frequently in Anna Ancher's paintings, there is no figure establishing eye contact with the viewer. As a result, one is able to survey the room apparently unobserved, find one's place in the blue room at Brøndum's Hotel, and allow oneself to become absorbed by its meditative peacefulness. In such a painting the Impressionist moment is transformed into an eternity, in which the extension of time materializes as light and colour.

As in her other paintings of domestic interiors, Anna Ancher works quite consciously with incoming light in the form of cones of light rays, of great importance for the balance of the composition. The room is filled with light, affording the artist rich opportunities of demonstrating her mastery of colour in the encounter between the bluish and reddish orange pigments. Even her daughter Helga is observed and represented "only as colour." Her yellow hair, blue apron, and golden brown skirt repeat the room's dominant colours, whereby she merges with the room and the overall colouristic effect.

The many oil sketches occupy a special place in Anna Ancher's artistic production.[8] Though numerous, they became publicly known only after the death of her daughter Helga in 1964, when they formed part of the Helga Ancher Fund, together with the artist's entire home. Many of these sketches were, however, displayed in the home of Anna and Michael Ancher, being well known to their family and artist friends, and have undoubtedly contributed to Anna Ancher's increased reputation among artists. We do not know if she considered them finished works of art. The fact that she chose not to exhibit them suggests that she regarded them primarily as studies, notations, a kind of memory store to draw on for the more finished works. She may also not have exhibited them because she was aware that the Danish public hardly would have appreciated their great colouristic and formal radicalism. Indeed, many are exclusively studies and examinations of colour, in which an individual colour, or a series of contrasted complementary colours, appears to be the principal motif. When confronted with a work such as *Interior with Chair and Plant* (Skagens Museum), with its remarkable colouristic intensity and formal reduction, one must ask oneself if it does not belong to classic Modernism, rather than the Naturalism and Impressionism with which Anna Ancher's art is generally compared.

In Danish painting of the decades before the turn of the century 1900, only Theodor Philipsen and Anna Ancher may be said to have employed an Impressionist

8. **Anna Ancher** (1859–1935): **Sunshine in the Blue Room**, 1891.
Oil on canvas, 65.2 x 58,8. Skagens Museum, 222.

style of painting in a great number of works. With other artists, such as P.S. Krøyer, Albert Gottschalk, Thorvald Niss, Lauritz Tuxen, Viggo Johansen and others, one sometimes comes across works with Impressionist tendencies and formal elements. Often in the form of a combination of rapid and sketchy brushwork, pure colours, and colour shading. Three characteristics usually expected of a typical Impressionist work, and often mentioned as synonymous with Impressionism. Yet, it is not reasonable to translate the term Impressionism by the above mentioned elements, either in combination or individually. All three might just as convincingly be used to describe a Naturalist work, aimed simply at representing a motif as true to nature as possible. Apart from a naturalistic point of departure, and the basic qualities shared by Impressionism and Naturalism, several conditions must be satisfied before one is able to speak of a consciously executed Impressionist work. The painting must be based on a specific awareness of colour theory and practice, as well as on the artist's desire to allow the painting as a whole to become subordinated to an Impressionist way of seeing and painting style. In the works of Philipsen and Anna Ancher we frequently encounter this desire to allow the painting to convey the purely painterly, the materialization of light and colour. In the work of Krøyer, Gottschalk, and Niss, the Impressionist elements are a part of the Naturalist vocabulary of form and colour, and, thus, generally subordinated to a message of content.

105. **Albert Gottschalk** (1866–
1906): **From Frederiksberg
Bakke, Winter,** 1894. Oil on
canvas, 45.8 x 65. Den Hirschsprungske Samling, Copen-
hagen, 3113.

However, there are individual works by Krøyer and, especially, by Gottschalk, which seem principally concerned with a purely painterly representation of the moment, though the overall impression of their art is one of a primarily Naturalist evocative painting.

The Short Flowering of Impressionism
That Impressionism achieves a relatively late breakthrough in Denmark is, above all, due to the fact that first-hand knowledge of the movement is very limited in the years before 1890. Prior to the Copenhagen exhibition of Scandinavian and French Impressionists in 1889, and the visits of many Danish artists and art critics to the 1889 World's Fair in Paris, few people had a qualified understanding of the aims of Impressionism. Perhaps only two individuals, Philipsen and Mette Gauguin, could claim more than a purely superficial insight into Impressionism's aims and means. For a majority of Danish painters, contemporary French art was identical with the work of the Naturalists Bastien-Lepage, Jules Breton, Leon Bonnat, and Raffaëlli. These same artists, together with the Academist painters Cabanel, Carolus-Duran and others, were selected by the brewer Carl Jacobsen, aided by P.S. Krøyer and Lauritz Tuxen among others, to be shown at a large-scale exhibition of French art in Copenhagen in 1888. Posterity has lamented the fact that the exhibition included

only few works by the Impressionists, including two seascapes by Monet. However, the selection becomes understandable when one considers how little known and recognized the Impressionists were. The art critic Emil Hannover, an eloquent spokesman for the Symbolists after 1890, has described in his memoirs just how unaware he and his contemporaries were. Hannover visited Paris in 1886, writing home enthusiastically about that year's official Salon: "while I seem to have completely neglected to visit the French Impressionists' exhibition, organized for the eighth time in the spring of 1886, this time in the Rue Lafitte. [...] Had I gotten to know them by as early as 1886, and had I already at that time introduced them here at home, the art world of Copenhagen, and I myself, would, in 1888, have been capable of a more reasoned attitude vis-à-vis brewer Jacobsen's French art exhibition. None of us had advanced any further at that time than being able, at most, to reject the purely Academist painters such as Bougereau, Cabanel, and Carolus-Duran. For us Danes, the high watermark of contemporary French art was Bastien-Lepage."[9] To the Danes, Albert Besnard's fashionable portraits, with their equilibristic technique, seemed the boldest expression offered by contemporary art: "we were entirely unaware that much more daring things had been attempted earlier in Paris and that a collective action had revolutionized the pictorial arts."[10]

When the Danes, in the wake of Philipsen's Danish Impressionism and the "discovery" of the French Impressionists in 1889, were finally capable of assimilating the new artistic developments, these were overtaken by an even more recent development, Symbolism, which, more than Impressionism, corresponded to the thinking of the younger artists. Just how rapidly the expectations of the new and unfamiliar superseded this recognition of Impressionism is revealed by the 1889 correspondence of the Danish painter Johan Rohde. In March he writes to his friend Emil Hannover in Paris, asking him "are you seeing something of the latest art, what is it like? Write to me about it. Let us know something of those artistic currents even more recent than the Impressionists. Explain to us who the 'Intentionists' are, isn't that what they call themselves?"[11] Later that year Rohde has an opportunity to visit the Paris World's Fair and, from the mention of Monet in his letters home, one clearly sees how Rohde is captivated by Monet's display of colours, though he also feels the absence of something above and beyond the painterly expression: "These are colours I could not get from my supplier, colours that, in these ingenious combinations, have an indescribable impact, but I search in vain for paintings, personal visions, or even a little mood painting, of the kind Millet is able to produce with a couple of gray pastel crayons on a coarse piece of paper."[12] In the same period, an ambition to isolate Danish art from the influence of Impressionism developed within more conservative Danish circles. United around the influential art historian, curator, art critic, etc., Julius Lange, many tried to warn of the consequences of an art that allowed itself to become consumed by the period's great interest in the material world, rather than in high ideals and universal sentiments. In his influential text, *Plein-Air Study. Painting. The Art of Remembrance* of 1889, Lange confronts "The new painting," "Impressionism in the wider sense," with its opposite, "the art of remembrance."[13] For Lange, the *plein-air* study is important as an immediate sensory experience, though not in its own right. Its value lies primarily in its ability to

190. **Johan Rohde** (1856–1935): **Self-Portrait.** Oil on panel, 43.2 x 32.7. Den Hirschsprungske Samling, Copenhagen, 3156.

sharpen the artist's powers of observation in relation to external reality, thus becoming a part of a store of memories he or she is able to activate in executing the final work of art. The role of the study is that of a servant in relation to his master, the studio painting, an imaginary piece and a "memory image" of universal relevance.

A few years later, in his essay "Norwegian, Swedish, Danish Figure Painting" (1892), Lange deepened his criticism of a study-based art: "It is a fact that the new painting often concerns itself with separating that which one is able to observe from that which one is able to comprehend through observation. We possess a profound knowledge of the use of our eyes, if only we would open them—no matter what is being observed. [...] But the emphasis on the purely painterly, that of which painting alone is capable in relation to all the other arts, has gone too far. [...] To this observer it is obvious that any attempt to Separate and Divide, as well as Abstract, the souls' activities will fail in the long run, and that the ambition to turn the art of painting into pure painting will do most damage to painting itself."[14]

The Symbolist and Post-Impressionist Breakthrough

If I discuss Julius Lange's resistance to Impressionism, it is because he embodies a certain preference for a Late Romantic aesthetic, still quite strong in the 1890s, and, not least, because his opinions converge with attitudes that, during the same period, develop among young Danish artists oriented towards Symbolism. After almost two decades of the modern breakthrough and worship of a Positivist worldview, many artists reacted against Naturalism's preference for objective truths capable of being immediately registered, measured, and weighed, at the expense of the potential development of art and the unfettered imagination.

Artists such as Johan Rohde, Vilhelm Hammershøi, J.F. Willumsen, and the couple Agnes and Harald Slott-Møller, shared this aspiration for a more evocative-oriented and decorative art. At Johan Rohde's initiative, these artists came together in 1891 to organize The Free Exhibition.[15] Among the founders was also Christian Mourier-Petersen, and the group was soon enlarged to include artists such as Joakim Skovgaard, Kristian Zahrtmann and Theodor Philipsen. The Free Exhibition offered a refuge for the new art, a place where the members themselves were responsible for what was exhibited, as opposed to the annual censured exhibitions at Charlottenborg, which, over the years, through unfortunate censorship, had come to occupy a relationship of opposition to the younger artists. The presence of Philipsen and Zahrtmann shows that The Free Exhibition comprised many different forms of expression, and that the community on which it was founded was oriented more toward art politics than ideas. Still, The Free Exhibition became synonymous, to a great degree, with the Symbolist breakthrough in Denmark. This is primarily due to the fact that this was where the Symbolists were allowed to exhibit their works, but also that the most important spokesmen for The Free Exhibition, Emil Hannover and Johannes Jørgensen, adopted Symbolism with great engagement and sympathy.

Like Julius Lange, the young Symbolists experienced Naturalism and Impressionism as an art historical cul-de-sac. No one expressed it more clearly than

Mogens Ballin, who wrote home from Paris in 1891 that the young Symbolists were gravediggers, with "a big, repugnant corpse to bury—a corpse with the audacity to claim it is not dead and, at times, so lively that we almost believe it. But no! Believe what you will: Naturalism—that is the name of the corpse—is dead."[16]

A few years later, the same view was published in the Danish journal of art and literature *Taarnet*. A journal that, in spite of its short life span, from October of 1893 until September of 1894, had great influence on the breakthrough and spread of Symbolism, not only in Denmark, but in all of Scandinavia. Articles by Johannes Jørgensen and Simon Koch proclaimed the fall of Naturalism to the advantage of Symbolism and the images of the soul. Instead of "Naturalism's sad tinkering and focus on detail, leading to the charming examination of whether this umbrella, too, was correctly drawn, or the colour of this spittoon true" (Simon Koch), one wished for "a pictorial language that, in earthly hieroglyphics, will speak of Eternity" (Johannes Jørgensen).[17] Rooted in reality, art should reach unto the heavens.

As Jørgensen wrote in his illustrative article "Symbolisme," published in the December 1893 issue of *Taarnet*, Symbolism involved "a belief in metaphysics, in another world, in the beyond."[18] The Symbolists' hope for a spiritual breakthrough that would replace Georg Brandes' modern breakthrough became, in Jørgensen's interpretation, the claim of a religious breakthrough. Jørgensen's definition of Symbolism is not false, just misleading in relation to the great volume of literature and art that did not live up to his religious demands. Jørgensen's Symbolism is in fact, as far as the visual arts are concerned, mainly valid for those artists with more or less strong ties to the circle of Paul Gauguin, Émile Bernard, and the Nabis, above all, Mogens Ballin, Ludvig Find, Gad F. Clement, and J.F. Willumsen. With Willumsen as the important exception, they united around a spiritually animated worship of beauty, closely associated with Symbolist literature, though, at the same time, far from the much more reality-oriented form of Symbolism also practiced in Denmark, by artists such as Ejnar Nielsen, Vilhelm Hammershøi, and L.A. Ring. In return, Jørgensen's definition of Symbolism, as regards the Danish artists, can generally be identified with those artists who adhered, more or less, to a Synthetist formal vocabulary, and may thus be regarded as the most important representatives of Post-Impressionism, the theme of the present exhibition.

The Loner Willumsen
The Danish artists' encounter with the work of Gauguin in Copenhagen, and their time spent together with the master himself in Paris and Brittany, was of major importance for the way in which they assimilated the Synthetist ideas. That is equally true for J.F. Willumsen, the Danish artist most often compared to Gauguin.

Willumsen himself readily emphasized the importance of Gauguin, something he would bitterly regret later on, as this made him seem less independent than was acceptable to his powerful ego. However, in spite of Willumsen's reluctance to acknowledge it, there is no doubt that his meeting with Gauguin in Brittany in 1890 greatly influenced Willumsen's decision to devote himself to wood sculpture, as clearly demonstrated by his first polychrome wood sculpture, *A Cocotte Hunting in Montagnes Russes*. During the time Willumsen and Gauguin spent together in

Above, to the left: 76. **Paul Gauguin** (1848–1903): **La Luxure**, 1890. Wood and metal, 70 x 15 x 7. J.F. Willumsens Museum, Frederikssund, G.S. 14.

Willumsen and Gauguin made each other's acquaintance in Paris in 1890. In the autumn of the same year, Willumsen received this sculpture in exchange for his own painting *Breton Woman Walking*.

Above, in the middle: 74. **Paul Gauguin** (1848–1903): **Woman from Brittany,** 1890. Pencil, pastel and charcoal on paper, 27.4 x 22. J.F. Willumsens Museum, Frederikssund, G.S. 582.

The large female figure in the drawing is a study after Willumsen's painting *Two Women Walking, Brittany*, executed in Pont-Aven in 1890.

Above, to the right: 79. **Paul Gauguin** (1848–1903): **Invitation from Paul Gauguin to J.F. Willumsen,** 1891. Ink, 17.2 x 11.3. J.F. Willumsens Museum, Frederikssund.

Opposite page: 217. **J.F. Willumsen** (1863–1958): **A Cocotte Hunting in Montagnes Russes,** 1890. Painted and carved wood, 100 x 60.5. J.F. Willumsens Museum, Frederikssund, Acc. 507.

Pont-Aven in 1890, Gauguin presented Willumsen with his wooden statuette *La Luxure*. As a return favour Gauguin received Willumsen's painting *Breton Woman Walking Towards the Beholder*. This exchange of art works suggests a relationship of mutual respect. One also has to give Willumsen credit for the fact that art historians have not yet been able to point to a dependency when it comes to his painting. On the contrary, one is constantly struck by Willumsen's originality.[19] This is true also of a work such as *Two Breton Women Parting After Having a Chat*, frequently associated with Gauguin, who had similarly created a series showing Breton women wearing traditional outfits. By the way, Bernard, Serusier, Mogens Ballin, and a great number of other artists who, in the years around 1900, spent a shorter or longer period of time in Brittany did the same. As opposed to Gauguin's suggestive, psychically charged space, Willumsen experiments with a completely different set of dynamics and expression, combining Cloissonism's strongly outlined colour planes with a more Nordic-Germanic expressiveness. The two figures rotate around an invisible axis, and the movement and inherent energy seem, on the whole, to be the main theme of the painting.

Similarly, it is difficult to discern Gauguin's influence in other works by Willumsen from the early 1890s. Like Edvard Munch, Willumsen goes his own way, and Johannes Jørgensen was thus entirely right when, as early as 1893, in a review of Gauguin and Van Gogh at The Free Exhibition in Copenhagen, he rejected the connection with Gauguin. In the exhibition catalogue, the French artist was described as "Willumsens's teacher and master," occasioning the following commentary by Jørgensen:

"The distance separating them seems, at first glance, to be considerable; hardly any of the French artist's paintings remind us of J.F. Willumsen, or tempt us into assuming a master-pupil relationship between him and Gauguin. They both belong

218. **J.F. Willumsen** (1863–1958): **Breton Woman Walking Towards the Beholder**, 1890.
Oil on canvas, 64 x 57.5. J.F. Willumsens Museum, Frederikssund, Acc. 1230.

219. **J.F. Willumsen** (1863–1958): **Two Breton Women Parting After Having a Chat,** 1890.
Oil and tempera on canvas, 100.4 x 93.2. Nordjyllands Kunstmuseum, Aalborg, NK 811.

to the same artistic movement, but each occupies his own space on the fringes of a common current."[20]

The Danish Synthetists—Ballin, Clement, and Find

In Denmark Synthetism quite rapidly turned into a few individuals' personal crusade. Consequently, several less spiritually oriented artists, such as Ludvig Find and Gad F. Clement, soon sought out other, more earthly roads, ending up in an area to which many French Synthetists had turned—namely, a Post-Impressionist painting of domestic interiors and portraits as practiced by Pierre Bonnard and Édouard Vuillard.

For many of the Synthetists this return to reality was the only possible solution, both in human and artistic terms. Their religious engagement was not as unconditional as that of Émile Bernard or Paul Sérusier, or of such subversive force as that of Mogens Ballin, or the Dutch artist Jan Verkade. For a majority of Danish artists, the association with the Nabis was based as much on the temptation for a young, not yet established artist to belong to a community of rebels resembling a brotherhood, as being a religious matter. Already by the mid-1890s, when individual artists began adopting a more independent profile, their social conditions changing, the Nabi circle lost its importance. However, as Mogens Ballin's landscapes from Brittany convincingly demonstrate, their radical departure from Naturalism not only paved the way for the early Modernism of Picasso, Matisse, and their circle. With its planes of bright colour, strong outlines, and desire to translate a sentiment, a mood, into an anti-naturalistic visual language, it is, indeed, synonymous with the earliest phase of Modernism.

Mogens Ballin traveled to Paris as early as 1889, and, carrying a letter of introduction from Mette Gauguin, soon became a part of the avant-garde artistic milieu. Yet, it was only in March of 1891, when Ballin met Jan Verkade at the farewell party for Gauguin before his departure for Tahiti, that his artistic development really gathered momentum. Verkade talked about his impending trip to Brittany with Sérusier,

196. **Paul Sérusier** (1864–1927): **Landscape, Brittany**, 1891.
Gouache, 25,5 x 51. Private collection.

11. **Mogens Ballin** (1871–1914): **Landscape, Brittany**, 1892.
Tempera on paper, 34 x 53.3. Private collection.

9. **Mogens Ballin** (1871–1914): **Landscape. Brittany**, 1891–92. Oil on canvas, 56 x 64. Private collection.

and Ballin, anxious to become more closely acquainted with a region fabled among the Nabis, was, after polite inquiry, asked to join their company.

Serusier's *Landscape. Brittany* was presumably executed in connection with this journey, in the summer of 1891 to be precise, during a stay in the village of Huelgoat, where Sérusier, theoretically as well as practically, through his works, introduced Ballin and Verkade to the formal principles of Synthetism. Their landscapes from this period bear witness to the degree to which the two artists followed Sérusier's instructions to purify and intensify the colours of nature, being so close in their examination of the potential of the new expression that they are often difficult to tell apart. Sérusier probably presented Ballin with his *Landscape. Brittany*, and the following year, when Verkade and Ballin were back in Brittany, living in the small village of Saint Nolff, Ballin produced a variation on Sérusier's painting. An exercise in translating and interpreting Sérusier's instructions.

Although Mogens Ballin, both artistically, in terms of his ideas, and his personal contacts, was the most wholehearted Nabi among the Danish artists, it was to a greater degree Gad F. Clement who, according to Emil Hannover, became "the

preacher of the Gospel of the new art."[21] In 1890–91 Clement accompanied Ballin to France, and was introduced by him to the latest anti-Naturalist currents. However, individual landscape paintings from Brittany by Clement, such as *Garden in Brittany*, were not based on the latest Synthetist formal experiments. Here he seems, to a greater degree, to have taken as his starting-point Gauguin's Impressionist works, which he knew from Mette Gauguin's collection, though a certain stylization of the poplars on the left also reveals his attempt to assimilate the latest currents. Later on, probably in the summer of 1892, when Clement returned to Brittany, he had completely adopted the formal language of Synthetism. A painting such as *Landscape from Brittany with Resting Girl* convincingly distills the formal principles of Synthetism, establishing a connection with the contemporary landscapes of Ballin and Serusier. After his return to Copenhagen, Clement established himself as a knowledgeable spokesman for Synthetism, and his Copenhagen studio, initially shared with Ballin, then with Ludvig Find, became the favorite gathering place for the Danish Nabis and the group associated with the journal *Taarnet*.

Clement's principal work from this period is the *Decorative Painting, The Vision of St. Francis* (1892–93). For the Nabis, St. Francis' vision was synonymous with that acknowledgment of a higher reality they sought to achieve through their art. Consequently, the Nabis' images are filled with saints and Christ-identifications, Gauguin being the artist who most frequently staged his own identification with Christ. But also Mogens Ballin represented himself as prophetic visionary in a self-portrait.[22]

Clement found his prototypes among Gauguin's Christ images, especially *Christ on the Mount of Olives* of 1889 (The Norton Gallery of Art, West Palm Beach), while the stylized flower-strewn landscape with women dressed in white seems, rather, to refer to similar motifs by Émile Bernard and, especially, Maurice Denis.[23] Comparisons with Gauguin's self-portrait of 1889 (The National Gallery of Art, Washington, D.C.) and *Self-Portrait with Yellow Christ* of 1889–90 (Musée d'Orsay, Paris), suggest that Clement may also have applied Gauguin's idealized facial

Above: 34. **Gad F. Clement** (1867–1933): **Garden in Brittany**, 1891. Oil on canvas, 93 x 79.8 (with frame). John J. A. Hunov's Collections, Copenhagen.

Opposite page: 36. **Gad F. Clement** (1867–1933): **Decorative Painting. St. Francis' Vision of the Three Holy Women**. Pastel on paper mounted on canvas, 161 x 110. John J. A. Hunov's Collections, Copenhagen.

Mogens Ballin (1871–1914):
Gauguin as a Prophet. Oil on canvas, 72 x 55. Private collection.

features to his St. Francis. That Gauguin was regarded as a prophet by his "disciples" is also evident from the portrait of *Gauguin as a Prophet,* probably by Mogens Ballin. A painting closely related to Gauguin's self-portrait and, especially, to *Christ on the Mount of Olives,* which Ballin would have had an opportunity to view in Paris, as it was in Gauguin's collection until March of 1891.[24]

An artist who had studied Clement's *Decorative Painting* in detail was Ludvig Find. In Find's principal Symbolist work, *Portrait of a Young Artist,* as in Clement's

Ludvig Find (1869–1945):
Portrait of a Young Artist,
1893. Oil on canvas. 150 x 128.
Skovgaard Museet, Viborg,
Denmark.

work, the slender trunk of a young tree grows along one side of the picture, and in both works the trunk divides at the centre, a single branch extending across the surface. Find dressed his young artist in a buttoned coat of simple cut, not unlike St. Francis' monk's robe, and, like Clement, Find chose to emphasize the stylized foliage as a decorative element.

Unlike Ballin and Clement, Find did not travel to Paris and, thus, did not experience the Nabi milieu at close quarters, and although he was probably deeply religious, Catholicism remained unfamiliar to him. However, his ability to translate his friends' knowledge of the Nabis' aims, allowed him to paint this initiated portrait of an artist. Painted in Naestved on Sydsjaelland, at a great distance from the Nabis' preferred spots, the *Portrait of a Young Artist* has, nevertheless, become one of the movement's key portraits. A portrait that captures the essential element of the Nabis' self-image: the specially chosen one possessing the gift of prophecy and, thus, capable of interpreting life's true metaphysical essence in the surrounding nature and everyday life.

Clement titled his painting *Decorative Painting*. Ludvig Find might, even more justifiably, have chosen this title for his own *Portrait of a Young Artist*. Using the decorative foliage of a chestnut tree and a background of green grass, a blue stream, and brownish soil that seems to rise up, functioning more as a decorative backdrop than suggesting spatial illusion, Find has created one of Synthetism's most surface-oriented paintings. As everything exists only on the surface, there is no spatial differentiation between the brown leaves of the chestnut tree and the brown soil of the "background."

Ludvig Find's landscape painting *Trees by the Shore* of 1893 is more naturalistic than his *Portrait of a Young Artist*, though with its own melancholy atmosphere, a certain feeling of discomfort reminiscent of certain works by Prince Eugen. Tree trunks and foliage are represented in a stylized manner to a certain degree, investing the motif with a decorative emphasis on outline, though less so than in the *Portrait of a Young Artist*.

The Symbolist period was short for both Find and Clement. Already during a trip to Italy in 1893–94, they became greatly interested in Italian Renaissance art, its clarity and compositional severity soon replacing all Symbolist fantasies. Around the turn of the century, they turned towards a more reality-based formal language, as well as a wider selection of motifs, including, in addition to portraits and landscapes, elaborate flower pieces and domestic interiors. When Ludvig Find traveled to Paris for the first time in 1902, he was greatly inspired by the art of Vuillard and Bonnard, initiating a renewed study of French painting. A light-filled late Impressionist style of painting and a selection of motifs including primarily images of children, characterize most of Find's artistic production after 1900.

Johan Rohde and Relations with "the bizarre Dutchman" Van Gogh
In addition to the Synthetists mentioned earlier, several Danish artists deserve attention in the present Post-Impressionist context. Above all, Johan Rohde, whose contribution as a pioneering art critic, exhibition organizer, and later art craftsman, has often overshadowed his art. His *Summer Night at Tønning* belongs to a group of

works executed in connection with a longer journey in 1892, a journey that put the already well-oriented artist in contact with the latest currents in contemporary European art. His *Diary of a Journey in 1892*, published posthumously, includes a description of the journey in the form of diary entries, an account of Rohde's many visits to museums and exhibitions, as well as his encounters with several leading artists, among others, Odilon Redon, Maurice Denis, and Paul Sérusier.

Rohde's paintings are always based on reality, but their true value lies primarily in their emphasis on mood, and awareness of painting as an abstract phenomenon built on the interaction of colour, line, space, and surface. This is characteristic of *Summer Night at Tønning*, as well as many of the artist's later paintings of landscapes and architectural views from Denmark and Italy.

Rohde transmitted his great knowledge about recent French art to his colleagues in Copenhagen by, for example, exhibiting his own exclusive art collection. Furthermore, he initiated the legendary exhibition of 29 works by Van Gogh and 51 works by Gauguin as part of The Free Exhibition of 1893. An exhibition that, together with the show of French Nabis at the Kleis Gallery in Copenhagen organized in the same year, was capable of placing the visual expression of the young Danish artists in an international perspective. Johan Rohde's friendship with Edvard Munch, and his great effort to secure Munch's scandalous 1892 Berlin exhibition for Copenhagen, should also be mentioned. Rohde was able to exhibit 54 of Munch's

189. **Johan Rohde** (1856–1935): **Summer Night at Tønning,** 1893. Oil on canvas, 86 x 111. Nationalmuseum, NM 1514.

paintings in the buildings used by The Free Exhibition in the spring of 1893, among others, *Death in the Sickroom, Puberty,* and *Melancholy.*

On his 1892 trip to Paris through Holland and Belgium, Rohde for the first time viewed works by Van Gogh. This happened at an Amsterdam art dealer's, and Rohde himself described the two works as "the best contemporary art I have seen so far on my trip—and probably the best I will see."[25] Rohde's knowledge of "the bizarre Dutchman" stemmed from a fellow art student, Christian Mourier-Petersen, who, in several letters addressed to Rohde in 1888, had written about his time spent in Van Gogh's company at Arles. Mourier-Petersen had painted side-by-side with Van Gogh at Arles, and, especially, his painting *Flowering Peach-Trees* is inconceivable without a thorough knowledge of the series of flowering fruit trees Van Gogh executed during his stay in Arles. When Mourier-Petersen went to Paris in May of 1888, he rented a studio from Theo Van Gogh, keeping in touch with Van Gogh at Arles through a series of letters. In Paris Mourier-Petersen established contact with Toulouse-Lautrec, among others, and after his return to Copenhagen in 1890 he was able to communicate his impressions of the latest art to Johan Rohde in

a detailed and insightful manner. Apart from a few paintings of domestic interiors of the 1890s, somewhat reminiscent of Degas, Mourier-Petersen's close ties with the period's most progressive artistic milieu gave a rather meager return, his later works being quite conventional, in spite of their fine colouristic qualities.

That other, perhaps more receptive, artists might have used a corresponding first-hand knowledge of Van Gogh's art in a more productive manner, is demonstrated by the Funen painter Peter Hansen's youthful work *A Field of Waving Rye.* Together with Mourier-Petersen's *Flowering Peach-Trees,* this is one of the few Danish paintings referring directly to Van Gogh, in particular, to the Dutchman's *Landscape from Saint-Rémy* of June 1889. At Johan Rohde's initiative, the painting was purchased at The Hague in 1892 on behalf of two Danish art collectors—the wholesale merchant Oscar Wandel and the Department Secretary H. Chr.

Vincent Van Gogh, Flowering Peach-Tree, 'Souvenir de Mauve', 1888. Oil on canvas, 73 x 59.5. Kröller-Müller Museum, Otterlo.

Christensen. At the drawing of lots between the two collectors the painting went to Christensen, quickly becoming an attraction among Danish artists.[26] Furthermore, as Van Gogh's painting was one of the principal works in the 1893 exhibition of Gauguin and Van Gogh, Peter Hansen had a good opportunity of studying it more closely. That he did so is demonstrated not only by his composition and colours, but also—and this is perhaps more interesting—by important details such as the billowing rhythms of the bundled ears and the restless clouds in the blue sky. When donated by Christensen to the Statens Museum for Kunst in 1905 Van Gogh's painting became the first Impressionist or Post-Impressionist work to be owned by a Danish museum.

Although Peter Hansen's point of departure was Van Gogh's painting, his attitude towards the motif and his painting style are far removed from Van Gogh's

107. **Peter Hansen** (1868–1928): **A Field of Waving Rye,** 1894. Oil on canvas,
85 x 115.5. Statens Museum for Kunst, Copenhagen, KMS 3800.

Vincent Van Gogh (1853–1890): **Landscape from Saint-Rémy,** 1889. Oil on canvas,
70.5 x 88.5. Ny Carlsberg Glyptotek, Copenhagen, SMK 1840.

68. Paul Gauguin (1848–1903): Jar in Glazed Stoneware Shaped Like a Lumpfish, 1889–90. Glazed stoneware, h. 22. Det Danske Kunstindustrimuseum, Copenhagen, B 3/1931.

After the last Impressionist exhibition in the spring of 1886 Gauguin began collaboration with the ceramicist Ernest Chaplet's workshop. Gauguin hoped that producing ceramics would improve his financial situation. Most of Gauguin's ceramics from the years 1886–87 have figurative decoration with motifs from Brittany. Financially the project was not a success. Many of Gauguin's ceramic pieces have long been in Danish collections.

dynamic, spiraling brush strokes and the energetic force of the composition itself. Peter Hansen's manner is more closely related to the approach and style of Philipsen's Danish Impressionism, as is especially evident in the representation of the billowing rye, where the artist, using short brush strokes, creates a rhythmic, vibrating field of golden ears and green blades. The Impressionist influence is also visible in the grayish violet shading of the clouds and, more generally, in the contrast between the blues and violets of the upper part of the composition and the predominantly golden and yellowish green tonalities of the lower part.

Early Acquisitions and Art Collections

French Impressionist art was not collected by the great Danish art collectors and museums while the movement was still functioning as a catalyzing force for the latest art. By the time Wilhelm Hansen, Christian Tetzen-Lund, Helge Jacobsen and others were assembling their impressive collections of recent French art, during and after World War I, Impressionism was already part of the history of art. More about that later. First, a few words about the art collections and acquisitions of the 1880s and 1890s, which played an important role in contemporary Danish art.

Most important was undoubtedly Paul Gauguin's collection of French Impressionists. When Gauguin left Denmark in 1885, he left his collection in the care of his wife Mette, and thanks to the research of art historian Merete Bodelsen we have good knowledge about its make-up.[27] Together with Gauguin's own works, to which new works were added on several occasions after 1885, the collection had great importance for the knowledge of Impressionism and Post-Impressionism during the following decade.

Due to strained personal finances, Mette Gauguin was forced to sell off numerous works, mainly to friends and acquaintances. However, they remained in Scandinavia, forming the core of several Danish exhibitions of French Impressionists during the following decade. At the Art Association's 1889 exhibition of Scandinavian and French Impressionists, the Danish display consisted almost exclusively of works from Gauguin's collection. At The Free Exhibition show of Gauguin and Van Gogh in 1893 most of the works by Gauguin came from Mette Gauguin.[28] As demonstrated by the exhibition catalogue, several paintings now belonged to Danish artists and art collectors, such as Theodor Philipsen, Johan Rohde, Emil Hannover, Mogens Ballin, and, not least, Mette Gauguin's brother-in-law, Edvard Brandes, listed as the owner of six paintings, a fan, and a piece of ceramics.[29] Due to an error, the painter Niels Skovgaard is not listed as the owner of number 155, *Landscape from Osny*, even though Skovgaard had purchased the painting as early as 1889. Furthermore, one notes that the Swedish painter Richard Bergh is listed as the owner of number 152, *Landscape from Brittany* (ill. p. 78, cat.no. 72), purchased from Mette Gauguin in 1892, when Bergh was in Copenhagen for the Art Association's exhibition. During the exhibition further works were sold to, among others, the painters Joakim Skovgaard, Georg Achen, and Johannes Wilhjelm.

Much later, in 1911, when the Art Association organized an exhibition in Copenhagen of contemporary French art in Danish ownership, another opportunity was provided to view a great number of works from Gauguin's collection. As

64. **Paul Gauguin** (1848–1903): **Double Vessel with Modelled Breton Girl**, 1886–87. Unglazed stoneware, h. 15. Det Danske Kunstindustrimuseum, Copenhagen, 44/1976.

65. **Paul Gauguin** (1848–1903): **Jug in Unglazed Stoneware with Breton Girl, Geese and Crab on Lid,** 1886–87. Unglazed stoneware, h. 24.4. Det Danske Kunstindustrimuseum, Copenhagen, B16/1943.

66. **Paul Gauguin** (1848–1903): **Jug in Unglazed Stoneware with Bust of Degas-like Woman**, 1886–87. Unglazed stoneware, h. 21.6. Det Danske Kunstindustrimuseum, Copenhagen, B17/1943.

67. **Paul Gauguin** (1848–1903): **Jug in Unglazed Stoneware with three Handles and Breton Girl,** 1886–87. Unglazed stoneware, h. 13,6. Det Danske Kunstindustrimuseum, Copenhagen, B15/1943.

Paul Gauguin (1848–1903):
Seascape from Brittany, 1886.
Oil on canvas, 75 x 112. Private
collection.

revealed by a handwritten inventory, the circle of owners had by then been further enlarged, Mette Gauguin now being listed as the owner of only nine works by Gauguin and a few by Guillaumin. Also exhibited were several works not derived from Gauguin's collection, but belonging to Danish artists, including Ballin and Clement, who, in the early 1890s, had been in contact with Gauguin, Bernard, and the Nabis in Paris.

Among the Danish artists and art collectors who acquired works by Gauguin in the years around 1890 are several who were, at that time, leaders in the effort to develop Danish art in the direction of a more contemporary idiom, principally Philipsen, Rohde, Hannover, the brothers Skovgaard, and Mogens Ballin. Philipsen, whose contacts with Gauguin paved the way for showing so many of his works in 1893, acquired his first painting by Gauguin in 1885. This was the *Road to Rouen (II)* of 1885, a version of a painting from 1884. Gauguin presented the painting as a gift to Philipsen, who wrote on the back of the canvas "Property of Th. Philipsen. Gauguin gave me this painting." The painting had great significance for Philipsen, providing, as it did, a practical example of the Impressionist painting technique Gauguin had advised Philipsen to employ, and one may assume that Philipsen consulted it diligently during the following year while working on his pioneering Impressionist painting, *A Late Autumn Day in Dyrehaven. Sunshine.* Indeed, close examination of the painting technique of the two works reveals great similarities.

Later on, in 1892, Philipsen confirmed his understanding of Gauguin's Impressionist art by purchasing *Woman Sewing* of 1880 (ill. p. 142). The purchase truly delighted Gauguin, surely not only because Philipsen paid 900 Danish kroner for it, but also because he still had a great deal of respect for the Danish painter.[30] At one time Philipsen decided that the painting would go to The Louvre after his death, but he subsequently changed his mind and instead bequeathed it to the Statens Museum for Kunst in 1920.[31]

Another Gauguin painting that had a great impact on Danish art of this period is his *Seascape from Brittany* of 1886. Johan Rohde purchased the painting from Mette Gauguin in 1892, in exchange for one of Rohde's paintings, which Mette had seen at The Free Exhibition. Johan Rohde had a small, but superb, collection of primarily Symbolist art, partly acquired during his journey to France, Holland, and Belgium in 1892. Among other things, he bought Van Gogh's drawing, *A Garden at Arles* of 1888, from the Parisian paint-seller Tanguy. He quickly forwarded the drawing to Copenhagen, where, together with Gauguin's *Seascape from Brittany*, it became the object of much discussion over the next few years among the many Scandinavian artists visiting Rohde in the hope of an introduction to the latest artistic currents.[32] As Emil Hannover wrote about Rohde in the journal *Politiken* on March 26th, 1893: "Recently returned from a major journey abroad, his trunk filled with samples of what is most modern in modern art, whereby his comfortable living room at Nyhavn, during the course of the winter, has been a pilgrimage site for all who long to see the sun of the new art rise in this country."

Mogens Ballin should also be mentioned among the art collecting artists. Exactly when he purchased his fine Gauguin painting, *Shepherdess from Brittany*, is not known, but it may have been among the paintings sent from Paris to Mette Gauguin in Copenhagen. Another, perhaps more likely possibility, is that Ballin bought it in Paris. The most likely place would be Gauguin's auction, the "Vente Gauguin," held on February 23rd, 1891, which Ballin attended. As the painting is not mentioned in the catalogue, however, he must have bought it directly from Gauguin.[33] At the "Vente Gauguin," the musician Fritz Bendix purchased the painting *Amongst the Lilies* of 1889, at the suggestion of Ballin and Gad F. Clement. A few weeks later, on March 8th to be precise, Ballin and Clement accompanied the composer Carl Nielsen on a visit to the paint-seller Père Tanguy, where Bendix purchased Van Gogh's *A Corner in the Garden of Saint Paul's Hospital* of 1889.[34] This, by the way, was the first painting by Van Gogh purchased for Denmark. In 1910 Bendix tried to sell the painting to Statens Museum for Kunst and Nasjonalgalleriet in Oslo. Both said no and today the present owner is unknown.

Ballin was also directly involved in the first (overlooked in the literature) acquisition of a Cézanne by a Danish museum. He had in fact himself purchased a small Cézanne still-life from Père Tanguy in Paris around 1890, later sold to the Statens Museum for Kunst in 1912. The Museum, which later chose to deposit its collection of contemporary French art at the Glyptotek, in 1928 took the unusual step of sell-

31. Paul Cézanne (1839–
1906): Portrait of the Artist's
Wife. Oil on canvas, 59 x 50.
Nationalmuseum, NM 6348. Gift
from Grace and Philip Sandblom
1970.

This painting was, for a period,
part of Wilhelm Hansen's art collection at Ordrupgaard.

ing the painting to an art dealer in Berlin, where it was later re-sold, and now belongs to the Cincinnati Art Museum.

In accordance with an agreement with the Director, Karl Madsen, Ballin offered Cézanne's still-life, together with a series of other French Post-Impressionist works, to the Statens Museum for Kunst. In the Museum's letter archives is an inventory of these works, apparently comprising the major part of Ballin's collection of French art. Gauguin's *Shepherdess from Brittany* is not included in the list. Apparently Ballin did not wish to part with the painting, which was sold only in 1917 to the great art collector Tetzen-Lund, years after Ballin's death in 1914. Helge Jacobsen later bought the painting, donating it to the Glyptotek in 1927. In Ballin's collection we also note Maurice Denis' *Madonna and Child with the Infant St. John* of 1898, which also, via Helge Jacobsen's collection, ended up in the Glyptotek. Incidentally, this was a late acquisition, purchased directly from Denis, which shows that Ballin stayed in touch with his old Nabi friends. On the list are also three works by Ker-Xavier Roussel, two by Vuillard, and one by Bonnard, as well as numerous litho-graphs and woodcuts by, among others, Gauguin, Degas, Redon, Bonnard, Vuillard, and Manet. In a letter accompanying the inventory, Ballin also mentions five or six woodcuts by Vallotton and lithographs by Daumier. In other words, Ballin offered the Statens Museum for Kunst a small, but superb collection, though apparently only the Cézanne and nine woodcuts by Gauguin were deemed worthy of a museum collection.[35]

Great Art Collectors and Collections
Already at the end of the 19th century important private art collections were being assembled in Denmark. The brewer Carl Jacobsen founded his collection of Antique and 19th-century French sculpture, the tobacco merchant Heinrich Hirschsprung assembled his collection of Danish 19th-century art, and the estate owner Johannes Hage his extraordinary collection of foreign Old Masters. Three very different art collections and collectors, yet, all agreed that the general public and future genera-tions should be able to enjoy their collections. The result was the Ny Carlsberg Glyptotek (1882), Den Hirschsprungske Samling (1907), and Nivaagaards Malerisamling (1908). They were important models for those collectors who, in the decades after 1900, created an enormously active collecting environment in Copenhagen. An art market with low prices, especially during World War I, and good economic conditions, allowed primarily the businessman Herman Heilbuth, the engineer, politician and businessman Johannes Rump, the wholesale merchant Christian Tetzen-Lund, the financier Wilhelm Hansen, and Helge Jacobsen, son of the brewer Carl Jacobsen, to assemble their large collections in just a few years. Only the last three collectors are relevant in an Impressionist and Post-Impressionist con-text. Heilbuth was mainly interested in Old Masters, while Rump, on the contrary, was oriented towards the latest developments in French art: Matisse, Derain, and others. From this perspective, Wilhelm Hansen's and Helge Jacobsen's collections, with their emphasis on Impressionism, seem the most conservative, while Tetzen-Lund's collection, including many key works by Cézanne, as well as by Gauguin, Matisse, and Picasso, seems the most farsighted.[36]

Camille Pissarro (1830–1903): **Flowering Plum Tree, Éragny. The Home of the Artist,**
1894. Oil on canvas, 60 x 73. Ordrupgaard, Copenhagen.

Wilhelm Hansen, who made his fortune in the insurance business, began collecting Danish 19th-century art already in the early 1890s, above all Golden Age painting and artists of his own generation, such as L.A. Ring, Vilhelm Hammershøi, and, not least, one of the Funen Painters, his fellow student, Peter Hansen. No doubt his conversations with Peter Hansen contributed to drawing Wilhelm Hansen's attention away from Danish to more recent French art. At the same time, Peter Hansen's roots in the tradition of Danish Naturalism surely contributed to Wilhelm Hansen's lack of interest in classic Modernism, remaining in what might be termed the French sphere of interest of Philipsen and the Funen Painters. Wilhelm Hansen's ambition was to create a representative collection of French art from Corot to Cézanne.[37] That he actually succeeded in assembling a collection of French art regarded as the best in Europe outside of France in just two years, between his initial purchases of Impressionist works in 1916, and his final public presentation of the collection on September 14th, 1918, reveals something about the period's fabulous opportunities, and about Wilhelm Hansen's single-mindedness and talent for tracking down and purchasing objects of the highest quality. Among his advisors were Théodore Duret, companion in arms of Manet and the Impressionists, and Wilhelm Hansen was in close contact with the leading Parisian art dealers and collectors, such as Ambroise Vollard and Alphonse Kann.

The creation of a consortium in 1918 together with Herman Heilbuth and the Winkel & Magnussen firm of art dealers was of vital importance for the collection's expansion. The aim of the consortium was to work towards the goal of "acquiring good quality, and outstanding, art for Scandinavia" through the purchase and reselling of art works. From time to time, the consortium succeeded in acquiring entire private collections, like those of Viau and Flersheim, while, at the same time, failing to acquire Auguste Pellerin's remarkable Cézanne collection at the last moment. The consortium negotiated the purchase of seventy paintings by Cézanne at the price of three million francs, but when it became apparent that Pellerin was interested in selling only fifty paintings for the same price, the consortium withdrew its offer. Unfortunately![38]

Like his great predecessors, Wilhelm Hansen wished for his collection to become accessible to the general public. Following its presentation in 1918, the collection was thus opened to the public once a week. To further increase the knowledge of French art, Wilhelm Hansen founded the Association for French Art the same year. With Hansen as President, a series of important retrospectives of, among others, Manet, Matisse, Gauguin, and Degas, were organized in the following years. Exhibitions frequently shown also in Stockholm and Oslo, entirely in line with the aims of the consortium.

Unfortunately, Wilhelm Hansen was also affected by the repercussions of the 1922 crash of the Landmandsbanken, mainly because the consortium had financed all their loans through the bank. To rid himself of debt as quickly as possible, Hansen sold off a large part of his collection of French art, as many as 76 works, among which were several key works by Cézanne, Monet, Manet, Gauguin, Renoir, and Degas. Foreign collectors, including the Swiss Oskar Reinhart and the American Albert C. Barnes, purchased a great number of these works. It should be mentioned

that Wilhelm Hansen had first offered the entire French collection to the Danish State for just one million Danish kroner. But not even this time the State was persuaded to act! Fortunately, Helge Jacobsen purchased 19 paintings and drawings, subsequently donating them to the Glyptotek.[39] Free from debt in less than a year, Wilhelm Hansen began replacing lost works by, for example, acquiring such essential works as Manet's *The Garters*, Renoir's study for *Le Moulin de la Galette*, Pissarro's *Flowering Plum Tree*, and, not least, Degas' study for the *Portrait of the Bellelli Family*.

In accordance with the original intention at its public presentation in 1918, at the death of his wife Henny Hansen in 1951, the collection was bequeathed to the Danish State, together with the buildings and park. The Ordrupgaard Collection opened as a museum just two years later.

Helge Jacobsen's father, the brewer Carl Jacobsen, did not think much of Impressionism, and even less of what came after. In 1903 he wrote to Helge about Manet: "Manet is a celebrated French painter, the founder of Impressionism. A couple of his paintings are in the Luxembourg Museum, being highly valued by the devotees of Impressionism. In my eyes they are merely ugly, mannered, affected."[40] Consequently, Helge Jacobsen waited until after his father's death in January of 1914 to show his interest in Impressionism and, not least, his talent for acquiring few, but vitally important, works by the movement's key artists. He did not wait long, however. Already in connection with the great exhibition of French art organized by Karl Madsen in May of 1914 at the Statens Museum for Kunst, Helge Jacobsen arranged the purchase by the Ny Carlsberg Foundation of, among others, Manet's *Absinthe*

Alfred Sisley (1839–1899): **The Flood. Seine at Bougival,** 1873 . Oil on canvas, 50 x 65.5. Ordrupgaard, Copenhagen.

Drinker, Sisley's *The Flood*, and Monet's *Shadows on the Sea*, ensuring their donation to the Glyptotek.

During the exhibition, an overview of the greatest achievements in French art from David to Matisse, the Statens Museum for Kunst added Manet's sketch for *The Execution of Emperor Maximilian* and Sisley's *The Water-Power Works, Bougival* to its collection of French art. Since the acquisition in 1905 of Van Gogh's *Landscape from Saint-Rémy*, the Museum had bought Gauguin's *Garden in Snow* (1907), *Figures in a Garden* (1910), *Still-Life with Flowers* (1912), and *Landscape from Pont-Aven* (1912), all in Danish private possession. In addition, a painting by Armand Guillaumin had been purchased from a private Danish owner in 1911, and, as mentioned earlier, Cézanne's *Still-Life* from Mogens Ballin. In other words, a small, but superb, collection of recent French art had been assembled in the years leading up to World War I. However, the Museum did not have sufficient economic resources to compete with the great private Danish collectors during, and immediately after, World War I, and, since the Director, Karl Madsen, was more enthusiastic about foreign Old Masters, the Museum's acquisitions of French art were limited to a series of donations. These included, for example, several works by Guillaumin and Pissarro, as well as Gauguin's *Woman Sewing*, bequeathed by Theodor Philipsen in 1920. However, these were chance occurrences. When Helge Jacobsen in 1922 purchased 19 works from Wilhelm Hansen's collection for the Glyptotek, he had occasion to propose a mutual deposition agreement with the Statens Museum. The Museum would receive a series of fine Old Master paintings, especially Italian, and would, in exchange, deposit its collection of French 19th-century art at the Glyptotek. Thus, by transferring his own collection of French art to the Glyptotek in 1927, Helge Jacobsen had secured a rather prominent collection of French Impressionism and Post-Impressionism for the museum.[41] The agreement with the Statens Museum for Kunst was later followed by further depositions, as the Museum, primarily through bequests, acquired works by, among others, Manet, Pissarro, Sisley, and Degas.

Compared to the collections of Wilhelm Hansen, Helge Jacobsen, and Johannes Rump, which were largely transferred to museum ownership, Christian Tetzen-Lund's collection was not of great significance for posterity. In return, Tetzen-Lund had great influence on contemporary Danish and Scandinavian artists through his activities as an art patron and his large collection of French art.[42]

During the years 1909 to 1916, Tetzen-Lund purchased almost exclusively paintings by young Scandinavian artists, often in such great quantities that it must be understood as a gesture of financial support. As an example may be mentioned that, over the years, he bought about 30 paintings by the Dane Aksel Jørgensen and nearly 50 by the Norwegian Ludvig Karsten. Add to this an important number of works by, among others, Edvard Weie, Harald Giersing, Jens Adolf Jerichau, Henrik Sørensen, Per Krohg, and Isaac Grünewald. This contact with the young artists presumably contributed to Tetzen-Lund starting to build up his legendary collection of French art in the spring of 1916. In any case, he was quite knowledgeable about the latest artistic currents and, from the outset, bought works by Picasso and Derain, as well as by older French artists, such as Delacroix, Daumier, and Courbet. Furthermore—and this is what makes him relevant in the present context—he began assembling an important collection of Impressionists and Post-Impressionists. Among the Impressionists he was principally interested in Pissarro and Renoir, while Cézanne, Gauguin, and Van Gogh, constituted the core of his collection of Post-Impressionists. At its most extensive, in the 1920s, the collection comprised some 900 works, of which no less than eight were by Cézanne, eleven by Van Gogh, twenty by Matisse, twenty by Picasso, and twenty by Derain. He also owned Renoir's preparatory study for the *Moulin de la Galette* (later sold to Wilhelm Hansen), two primeval forest scenes by Henri Rousseau, and a painting by Giorgio de Chirico.

A large part of this impressive collection had already been acquired when Tetzen-Lund opened his collection to the general public on January 2nd, 1917. Before November 2nd, 1924, one could visit the collector's home in the Palaegade 6 in Copenhagen every Monday afternoon, from October to April. The guest book reveals that it was above all the artists who benefited from the collection. Of the circa 4 000 visitors, 800 were artists. In addition to the young Danish artists, the visitors included Edvard Munch and Ludvig Karsten, the Swedish art historian

Ragnar Hoppe, and Herwarth Walden, editor of *Der Sturm*. In the last years of World War I and immediately after the war, when it was difficult for, especially, Swedish and Norwegian artists to travel to Paris, the Tetzen-Lund collection became an important source of inspiration, keeping the young Scandinavians informed about the latest currents in French art.

Apparently Tetzen-Lund wished for the transfer of part of his collection to public ownership, however, due to disagreements, mainly between Tetzen-Lund and the Statens Museum for Kunst, this never occurred. Thus, the absolutely most farsighted and, when it comes to contemporary art, qualitatively best of the great private Danish collections, was sold and dispersed abroad. To view the many key works by Cézanne and Picasso once owned by Tetzen-Lund, one must now visit foreign museums, apart from a few works by Gauguin and Matisse purchased by Helge Jacobsen for the Glyptotek and a series of key works by Matisse which, through Johannes Rump's efforts, ended up in the Statens Museum for Kunst.

Yet, no matter how much one may regret the loss of so many, now internationally recognized works, a prominent collection of French Impressionism and Post-Impressionism still exists in Denmark, thanks to Gauguin's art collection and the efforts of the great art collectors. A collection that, being representative and of high quality, is equal to the great international collections established outside of France during the course of the 20th century. Furthermore, this collection offers extraordinary opportunities for a broader perspective on Danish art of this period, and for an appreciation of not only the obvious relationships, but also the Danish artists' regional distinctiveness.

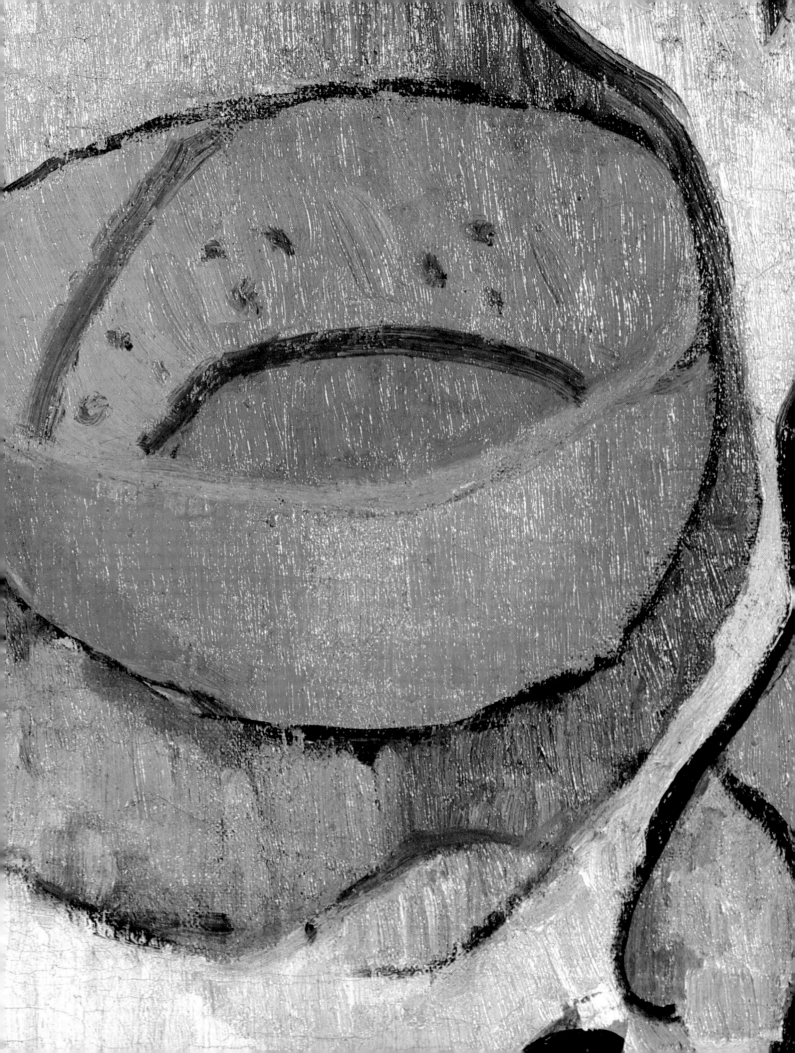

Norwegian Impressions
Nils Messel

"Words that are common currency at any given time are generally the most unclear of all. Consequently, hardly two individuals have the same understanding of Impressionism, defining it in the same way—if it can be defined at all. But everyone makes use of the term—something that only leads to general confusion." Andreas Aubert, 1883.[1]

DURING MOST OF the nineteenth century, Norwegian artists had looked to Germany for inspiration. They studied in Dresden, Düsseldorf, Karlsruhe, and Munich. Around 1880 they began to orient themselves towards France, and Paris became the city they preferred for their studies. Within the space of a few years, it was generally recognized that the influence of contemporary French painting had a liberating influence on Norwegian painting. A Norwegian "Golden Age" generation was emerging, painters like Erik Werenskiold, Christian Krohg, Gerhard Munthe, Frits Thaulow, Eilif Peterssen and Harriet Backer, to name just a few. What this new influence actually was, and how it was absorbed, immediately becomes more difficult to discern. However, Jens Thiis, our nation's leading art historian and the first Director of the Nasjonalgalleriet, did not hesitate: "Like streaks of migratory birds in autumn they flocked to Paris in 1879," he wrote poetically in his *Norwegian Painters and Sculptors*, the first truly comprehensive Norwegian work of art history (1904). Thiis strongly suggests that Impressionism, which the Norwegians supposedly encountered at the International Art Exhibit in Munich in that year, was a contributing factor in their choice of a new destination. "Because the moment marked by this exhibition is of critical importance for our national history of art—it is the moment when Norwegian painting, dependent since half a century on German art, makes a fresh start, drawing closer to French art." It is true that Thiis had neither studied the exhibition catalogue nor been present at the event itself. In other words, he had received his information at second hand from, among others, the Norwegian painter Erik Werenskiold, who had actually seen the exhibition: "To what extent the Impressionists participated is difficult to say, since the German critics thought it hardly worth their while to mention the names of painters like *Monet* and *Pissarro*, even though they were represented in the exhibition. *Manet* apparently did not participate. I can only name *Caillebotte* with certainty, the friend of Manet and Renoir and patron of the Impressionists, who has bequeathed his marvellous collection of their paintings to the Luxembourg Museum—and who is an excellent painter himself, one of those whom Werenskiold noticed in the exhibition."

Unfortunately, both Thiis and Werenskiold were mistaken. None of the artists today associated with Impressionism were represented in the Munich exhibition, so important to the Norwegians, not Monet, not Pissarro, not even Gustave

156. **Edvard Munch** (1863–1944): **Spring Day on Karl Johan Street,** 1890 (detail). Oil on canvas, 80 x 100. Bergen Art Museum, Bergen Billedgalleri, BB.M531.

Caillebotte. As early as the turn of the century, thus, Impressionism was beginning to occupy a dominant position in the historical consciousness. It was considered exceptionally important, even when it comes to circumstances it could not possibly have influenced directly.

It might have been the easiest to deny there ever was a fruitful relationship. That Impressionism left no traces in 19th-century Norwegian painting, that Thiis and other Francophile writers sympathetic to the movement were mistaken, not only as regards the Impressionists' participation in the Munich exhibition, but also when it comes to the general perception of the movement's beneficial influence on Norwegian painting? Indeed, in Paris the Norwegians sought the guidance of minor masters, demonstrably fancying Bastien-Lepage more than Monet. And if Impressionism is exclusively equated with a clearly defined style of painting, a technique involving short parallel brush strokes and pure unadulterated colours, one might easily dismiss the whole phenomenon. Such direct stylistic borrowings occur only sporadically in Norwegian painting. And yet, the situation is probably not that simple. Let us assume that Thiis was right in supposing that Impressionism was important for Norwegian art, even when his enthusiasm led to certain art historical short-circuits. And he was slightly mistaken about the actual circumstances. Let us assume for a moment that the vitality of Impressionism and its revitalizing force reached Norwegian shores. Our question, then, must be how did this come about.[1]

Another art historian and contemporary witness was Andreas Aubert. In January of 1895, when it became known that Claude Monet would visit Norway, Aubert mentioned his impending visit in the *Dagbladet*. The Norwegians had so many reasons to feel grateful to the French he wrote enthusiastically: "… Claude Monet, the bold conqueror, one of the creators of a new kind of painting, for which our young art owes him a large debt of gratitude. Claude Monet's youth has turned into a new youth for our painting, to new blood in its veins."[2] Although Aubert often expressed himself in slightly high-minded and metaphorical terms, we really have no reason to doubt his words. By this time, he had for more than 15 years served as an enthusiastic spokesman for, and interpreter of, his generation, "the Golden Age generation." He had long hesitated between becoming a painter himself and pursuing art theoretical studies, and now enjoyed a great reputation as one of our leading art critics. He had years of studies in Paris behind him. There were those who felt he was far too one-sided and biased in his support of the Naturalists, while holding the slightly older "Düsseldorfers" responsible for all that was bad and false in contemporary painting. Those schooled in the German tradition were, according to Aubert, still rooted in German Romanticism and, consequently, unable to approach Nature, while those schooled in the French tradition had studied French Naturalism and Impressionism, cleansed their palette, and approached Nature at a great stride, above all the Norwegian landscape. It was as simple as that.

A foreigner had once asked him if he did not find the Nordic landscape a bit too painterly, everything appearing so glaring and sharp in the strong light? Aubert had answered: "… That I loved our landscape, that I found it prodigiously beautiful. Yet, that we must learn how to capture this beauty. *This* we could not learn from Nature herself, but only from French art. And, little by little, I have come to realize that

Impressionism, with its strong and sharp colour contrasts, is the right means. In the same way that, in France, it is an up-to-date protest against all their anemic, sickly art, for us it is a timely means to solve tasks we could not otherwise have solved—a means, nothing but a means, and not without risk."[3]

Thus, Aubert did not regard Impressionism as an end in itself, but as a means by which our artists might render a truer impression of Norwegian nature. Furthermore, it is interesting to note that Aubert is also reminding us here that Impressionism might serve a different function depending on the place and cultural conditions—in Paris it had more relevance as an artistic protest movement, while in Norway, on the outskirts of Europe, it had a different raison d'être, as an aid in contemporary Naturalism's continual conquest of reality. Aubert was right, of course. French Impressionism was probably somewhat easier to identify and understand as a protest movement. France was the home of Cabanel and Bouguerau and *l'Art officiel* and *le Salon* and the Academy's *Prix de Rome*, and all that was backward. In the young nation of Norway there were few such redundant institutions to attack. We had barely established a national school of painting, much less an Academy of our own, and were continuously searching for a national expression. Consequently, there were few established and traditional aesthetic truths that the new art might oppose. Granted that the young Naturalists had, of course, labeled the previous generation old-fashioned Romantics unable, literally speaking, to see the light. Yet this was probably more of a conflict between different generations, than between opposing artistic principles. Furthermore, ever since J.C. Dahl had staked out his *naturvei* at the beginning of the century, the Norwegians had a predilection for landscape painting in a realistic Dutch/Nordic mode. And, as is well known, the slogan at Düsseldorf was "nur nach der Natur." Long before the term Impressionism was coined, direct impressionistic nature studies had been a fundamental part of their working method. When confronted by Claude Monet's youthful works, Aubert noted that they might easily pass for the work of a "Düsseldorfer," or a Dane![4]

The Norwegians were surprisingly well oriented about contemporary French art.—One notices the great curiosity of the northerners visiting the French capital, hungry for art and culture. "The Louvre and the Luxembourg Museum do not provide a complete overview of the new, or most recent, French art," complained Aubert, experienced in the ways of the world, as early as 1883.[5] "As much as these galleries own, one still regrets the absence of a more complete representation of several of the most remarkable artists, as, for example, Daubigny, Millet, Corot, Meissonier, Rosseau [sic!], and others." He had, of course, searched the public collections in vain for the very latest: "One is unable to find anything at all by the Impressionists."

As indicated by Aubert's heartfelt sigh at the opening of his article, there was obviously great disagreement about the meaning of the term Impressionism. Generally speaking, Impressionism was understood in Norway, with few exceptions, as a continuation of the immensely popular Realism and *plein-air* painting. This naturally complicates all attempts to define, and measure the impact of, any potential Impressionist influence. Few Norwegians, if any, during the second half of the 19th century, doubted the superiority of French art. Even though the Norwegians had studied in Germany, they had barely paid attention to German Idealism. It was

209. **Erik Werenskiold** (1855–1938): **Shepherds I**, 1882. Oil on canvas, 40 x 60. Private collection.

Werenskiold had viewed Impressionist art at Paris in 1882, and wrote about the movement in *Nyt Tidsskrift* the same year. In his painting *Shepherds I,* executed in the summer of 1882, he came close to the sketchiness of Impressionism, with a motif from the Norwegian countryside. Werenskiold exhibited a slightly larger version of the same motif at the Paris Salon in 1883, a painting now owned by the Nasjonalgalleriet in Oslo.

French Realism and Naturalism—the terms were used interchangeably—that had fascinated our painters for some time, at least since the 1860s. We were preoccupied by those artists who, in later art historical writings, were proclaimed as the precursors of Impressionism, the landscape painters of Barbizon. The Naturalistic landscapes of Corot, Courbet, Rousseau, Daubigny, and Millet, were held up as masterly and exemplary also by the Norwegians. Their works, occasionally reminiscent of sensitive and direct sketches, bore witness to aesthetic ideals close to those of the Norwegians—be it of Late Romanticism or Early Realism. Our first Professor of Art History, Lorentz Dietrichson, claimed that "the new Colourist-Realist movement" had won the decisive battle of European painting by as early as the mid-19th century. Dietrichson writes (1879): "The cutting edge was to be found in d'Aubigny's, Corot's, and Rousseau's landscape paintings. The New Age announced itself like a conquering hero, sweeping away the dead leaves, and our brains were on fire, those of us who were young in those years. What were Andreas Achenbach's assemblages of motifs to us, when measured against d'Aubigny's simple, but perfectly painterly mood, if only in the depiction of a field or a gravel road—what was Kaulbach's whole staircase, when measured against those six inches of Meissonier ..."[6]

An early sign that the Impressionist phenomenon had begun to arouse interest in Norway already by the early 1880s, is Erik Werenskiold's enthusiastic article "The Impressionists," written in the summer of 1882, during a longer period of study in Paris.[7] Werenskiold was at that time fast establishing himself as one of Norway's leading painters, highly regarded by the critics and celebrated by his colleagues for his faithful Naturalism. He praised the new French movement for bringing full day-

210. **Erik Werenskiold** (1855–1938): **A Ditcher.** Oil on canvas, 111 x 93.8.
Statens Museum for Kunst, Copenhagen, KMS 1329.

light and sunshine into painting, as should every Naturalist and devotee of *plein-air* painting. As Werenskiold saw it, the movement was "nothing but a developed form of Naturalism, embodying a more advanced conception of nature."

Werenskiold had seen two of the Impressionists' annual exhibitions, in 1881 and 1882. He had to admit that much of what was shown was both unusual and incomprehensible, in terms of both composition and colour—"landscapes with red grass and green skies, blue trees and yellow water, or just blue, the most infamous, loud Parisian blue"—but the exhibition was, nevertheless, very important: "The fact remains that it puts on display a movement that is exerting an increasingly noticeable influence on contemporary French art, and is represented by several of France's leading artists." According to Werenskiold, writing in 1882, the best known Impressionists were Édouard Manet, Claude Monet, Edgar Degas, de Nittis, Jean-François Raffaëlli, Gustave Caillebotte, and the illustrator Daniel Vierge. The will to "… render the impression—l'impression—the immediate, fleeting impression of nature on our senses," was the most important characteristic of the movement, "in other words, to represent objects, not as we *know* them, but as they *appear*. For example, they do not depict every single pin of a spinning wheel, but merely intimate them, in an effort to capture the very trembling, fleeting, indefinite nature of the movement." When outdoor objects are experienced as blue and bare, he paints them exactly like that, not warm and brown like tradition would have it. "And this is, of course, only proper; since painting should make its impact by illusion. It must, therefore, make an impression corresponding as closely as possible to that of Nature herself."

In the spring of 1883 the turn came to Andreas Aubert to be greatly impressed. His curiosity was finally sated. It was then that Claude Monet had his first large solo exhibit at the Galerie Durand-Ruel in the Boulevard Madelaine, showing as many as 56 paintings. The encounter resulted in a comprehensive article, published in the *Aftenposten* in the late autumn of that year.[8] Not long before, Aubert had seen an exhibition by the landscape painter Eugène Boudin at the same gallery. In his opinion, a comparison between Boudin and Monet was illuminating: no new words were needed to describe Boudin's paintings. Here the form was familiar, and the paintings must be described as studies and sketches, swift and elegant, with a feeling for the whole, for the effects of air and light. Similarly, Monet's paintings from the 1860s and '70s were not difficult to characterize as self-confident, broadly executed sketches. The earliest might easily pass for the work of a naturalistic "Düsseldorfer," or a Dane—they were boldly and surely executed. Only the paintings executed by Monet in his later years required a new art critical terminology. Aubert writes: "And so we stand in front of the canvas, observing something akin to stains of red, green, blue, yellow, of all the colours of the palette. What sort of a rage is this? What does it signify? We realize that this is a vase of asters. But—no! We step back in order to view it from a distance.—It works like magic: the vase shapes itself into firm, blue porcelain, the rosewood table top lies shining and blank with its streaks of colour, mirroring the asters, which tumble, light and airy, from the vase. The contradictions are dissolved into radiance and strength. But this sunset, is it not too insolent! Blue, reddish yellow, greenish, shouting side by side, boldly set down in long sweeping strokes like a pastel drawing: the colours chase each other like in a soap bubble. But the magic is repeated: the skies are burning. The sun is boiling in the golden green, radiant sea. The tide washes ashore in a long sky blue wave."

And so he went from one painting to the next. There was, among others, a picture of sunlight, boats and masts: "This is the very painting, so I have been told, that gave the movement its name." Aubert was continually struck by the Impressionists' ability to create a life-like feeling, a feeling of reality, "an illusion that one would have thought impossible from such a tangled heap, from such a web of colours: an illusion not usually transformed into …" Naturally, the impression of the whole was important, according to Aubert, but the radically new element was Monet's treatment of colour. "This is what I call the decomposing of colour—and, to a certain degree, of light. One might also put it this way: while the pigments are normally mixed, to varying degrees, directly on the palette, or the canvas, to achieve their final tonality, here they are, so to speak, mixed only in the viewer's eye; that which is separate and distinct—the red, the yellow, the green, the blue, etc.—blends together, helps to modify, and is modified by, the final symphony. Monet's colour genius produces effects that might conceivably be useful for physicists in their examination of optical phenomena. I recognize that a greater luminosity and a livelier play of light have in this manner been achieved here. Is this because the unmixed pigments possess a greater intensity, a brighter luminosity? Perhaps because the optical nerve is more intensely stimulated?"

For Aubert, who attended Taine's lectures in Paris and took an active interest in modern Positivism, it was, of course, fascinating to think that Impressionism might be explained by the natural sciences. "The method is not only founded on science," he later wrote,[9] "but also has its historical basis in the optical studies of the composition of light, which the one-hundred-year-old Chevreul has initiated, and others, like Helmholtz and Brücke, have developed further. Claude Monet has, indeed, confirmed by oral communication, that these scientific investigations are the very basis for his artistic experiments."[10]

Both Werenskiold and Aubert were important eyewitnesses to, and contemporary interpreters of, the history of our national art. However, there were those who argued that they sometimes got carried away by their enthusiasm and that, consequently, their thinking was somewhat muddled. Lorentz Dietrichson was of this opinion. He had been a Professor of Art History at the University of Christiania (Oslo) since 1875, and had long before been identified as the special enemy of the young Naturalists. The art world of the Norwegian capital was narrowly circumscribed and financial resources were limited. There was a frequent struggle over professional competence and power and public acquisitions. Dietrichson was no opponent of either Naturalism or Impressionism. Thanks to him the Nasjonalgalleriet acquired Claude Monet's *Rain Etretat*, as early as 1890. He had, however, been around for awhile, and was no longer as easily impressed by the latest trends. He was all the more easily provoked by the somewhat pretentious and one-sided pronouncements concerning the nature of art by members of the younger generation. Dietrichson's article "Impressionism" was intended as a reply to Werenskiold's above mentioned "The Impressionists."[11] According to the Professor, Werenskiold had delivered a very bad and poorly justified defense of the movement, having mostly

144. **Claude Monet** (1840–1926): **Rain,
Etretat,** 1886. Oil on canvas, 60.5 x 73.5.
Nasjonalgalleriet, Oslo, NG.M.00368.

Monet's painting *Rain, Étretat* was acquired
by the Nasjonalgalleriet in 1890, and
became the first Impressionist painting to
be acquired by a Scandinavian museum.

misjudged it. What perhaps provoked him the most was the claim that the Impressionists supposedly were the first to reveal Nature as it *really* was, and to teach us how it should be represented. Werenskiold was, in fact, condemning all earlier painting—"Until the year of Our Lord 1867, or thereabouts, no one, without exception, had observed how Nature 'appears,' everyone simply 'knew what she is' and painted her accordingly." Yet, the ability to see Nature as her true self was certainly not invented by the Impressionists, Dietrichson maintained sarcastically. And the Old Masters, be it the great Naturalists or the Idealists, Rubens or Raphael, knew perfectly well how to represent movement, though they kept the solid form and plasticity.

If Impressionism must be regarded as the extreme wing of Naturalism, as the ultimate product of a movement whose banner was inscribed "true to Nature," still, art is surely something distinct from Nature? Werenskiold had maintained that painting should make its impact by "illusion" and must, therefore, create an impression resembling that of Nature herself. Dietrichson found such statements absurd. "What we seek in a work of art is, in fact, not the illusion, which makes every picture = Nature, but, rather, the expression of a personal, spiritual conception of Nature." For an Impressionist painting to have its proper illusionistic effect, one would have to experience it in motion, at the speed of lightning and, preferably, through the window of a train compartment "going by at the speed of an express train." Yet, the Impressionists could not possibly have meant for their paintings to be viewed at such speed—"at the speed of a passing train"? And if the illusion itself was the ideal goal, then paintings of the same motif by different artists would surely be identical, and this ideal would end up abolishing the pictorial arts? "According to Mr. Werenskiold's theory, Impressionist paintings […] would actually become no more than a presumably soon-to-be mechanically reproduced unit of light impressions, colour photographs …"

Dietrichson had no difficulties in realizing that Impressionism had some interesting qualities: "… its peculiarity lies in the fact that it decomposes colour and, with ingenious energy, captures the fleeting moment in order to, using colour, allow the form to recede in favour of movement." However, he did not accept an interpretation of Impressionism in which the creative human being was banished in favour of some sort of objective imitation of the visible. All true art was dependent on the feeling subject and the seeing eye, "the artistic and soulful personality's conception of nature."

What is perhaps most interesting about Dietrichson's evaluation of Impressionism is that he really was not certain that the movement should be regarded as the extreme wing of Naturalism, having Nature as it's goal, as Werenskiold had claimed: "Looking at things differently, one might say that it is the Impressionists who are not representing Nature as they see her, but render Nature abstractly, that is to say, that the abstraction of which Mr. Werenskiold accuses the non-Impressionists, is in fact produced by the Impressionists themselves, only in reverse order: in reality, they are performing a work of abstraction, both in decomposing colour and in separating movement from form by means of colour—and this will no doubt become apparent to most of them when their enthusiasm about the initial experiments has evaporated." Dietrichson was not unwilling to concede a place to the Impressionists "among those who carry the future upon their shoulders," as long as they held on to

201. **Frits Thaulow** (1847–1906): **Flooding by the Seine,** 1893. Oil on canvas, 58 x 95. Private collection.

Thaulow's painting of Paris and the banks of the Seine is Realist, rather than Impressionist, in execution. Thaulow was, however, one of the relatively few Scandinavian painters who, like the Impressionists, depicted the modern city. Most Scandinavian artists working and studying in France in the 1870s and '80s concentrated primarily on motifs from the countryside around Paris.

what was passionately experienced and subjective, which he regarded as being at the heart of the whole Impressionist movement.

By combining the abstract qualities of Impressionism, like brushwork, colour, and rhythm, with the importance of the strong artistic personality's subjective understanding of Nature, Dietrichson here anticipates, in the early 1880s, ideas that later became commonplace in Post-Impressionist theory.

Someone will, of course, object that not even professors are ahead of their time, that he is merely hawking aesthetic ideals long since embodied by Late Romantic Einfühlungs-theories. And that is probably correct.

Among the rapidly emerging Golden Age painters, it was, above all, Christian Krohg who adopted Impressionism as part of his painterly expression. Like Werenskiold, Krohg had studied the Impressionists at close quarters, especially at the Impressionist Exhibition of 1882. The influence of Monet and Gustave Caillebotte resulted in a freer handling of the paint and bolder cropping of forms. Yet, the influence of Édouard Manet was probably even stronger (the northerners seem to really have become aware of Manet in connection with the great commemorative Paris exhibit in 1884). When Krohg exhibited his painting, *Look Ahead!*, Bergen Harbour, at our national Salon, the Autumn Salon of 1884, Aubert wrote an enthusiastic review. Faithful to his habit, he began by lamenting the lack of precision of the term Impressionism. "One has heard mention of the recently deceased Manet, as well as of Claude Monet; but any notion of them and their art must remain vague and uncertain, as long as something more concrete is lacking, to which it may be

116. **Christian Krohg** (1852–1925): **Look Ahead! Bergen Harbour,** 1884. Oil on canvas, 62.5 x 86. Nasjonalgalleriet, Oslo, NG.M.00967.

tied." Édouard Manet's influence, the starting-point of Impressionism, had by now reached Norway, Aubert stated, and Christian Krohg's *Look Ahead!* was an instructive example of "the goal of his [Manet's] endeavour, the essence of his style." In the cropping of the motif, the accidental nature of the movement, the bright and bold colour contrasts, the intensity of the light, the swift and powerful interpretation, in all of this there was something "truly Manet-like."

Aubert would, moreover, devote an entire study to the Frenchman, his article "Manet: A Contribution to the History of the Motif and the Colours in the New Age," published in the journal *Tilskueren* in Copenhagen in 1888. Krohg himself paid homage to Manet in his 1886 lecture, famous in the history of Norwegian art, "The Pictorial Arts as an Integral Part of the Cultural Movement."[12] The Realists had, according to Krohg, contributed much of value to the arts, but "… they began to kneel down before the details of Nature and worship them, forgetting that they themselves were a part of Nature, and, thus, equally worthy of adoration." The Realists were eventually swallowed up by their focus on details and inessentials. "But then Manet arrived on the scene—the French painter Manet." His goal was not essentially different from that of the Realists, but he possessed an entirely different kind of self-consciousness in his relationship with Nature and observed reality "… so that his every brushstroke bore the imprint of a definite *goal*, one of the *essential*

118. **Christian Krohg** (1852–1925): **At the Roof Balcony, Grønnegate**, 1889. Oil on canvas, 62 x 51. Lillehammer Kunstmuseum, LKM 167.

154. **Edvard Munch** (1863–1944): **The Olaf Rye Place in Oslo. Afternoon,** 1883. Oil on canvas, 48 x 25.5. Moderna Museet, Stockholm, NM 2400.

things being to finish a work—not to represent more than one was able to observe, never to look for something more to paint. What was not striking, not immediately apparent, he did not represent …"—It is obvious that the views of the young revolutionary Krohg were not far removed from those of Professor Dietrichson, both regarded contemporary painting as essentially individualistic and subjective, that being its moral raison d'être—"Manet said: only the *impression* must be captured, Nature's impression on us, the children of our age, and then one must put one's soul into the work, share one's hate and love, it's about living and hating and loving, for *in that way, in every single work*—be it a still-life, a landscape painting or anything else, one will have a small image of time, and when everything that is thus created is put together, one will have the large, final, unobstructed image of time, and that is what we are striving for." Naturally, Krohg used Émile Zola as a kind of witness about Manet. Zola had been Manet's principal defender and most ardent follower throughout the many years he was active as an art critic. Zola was a man who appealed to Krohg, and he readily quoted the Frenchman's many famous pronouncements about the intimate relationship between art and temperament, not least "What I look for most in a painting—it's a man, not a painting."[13]

Krohg ended his article with a complaint: "We, the generation of Norwegian painters to which I belong, are not Impressionists—unfortunately. We can only stand on the mountain and look down into the Promised Land. But no—we are not Impressionists. Far from it."

About this Andreas Aubert was apparently not in agreement with Krohg. It is precisely in connection with a painting by Krohg, exhibited at the Autumn Salon of 1887, that the art critic again feels inspired to write a new and extensive commentary on the subject of this new school of painting.[14] Under the headline *Impressionism and Colour Composition*, Aubert made the following statement: "Christian Krohg's *The North Wind* reveals a more uncompromising boldness in the use of the two basic principles of the Impressionist method than any previous work produced here in Norway. Never before was the accidental nature of vision more strongly emphasized in the motif, or a more violent colour decomposition employed as part of the technique. No matter how much the latter angers some people, its surprising result is perhaps of interest to everyone: nearly all colours of the rainbow; at a distance, indeed, at a very great distance, all comes together to produce a marvellous effect! […] When it comes to the experimental study of light Krohg is undoubtedly the leading Scandinavian artist. Even among the French, he is at the cutting edge. He makes his original contribution to the development."

Krohg is also credited with introducing Impressionism to the youngest artists of the 1880s. "Through several of our painters, above all, through Krohg, the Impressionist movement has increased the progress of our youngest artists," Aubert noted, "Hardly any of our most capable artists remains entirely outside its sphere of influence. Firstly, it has taught them to value the whole, and, secondly, it has given their colours greater life and intensity."[15]

Norway did not have an Academy of Art until 1909. After initial studies at the Royal School of Drawing, young artists were left to their own devices. Many sought out the informal artists' community at the "Pultosten," a centrally located building

155. **Edvard Munch** (1863–1944): **The Seine at St. Cloud,** 1890. Oil on canvas, 46.5 x 38. Munch-museet, Oslo, M1109.

156. **Edvard Munch** (1863–1944): **Spring Day on Karl Johan Street**, 1890. Oil on canvas, 80 x 100. Bergen Art Museum, Bergen Billedgalleri, BB.M531.

in the nation's capital, which housed a number of studios on its upper floors. (The property received its name after a cheese merchant who previously occupied the building.) Here the young artists were instructed sporadically by the older and more established painters, especially Krohg. And in the summer the young artists sometimes went to the "open air academy" at Modum, where they were taught by Frits Thaulow. He painted broadly and fleetingly, in a contemporary style, his motifs often being associated with *la vie moderne*, his colours with blond *plein-air* painting in the French mode. Most painters of this "in-between generation," however, were quite satisfied with "a talented eye, painting materials, and a piece of reality,"[16] and many ended up worshiping a sketchy, colourful Naturalism, never exploring the new possibilities of abstraction and formal experimentation, as did Munch. Soon enough artists like Jørgen Sørensen, Karl Jensen-Hjell, Kalle Løchen, Halfdan Strøm, Jens Wang, and others, would find themselves marginalized in our national art history, completely overshadowed by Edvard Munch, the most important artist influenced by Krohg. Apart from a few hasty "impressions" from the mid-1880s, it is primarily in a group of pictures of circa 1890 that Munch tries his hand at Impressionism. The main thoroughfare of our capital, the Karl Johan, our closest parallel to a French boulevard, here becomes the setting of a series of light-filled scenes of the local bourgeoisie in summer dress beneath colourful, Monet-like umbrellas, often cropped à la Degas, but probably mainly inspired by Pissarro's technique of vibrating lights. During a stay in Paris he painted the *Rue de Rivoli* and the *Rue Lafayette* (ill. p. 22, cat.no. 157) in a style showing all the formal attributes of Impressionism, and he also painted on the Riviera and in Nice. Possibly, Seurat and Pointillism also drew Munch's attention during his period of studies in France. If so, this would be an excellent example of how rapidly art had progressed and changed course already in this early phase of Modernism. By this time, Edvard Munch himself had for some time been moving towards an anti-realistic style of painting, geared more to communicating mental experiences than visual reality: "I started out as an Impressionist painter, but during the violent spiritual- and life transitions of my Bohemian period, I found that Impressionism did not provide an appropriate means of expression—I had to find a means of expressing what stirred in my soul [...] The first break with Impressionism came with the sick child—I searched for the expression (Expressionism)."[17] Furthermore, he spoke about his painting *Spring* of 1889, as a "farewell to Impressionism."[18] Munch thus regarded (at least in his later years) Impressionism as Naturalism's co-conspirator and, therefore, as not suited to communicating human feelings and imagination. As we all know, he desired to paint "not what I see, but what I saw."

Munch was not the only artist to turn towards a style of painting that, to a greater degree, rejected the eye's natural correction. A belief that the demand for visual observation embraced by Naturalism and Impressionism violated artistic freedom and imagination was rampant in all camps, both among the well established and the younger artists.[19] In 1889 the Danish art historian Julius Lange had thrown a firebrand of sorts. Although he was already a mature man and a friend of Lorentz Dietrichson, Lange was greatly respected by Norwegian painters. In his essay, *Plain-Air Study. Painting. The Art of Remembrance*, Lange was prepared to accept—with some hesitation—the emerging *plein-air* Realism, though he wished to beat his drum for an art more deeply rooted in the soul. "By contrast with Impressionism and an art based on open air studies, I wish to promote what might be called *an art of Remembrance*," Lange wrote. "Its birth takes place not in the daytime, when the light is blinding, when surprises from without jostle each other, hurried and restless—that, in any event, becomes merely a superficial art, an art without deep roots in the soul. It is born, rather, in the quiet and darkness, or at least when the external eye is *not* engaged in seeing, and the soul is at peace to make its selection from half-forgotten memories, then images appear before the inner eye, semi-clear, semi-obscure images out of the nourishing night of the unconscious, out of its dark, fertile soil."[20] Lange's contribution might perhaps be dismissed as old-fashioned Romanticism (—no matter how much he anticipates thoughts Edvard Munch would soon make his own). Yet, even the most fervent adherents of *plein-air* landscape painting were beginning to have their doubts. Perhaps the relationship between image and reality demanded a slight adjustment? The verbal attacks on the

158. **Edvard Munch** (1863–1944): **The Roulette Table I,** 1892. Oil on canvas, 54 x 65. Munchmuseet, Oslo, M266.

art of the eye were sometimes surprisingly vicious. (Even though they never completely rejected Realism as the foundation of painting.) Andreas Aubert soon began to speak of Naturalism as though it had shackled the artist, and came to prefer an art that opposed "soulless Naturalism's slavery of the 'concrete'."[21] Werenskiold would articulate similar thoughts. He wondered if Naturalism had perhaps signified "nothing but a small step—forward or to the side, perhaps even a short detour."[22]

Departing from Impressionism, several roads led ahead in Norwegian art. Munch moved towards a style of painting he believed was deeply rooted in the soul, an antirealistic art that opened up the possibility of a greater use of symbols and liberated line and colour from a purely descriptive function, making the form emotionally pregnant. On the whole, the wave of sentiment that engulfed Norwegian painting towards the end of the century, often labeled "New Romanticism," hardly concerned itself with the Impressionist analysis of the effects of sunlight and atmosphere on

46. **Thorvald Erichsen** (1868–1939): **Landscape**, 1894. Oil on canvas, 67 x 98. Lillehammer Kunstmuseum, LKM 44.

This painting is an example of the surface-oriented and decorative Synthetism that Erichsen developed during the first half of the 1890s. He had lived in Paris in the spring of 1893, and in the autumn of that year he socialized with some of the Danish Symbolists—Gad F. Clement, Ludvig Find, and Carl Frydensberg—most closely associated with Gauguin and the Nabis.

form. The imagination and dreams, the night's anguish and the subtle poetry of nature, were communicated through glowing sunsets and pale Nordic summer nights. Here, at the outskirts of Europe, there were other problems to solve than those formulated on bustling and sunlit Parisian sidewalks. The painter Christian Skredsvig put it thus: "Well, Paris is now in the grip of Impressionism—but these apostles of light—these priests of the sun, they are blind to the fact that the sun and its light are poor! Yes, for all their glowing publicity, of use only to a pauper! But on a summer night by the shallow Finnish lakes, or the deep dormant rivers and tarns of Norefjäll—the useless moon rises in the sky with dignity, building bridges of its ancient gold to faraway places, moving the boundaries across its dream landscape— that is painterly, for it is capable of being painted."[23]

During these years of intensive nation building, the young Norwegian nation was constantly searching for an art to call its own. An increasing number of Norwegian artists participated in international exhibitions, a breeding ground for nationalistic manifestations and confrontations. Here the Norwegians were met by foreign expectations about a different kind of painting, one that did not mirror foreign trends, but showed distinctly nationalistic traits. At the Scandinavian exhibit in Copenhagen in 1888, the noted French art critic Maurice Hamel had praised the Norwegians for bravely striking out to conquer reality. "It is all straightforward and healthy, giving a fresh impression that acts like a tonic for the senses." According to

Hamel, they had obviously learnt from the French, from, among others, Raffaëlli and Claude Monet—"Yet, at the same time, this art is deeply rooted in the Norwegian people and their land, and in that lies its true significance."[24] And Kitty Kielland noted, self-confidently, about the Norwegian pavilion at the 1889 World's Fair: "Soon I was happily convinced there was a freshness and a boldness, a daring quality in the colours and conception, something observed and experienced, that made our display distinctly *Norwegian*, as opposed to those of other countries [...] Where are the painters headed? Well, those who are ambitious want to observe our landscape and our way of life with the eyes of a Norwegian, with a fresh outlook, independent of foreign influence."[25]

What was considered nationally distinctive obviously changed according to the times and the prevailing aesthetic ideals. During the 1880s, the realistically unmediated, the direct and harsh, was emphasized, and these qualities corresponded closely with the Impressionist ideals. However, during the 1890s, when New Romanticism and New Idealism were fashionable, art was expected to mirror a more complex reality, not least, a national reality: Andreas Aubert became the theorist of the nationalistically oriented, liberal "Lysaker circle." Backed by Gerhard Munthe's recent Art Nouveau-influenced works, he spoke ardently of the need for our national art to return to its roots, in the land and the people. His study of ancient Norwegian culture, Norwegian folk art and "rose painting"—a kind of folksy decorative painting—had convinced him that *true* Norwegian art had a strongly anti-realistic character, that it was decorative, stylistically self-assured, rhythmic, ornamental, and constructive. These beliefs eventually formed the basis for a complete little national art ideology near the end of the century and the year of Norwegian independence in 1905. It is easy to see that these ideals were hardly compatible with Impressionism—at least not as it was generally understood at that time.[26] One might perhaps imagine that Impressionism was also put on the defensive in the name of nation building? That was, however, not the case: many years later, Erik Werenskiold attempted to increase the status of his art. In 1908 he had executed the first decorative painting in a series later known as *The Peasant*: "and now I realize that my thinking of a few years ago, when I speculated about decorative art, still holds true, and I believe it represents a new direction in art. It will lead us, in the most natural manner, from the wise and clear principles of decorative art, as we observe them in Babylonian-Assyrian, indeed, in Sumerian art, and all the way up to Impressionism, and it will still be just as frank and Norwegian—indeed, quite simply, an art of sill-and-potatoes."[27] Here we do well to remind ourselves once more of Andreas Aubert's didactic rule of memory: "Words that are common currency at any given time are generally the most unclear of all. Consequently, hardly two individuals have the same understanding of Impressionism, defining it in the same way." Aubert's words are still valid. As for himself, he insisted that Impressionism had led to a "new youth for our painting, new blood in its veins." But just how the organism benefited from this new blood, how this new vitality affected the nation's art, is still quite difficult to determine.

Following pages: 71. **Paul Gauguin** (1848–1903): **Landscape from Brittany with Cows** (detail), 1889. Oil on canvas, 92 x 74.5. Nasjonalgalleriet, Oslo, NG.M.01006.

French Paintings on Norwegian Soil
By Nils Messel

"AN OUT-OF-THE-WAY AND modestly funded museum, not backed by wealthy patrons." That was the Director's, Jens Thiis, characterization of the Nasjonalgalleriet when, in 1914, he attempted to explain why there had until then been so few opportunities to see French art in Norway.[1] At that time, however, the situation was beginning to change radically. During the course of the next ten years, we would experience a regular sea change when it comes to French art in Norway. Friends' associations, patrons, and private collections soon appeared in great numbers, not least thanks to the economic boom neutral Norway was able to benefit from during World War I.

Thiis' words, however, are still valid when it comes to the past. The economic circumstances had been quite limited. It is true that our attention had been directed towards France for several generations, long before Impressionism became a household word. Norwegian art had learnt a great deal from the French, ever since Late Romanticism had given way to the new Realism around the mid-19th century. Yet, Norway was a poor country on the outskirts of Europe, and our recently founded Nasjonalgalleriet had for a long time wished to use its limited resources primarily to establish a representative collection of Norwegian painting.

It is quite remarkable that, during the last few decades of the 19th century, a period marked by strong nation building, we still managed to acquire a few French art works, which later became important milestones in our national history of art. Inspired by the French Salon, the so-called Autumn Salon became an annual event in Norwegian artistic life beginning in the early 1880s. Even a few foreign artists were represented here. Already in the Autumn Salon of 1884 Paul Gauguin was represented with several paintings, among others, *The Flower Basket* and the *Portrait of Mette Gauguin*, while two years later visitors were able to enjoy two landscapes by Courbet and Daubigny.[2] In 1890 works by Degas, as well as by Monet and Pissarro, were exhibited.[3] This was the reason that the Nasjonalgalleriet purchased its first Impressionist painting, Claude Monet's *Rain, Etretat*. It is also worth noting that the suggestion to purchase the painting came from the Professor of Art History, Lorentz Dietrichson, who was in fact regarded by many younger artists as an old reactionary. Dietrichson was at that time President of the Board of Directors of the Nasjonalgalleriet. His proposal was accepted by a narrow margin of votes: three members voted in favour, two against. At the Autumn Salon of 1891 we find works by Carolus-Duran, as well as by Besnard, Roll, Rodin, and G.P. Jeanniot.[4] The Nasjonalgalleriet purchased a large park landscape by the latter.

During the 1890s there were also more privately organized exhibitions in the nation's capital. Especially at the Blomqvist Gallery visitors could enjoy a few French exhibits. In 1898 the Nasjonalgalleriet purchased two works there by Auguste

Édouard Manet (1832–1883): **At the Paris World's Fair in 1867** (detail). Oil on canvas, 108 x 196.5. Nasjonalgalleriet, Oslo, NG.M.01293.

56. **Paul Gauguin** (1848–1903): **Portrait of Mette Gauguin**, 1884. Oil on canvas, 65 x 54. Nasjonalgalleriet, Oslo, NG.M.00771.

Vincent van Gogh (1853–1890): **View of Arles from Montmajour.** Pencil and pen, 48.5 x 60. Nasjonalgalleriet, Oslo, NG.K&H.B.00068.

Rodin, *The Thinker* and *Danaïde*. It was also not unusual for our artists studying abroad to suggest the purchase of art works they had acquired abroad. Usually, though, such proposals went unheeded for lack of economic resources. In 1891, however, a painting of street life by Jean-François Raffaëlli was acquired. Raffaëlli was one of the painters whom Werenskiold had held up as one of the French Impressionists. The painting was purchased in Paris, at the suggestion of Frits Thaulow and Johannes Grimelund, who were both then living in France. The fine Van Gogh pen-and-ink drawing, *View of Arles from Montmajour* (1888), was acquired in the same manner—in 1905 the young Thorvald Erichsen had come into contact with someone in Copenhagen, who owned a fine drawing by Van Gogh that he wished to sell. Might this be of interest to the Museum?[5]—It is part of the story that the drawing had to be sent to Norway for a decision to be taken regarding its purchase. Fortunately, the members of the acquisitions committee were all enthusiastic.

These examples, however, are the exceptions rather than the rule, thus confirming Jens Thiis' characterization of the reduced Norwegian economic circumstances mentioned earlier. He was himself a true Francophile. Already in his monumental art historical survey, *Norwegian Painters and Sculptors* (1904–07), he devoted great attention to French art. A substantial portion of his later writings would be devoted entirely to French subjects.

In 1908 Thiis was appointed as the first director of the Nasjonalgalleriet. The newly appointed director enthusiastically began the process of securing funding and space for contemporary French art. Already during a trip to Paris in 1910, he bought a Van Gogh self-portrait. Paul Cézanne's magnificent *Still-Life* of 1886 was acquired in the same year with a financial contribution from Auguste Pellerin in Paris. In 1913 the Nasjonalgalleriet acquired two paintings by Gauguin, *On the Beach* (1889) and *Landscape from Brittany with Cows* (1889), previously in Norwegian private collections. These paintings formed an important supplement to the two early Gauguin paintings donated to the Museum in 1907.[6]

Yet, it was only around the time of World War I that French art was seriously introduced to Norway and the Nasjonalgalleriet. In that period large private fortunes were being created in Norway; especially the shipping trade and anything connected with maritime commerce enjoyed great success. The economic upswing and easy access to money also benefited the arts. The financial resources of the Nasjonalgalleriet could barely keep step with the economic progress. The price of French art soon skyrocketed, but so, fortunately, did the number of donations. A number of private individuals provided the Museum with large sums of money. Thanks to the young shipping magnate Tryggve Sagen, the Nasjonalgalleriet was able to benefit from a gift of 60 000 Norwegian kroner in 1916, for the acquisition of French art.[7] Works by Courbet, Degas, Gaugin, Renoir, Cézanne, and Friez were acquired. And another shipping magnate, Christoffer Hannevig, contributed 50 000 Norwegian kroner to the recently founded Association of Friends of the Nasjonalgalleriet. This Association would contribute more than any other source to the Museum acquiring French masterpieces of which one could otherwise only dream. One of the Association's invitations read: "Our remote location and limited economic circumstances have until now made it possible for us to purchase foreign art of major importance only rarely. This situation must now change. In the long run, even our domestic art is bound to suffer from a lack of contact with great international art, which is a prerequisite of our own. The general public, as well as the artists, should always have the opportunity to view foreign art of the highest quality."[8] The Association was officially founded in the autumn of 1917, and by the end of the following year they had already gathered a base capital of close to half a million Norwegian kroner. Among the many gifts of the "Friends" in the first few years should be mentioned Cézanne's *Seated Man* of the 1890s and Édouard Manet's *Madame Manet in the Winter Garden* (1876), both purchased in 1918. Cézanne's *Mont Sainte-Victoire* (1885–87), Claude Monet's *La Grande Jatte, Argenteuil* (c. 1875), and Edgar Degas' magnificent *La coiffure*, were all acquired in the following year. Possibly the most important painting ever acquired with the aid of the Association was Edouard Manet's *At the Paris World's Fair in 1867*, acquired in 1923. This painting had previously been in the possession of Tryggve Sagen. Symptomatically, it now belonged to a bank—the good economic times were disappearing for some of our patrons.

Another society, the Association for French Art, should also be mentioned as an active institution in the dissemination of French art. Indeed, the same enthusiasts were often members of the Friends' Association as well. Thus, Jens Thiis, Tryggve Sagen and Jørgen Breder Stang were among its members in 1919. The idea was to organize exhibitions that would tour Scandinavia. Similar associations were also

founded in Denmark and Sweden. The first exhibition organized by the Norwegian association was a comprehensive survey of works by Camille Corot at the Nasjonalgalleriet in the spring of 1919. The 56 works in the exhibition belonged to public and private collections in Sweden, Norway, and Denmark. In 1920 the turn came to Degas, while in 1921 there was an exhibit of works by Auguste Renoir, and in 1922 of Édouard Manet. These were followed by exhibitions devoted to Courbet, Daumier, and Guys in 1923, Matisse in 1924, and Gauguin in 1926. The eighth in this series of exhibitions, From David to Courbet, organized in collaboration with the French museums in 1928, was a comprehensive exhibit of 161 works. After that we loose sight of the Association.

During World War I numerous French paintings were purchased while they were being exhibited in Norway: as early as the autumn of 1914, Jens Thiis had mounted a comparatively broad exhibition of contemporary French art at the Nasjonalgalleriet. Several of the exhibited paintings had previously been shown in the comprehensive exhibit of French Painting in Copenhagen in the early summer.[9] Due to the troubled political situation in Europe, many of the paintings remained in Norway and were sold here. In 1916, in the midst of war, a new exhibition of French painting was organized in the Norwegian capital. The Exhibition of French Art at the Artists' Society was the brainchild of the energetic Walther Halvorsen. As a young man Halvorsen wanted to become an artist, and therefore went to Paris where he studied for a time at the Académie Matisse. However, he soon embarked upon a career as a journalist and art dealer instead. For many years Halvorsen resided permanently in the French capital, and through his marriage, as well as his friendships, he had established many useful contacts in French art circles. The 1916

exhibition included 125 entries, works by Picasso, Matisse, Bonnard, Signac, Marquet, Derain, and Dufy, among others. The paintings were, with few exceptions, for sale. The Nasjonalgalleriet purchased Matisse's *Portrait of Albert Marquet*, as well as a winter landscape by Marquet himself. In the New Year of 1918, Halvorsen organized yet another exhibition of French art at the Artists' Society.[10] And once again the Norwegian public, the well-to-do and the merely curious, were able to enjoy great art.

During and after World War I, a number of Norwegian businessmen, shipping magnates, and industrialists supplied Norway with paintings the likes of which have never been seen, before or after. Since the paintings ended up in the Nasjonalgalleriet, we are able to enjoy them to this day. Unfortunately, however, some of the private collections were of an even more fleeting nature than the fortunes that created them. In the interim period between the two World Wars several of the paintings disappeared abroad, and many are today key works in American, and some European, private collections and museums. As is frequently the case with private

Above: **Paul Cézanne** (1839–1906): **Portrait of a Seated Farmer,** 1898–1900. Oil on canvas, 54.6 x 45. The Metropolitan Museum of Art, The Walter H. and Leonore Annenberg Collection. Partial gift of Walter H. och Leonore Annenberg, 1993. (1997.60.2).
Opposite page: 22. **Paul Cézanne** (1839–1906): **Seated Man,** 1892–95 ca. Oil on canvas, 102.5 x 75.5. Nasjonalgalleriet, Oslo, NG.M. 01287.

collections, we have only limited information about their content, provenance and permanency. The French journal *La Renaissance*, which devoted its February issue of 1929 to "French Art in Norway," offers interesting and rare insights into this material. The reason the article was written was the above-mentioned exhibition From David to Courbet, organized by the Association for French Art in the summer of 1928. Following an introductory presentation of the collection of French paintings at the Nasjonalgalleriet, Jens Thiis and Walther Halvorsen are praised for their important role in the dissemination of French culture. The French journalist P. Jamot then takes us on a tour of the usually private salons of art collecting shipping magnates and industrialists. And Jamot delighted in being able to describe a series of representative French art works by Manet, Degas, Renoir, and Cézanne, among others.

The most important collection he was allowed to visit was that of the shipping magnate Jørgen Breder Stang (1874–1950). Stang's interest in art collecting was stimulated by the exhibition of French art in Copenhagen in the early summer of 1914, and since then he had been active as an art collector and supporter of both the Association of Friends of the Nasjonalgalleriet and the Association for French Art. In 1918 he had donated Auguste Rodin's large bronze sculpture, *Aphrodite Victorious*, to the Nasjonalgalleriet. The shipping magnate's patrician villa at Skillebekk in Oslo housed works by Delacroix, Courbet, Corot, Manet, Morisot, Pissarro, Van Gogh, Seurat, Toulouse-Lautrec, Picasso, Marquet, as well as several important works by Renoir and Cézanne. The most striking artwork displayed against the damask-covered walls was Paul Gauguin's *Where Do We Come From? What Are We? Where Are We Going?* of 1897. When it comes to Manet, the

Above: **Paul Gauguin** (1848–1903): **Where do we come from? What are we? Where are we going?**, 1897. Oil on canvas, 139 x 375 cm. Museum of Fine Arts, Boston, Tompkins Collection, 36.270.

To the right: Interior views of the home of Jørgen Breder Stang, photograph from *La Renaissance* no. 2, 1929. Stang assembled an extraordinary collection of French Impressionist and Post-Impressionist art in a short period of time. The most striking work in the collection was undoubtedly Gauguin's large *Where do we come from? What are we? Where are we going*, a painting here shown hanging above the sofa in Stang's salon. Also visible in the photographs are Cézanne's *The Card Players*, now in the Courtauld Gallery, London, as well as additional works by Cézanne and Renoir. Stang's collection was dispersed in the 1920s.

Nasjonalgalleriet owned the highest quality paintings, but for the rest Stang's collection was unmatched and not unlike a museum, as Jamot noted enthusiastically, "Stang's collection is so magnificent that it would be impossible to rival it."

By as early as the 1920s, however, Stang had begun to sell off his collection—even though he kept a few pieces throughout his life. Today we find his Gauguin painting mentioned earlier, as well as his Van Gogh landscape, *Ravine*, in the Boston Museum of Fine Arts. The Washington National Gallery of Art is the fortunate owner of Stang's second Van Gogh painting, namely, the beautiful *La Mousmé* (1888), showing a seated girl with a bouquet of flowers in her lap. Berthe Morisot's *Young Girl Braiding Her Hair* (1893), is owned by the Ny Carlsberg Glyptotek, Copenhagen. The Museo de Arte de São Paolo today owns Corot's beautiful *Italian Lady with a Mandolin*. Gustave Courbet's *Study for Girls on the Banks of the Seine* (1856), which Stang had purchased from Durand-Ruel, is now in the London National Gallery of Art, while Manet's large *Portrait of Carolus-Duran* (1876) can be admired at The Barber Institute of Fine Arts in Birmingham. Paul Cézanne's *The Card Players* (1893–96) is now in The Courtauld Institute Galleries in London, while the other two Cézanne paintings, *Bathers* (c. 1890, Rewald no. 747) and *Harlequin* (1888–90, Rewald no.621), are in private collections in, respectively, Paris and South America.

29. **Paul Cézanne** (1839–1906): **The Cardplayers**. Oil on canvas, 60 x 73. Courtauld Gallery, Courtauld Institute of Art, London, P.1932.SC.57.

123. **Édouard Manet** (1832–1883): **Georges Clemenceau**, 1880. Oil on canvas, 115.9 x 88.2. Kimbell Art Museum, Fort Worth, Texas, AP 1981.01.

The painting belonged for a period of time to the Norwegian artist, art-dealer, collector and writer Walther Halvorsen.

As regards other paintings by Cézanne in Norwegian collections, Jamot was also able to supply the information that the industrialist Christian Mustad owned the *Portrait of a Seated Farmer* (1898–1900, Rewald no. 827), and that Walther Halvorsen was the fortunate owner of some very fine paintings: *Portrait of Madame Cézanne* (1898–1900, Rewald no. 650), *Bathing Women In Front of a Tent* (1883–85?, Rewald no. 553), and *The Environs of Jas de Bouffan* (1885–87, Rewald no. 524). The paintings once owned by Mustad and Halvorsen are also no longer to be found on Norwegian soil. Mustad's Cézanne is in the New York Metropolitan Museum of Art, Halvorsen's Cézanne portrait can be admired in the Houston Museum of Fine Arts, his female bathers are in the Staatsgallerie in Stuttgart, and his landscapes from Provence long ago found their way into The Solomon R. Guggenheim Museum in New York. At least we know where they are.

Monet and Norway

Karin Hellandsjø

"I am living in a wonderful country and would like to be able to capture everything I see, but I have been very confused, and at the beginning I felt discouraged and could not get anything done. Now things are picking up, but I am worried about the weather, and I would be very happy if I were able to extend my stay somewhat. Therefore, I am impatiently awaiting your answer.¹"

CLAUDE MONET HAD been staying in Norway for about a month when he wrote this letter to his art dealer, Durand-Ruel, with a request to postpone the scheduled spring exhibit at the Parisian gallery, so that he might prolong his stay in Norway by a few weeks. He was granted another two weeks, but later complained repeatedly about not having arrived earlier, and that the two months at his disposal simply was not enough time to achieve his goal, to capture the Norwegian winter in his paintings. Indeed, he would experience only a small area of the country, the countryside around Christiania, and had to content himself with bringing back photographs of the western and northern parts of the country. He realized early on that he had misjudged the situation, and after barely a month's stay he wrote: "One would have to live here a whole year to do really good work, and even then, one would first have to explore and get to know the country."² Still, he hoped to be able to set down some of his impressions of a wintry Norway on canvas, and after his return to France he wrote: "I am not too dissatisfied with what I am bringing home."³ He had produced about thirty paintings.

That Claude Monet had so badly misjudged the situation may seem surprising. He had frequently undertaken such expeditions in search of new landscapes and motifs, not only in France, but also to more remote places, and two to three months was usually enough time to accomplish his goal. He also did not like being away from Giverny for too long, from his large family, his garden, and his regular work habits. But then again, he had never before undertaken a similar expedition. Norway, it is true, was an exotic destination for many Europeans at this time, but most people travelled there in the summertime, as recommended by the Baedeker travel guide, which Monet had acquired.⁴ Winter travel would prove something altogether different and filled with hardship, but then again, it was precisely winter and its particular light that Monet wished to explore and paint, being the very reason for his travelling so far north.

Monet's art is readily associated with flowers and water. However, in her article for the catalogue accompanying the 1995 Jubilee Exhibition dealing with the artist's Norwegian journey, Sylvie Patin, Chief Curator of the Musée D'Orsay, noted that winter landscapes actually make up an important part of his total artistic produc-

150. **Claude Monet** (1840–1926): **Sandviken, Snow Effect** (detail), 1895. Oil on canvas, 73 x 92. Næringslivets Hovedorganisasjon, Oslo.

Previous pages: 155. **Edvard Munch** (1863–1944): **The Seine at St. Cloud,** 1890 (detail). Oil on canvas, 46.5 x 38. Munch-museet, Oslo, M1109.

141. **Claude Monet** (1840–1926): **The Magpie,** 1869. Oil on canvas, 89 x 130. Musée d'Orsay, Paris, RF 1984–164.

This painting is an early example of Monet's interest in winter scenes. Monet was fascinated by the light- and colour problems that the snow-clad landscape offered.

tion.⁵ This is especially true of his work from the 1860s, and Patin distinguishes obvious parallels between the snow landscapes of Monet's youth and those produced in Norway thirty years later. Water, lakes, and snow were themes that had already preoccupied the young Monet, and which he returned to while in Norway, but due to the weather conditions his main subject was now snow.

There were several reasons why Claude Monet, in the mid-1890s, returned to the subject of the winter landscape, and even travelled as far as Norway to find it. Norway had long been a dream destination for Monet, as first recorded in 1890. How this desire was born, however, is unknown; several different factors probably played a role in it. Scandinavia and Norway were fashionable in France at this time, not least in literature and the theatre, where Ibsen, Bjørnson, and Strindberg, were counted among the great names of the age. Monet's library at Giverny shows that he shared this interest in Scandinavian literature, especially in the work of Ibsen. He read *Hedda Gabler* in 1892, and then *The Lady from the Sea, An Enemy of the People, The Pretenders,* and *Emperor and Galilean.* In 1896 he acquired *Love's Comedy, Ghosts,* and *A Doll's House.* He also subscribed to *La Revue blanche,* which, in its supplements, published works by Bjørnson, Strindberg, Hamsun, and Herman Bang. The Scandinavian influence was also great in contemporary French musical life. Edvard Grieg was the most popular foreign composer in France in the early 1890s, and his music was heard in every French bourgeois home. His music influenced Debussy, among others, and the critics singled out its nationalistic sentiment and the experience of a connection between Grieg's music and the natural beauty of his native country. Such impressions were further strengthened by the depictions of the country in the visual arts.

When Fridtjof Nansen finally returned home in 1886 from his three-year expedition to the North Pole, and was received as a national hero, his subsequent lecture tour of France and other countries turned into a veritable triumphal procession, and he was everywhere showered with praise. This reinforced the popular image of Norway as a nation. Norway was, in other words, a very popular country in France in those years: "The small Norwegian population emerges from the darkness, introducing itself to the rest of Europe, its hands full of the fruits of its renaissance ... In a time of drought and general insecurity, France turns towards foreign nations and imports. Norway exports its riches."[6]

In the wake of this enthusiasm, it has also been asserted that Claude Monet, who grew up in Normandy, in Le Havre, saw himself as an heir to the ninth-century Scandinavian conquerors of Normandy. In the year 885, Norwegian Vikings raided and conquered Rouen, a city that was to become the center of their Empire. According to Oscar Reutersvärd, Blanche Hochedé-Monet supposedly even said that Monet grew a beard and adopted a hairstyle to resemble a Norwegian Viking![7]

If there was a great fascination with all things Scandinavian in France at this time, the reverse influence was even greater. Not least as a result of a marked increase in Norwegian trade relations with France in the wake of the Napoleonic Wars, especially timber exports, cultural ties between the two countries were also strengthened, and Norwegian artists travelled frequently to France. The 1878 World's Fair received a lot of attention, and the stimulating influence of this event inspired many to settle in Paris for a shorter or longer period.

Monet was, in other words, hardly an unknown artist in Norwegian cultural circles. Andreas Aubert had introduced him and the Impressionist movement to the Norwegian public as early as 1883, and had later repeatedly pointed to the importance of Monet's art. At the initiative of Aubert and others, Pissarro, Degas and Monet, were all invited to participate in the 1890 Autumn Salon at Christiania, and in his review Aubert wrote of Monet: "I want to encourage all who wish to understand the basic principles of the colourist painting of our time, to at least make an honest attempt to grasp the meaning of his experimental art; for it constitutes the focal point of one of the most remarkable and spiritual movements in the visual arts of our times, internationally as well as nationally."[8]

And the Norwegians actually seized the opportunity: one of Monet's paintings in the exhibition, *Rain, Etretat* of 1886, was purchased by the Nasjonalgalleriet, and it is worth noting that this was the first acquisition of a painting by Monet by a public collection outside of France (ill. p. 214, cat.no. 144). No doubt this warmed the artist's heart, further stimulating his curiosity about this country in the far north.

Of decisive importance, however, being the immediate reason for his journey, was the fact that his stepson, Jacques Hochedé, was then living in Norway. In Rouen Hochedé worked with timber imports from Norway and he had traveled there to

145. **Claude Monet** (1840–1926): **Houses in the Snow, Norway,** 1895. Oil on canvas, 64.7 x 91.4. Private collection.

study Norwegian in order to further his business relations. He had arrived on the 25th of June 1894, and would remain in the country for one year, until the 27th of June 1895. Without his stepson's assistance during his stay in Norway, Claude Monet would never have been able to carry out his project. With his stepson in place, he was able to fulfill his dream of experiencing a northern winter, and begin his pursuit of its changing light and moods.

"… I have often accompanied Claude Monet as he searched for visual impressions. In reality, he was then no longer a painter, but a hunter. He marched off with children in tow, carrying his paintings, five or six with the same motif captured at different times of the day and having a different impact. He moved from one to the other as the skies changed. I have seen him set down on his canvas … a sudden shimmer of scintillating light. On another occasion he caught a handful of rain that was lashing the surface of the lake and literally threw it onto his canvas."[9]

Guy de Maupassant demonstrates how Monet, in his search for motifs, behaved much like an explorer. In addition, his account of 1886 describes precisely the painting of Etretat purchased by the Nasjonalgalleriet. Monet's Norway hunt would, however, present him with a different set of problems and turn out to be the most difficult expedition he had ever undertaken."

Worn out from an eventful five-day train- and boat trip, Claude Monet arrived in Norway, in the middle of a violent winter storm, on the 1st of February 1895, at eleven o'clock in the evening.[10] Jacques met him at the railway station, and he checked into his pension in town. Monet would experience an unusually cold and snowy winter in Norway. Large areas of Europe had been struck by unusually cold weather that year; the day of Monet's arrival in Christiania, for example, all Norwegian and Swedish ports were closed due to the ice. Paradoxically, Giverny was also blanketed by snow during the time that Monet was away in Norway, and the skates were taken out of storage.

Monet had come to Norway to meet the snow head on, and that was what most occupied him, but initially he felt overwhelmed and almost dejected. He had never imagined that there would be so much of it, that it would blanket the entire frozen landscape. He loved the combination of snow and water, and the possibility this created of a subtle play of light, but it would take some time before he felt intimate with the snow and allowed himself to become fascinated by its endlessly changing and subtle light effects. Immediately on arrival, he said about the journey: "… The landscape was mostly monotonous, and the constant snowfall, lasting all the way from Paris, was a bit tiresome in the long run," and about Christiania: "This country is surely infinitely more beautiful without the snow, or at least when there is not so much of it."[11]

All this snow would create frequent problems for him and give rise to a sense of frustration during his stay in Norway, but, at the same time, it did not take long for him to become enchanted with and fascinated by the winter landscape. "After the depressing arrival, it has been just endless rapture … So much of beauty I have observed from the top of these steep mountains looming over immense lakes, completely frozen and covered with snow! In these places the snow was more than a meter deep, and our sleigh glided over it, the sweating horse covered, like ourselves, in frost and ice. I have also seen enormous waterfalls, of one hundred meters, but completely frozen over, it is extraordinary."[12]

Monet wrote this in a letter home on the 9th of February, after a several days long excursion by horse and sleigh in the countryside around Christiania. Faithful to his habit he had, immediately upon arrival, made reconnaissance tours of the environs in search of suitable motifs. His desire to immediately get to work would, however, prove more difficult to satisfy than he had foreseen. He soon realized that the massive amounts of snow created limitations that he, a foreigner, would somehow have to cope with. "Jacques and I make fantastic excursions. I hardly know which way to turn, or what to do, so much beauty I get to see. I am looking for potential locations near an inn or the railway, but it is completely hopeless. Since I do not know how to ski, I am forced to find my motifs along plowed roads; for as soon as you leave the road, the snow is three meters deep. On skis you can go anywhere."[13]

He travelled incessantly, allowing himself to become fascinated, but also feeling discouraged by what he had undertaken "… I have now been here for eighteen days and have still not been able to work. I hope to get started soon, one needs a lot of time to understand things and really see them. Jacques is as kind as can be, but he was incapable of showing me the most typical locations, and for the first few days the snow and the fog, and the snow again, kept me from getting a closer look at things. This is an admirable country, but too remote to allow for a second visit here. And so, I sometimes feel sad and discouraged, seeing the days go by without being able to accomplish anything at all."[14]

After two weeks in the country he finally arrived at the Bjørnegaard Pension in Sandviken (today Sandvika), barely an hour's train ride from Christiania, a place recommended by his Norwegian colleagues and one that he immediately appreciated. The pension was run by Jenny Bjørnson, Bjørnstjerne Bjørnson's daughter in law, and was a lively and popular spot, a frequent haunt of the artists. The painter Gerhard Munthe and the Danish author Herman Bang were among those who stayed there at the same time as Monet. Not least because he spoke fluent French, it was Herman Bang that Monet had most contact with. His stepson, Jacques, usually accompanied him as an assistant on his daily painting excursions in the area, but he stayed at a pension in town and returned to his lodgings in the evening.

Although Monet now seemed to have found a place where he could catch up on his work, it still took him six days to get started. He explored the area in search of the "right spot," and also visited Christiania for the Holmenkollen race on the 18th of February. "We had to hire a sleigh and two horses ten days in advance; quite apart from the wonderful location where the race is held, the race itself is a very special event that I am very happy to have experienced. In addition to all sleighs from Christiania and the surrounding area, the whole population is present and everyone is on skis, the soldiers, the musicians, all are on skis … The race itself is one of the strangest events imaginable: they race down a slope of more than one hundred and fifty meters, then jump twenty to twenty-five meters straight out in the air … We left the inn at half past nine o'clock in the morning and did not return until seven o'clock. The procession of people returning home was a long one and, just imagine, the whole audience—thousands of people, sleighs and horses—stood on a lake. That should give you an idea of what ice really is."[15]

Finally, on the 21st of February, three weeks after his arrival in the country, we find him at work. The following four weeks were entirely devoted to work. Through his extensive correspondence we are able to follow its progress in detail. The workday was long: he awoke at six o'clock in the morning and left the house at eight. After a lunch break at two o'clock in the afternoon, he went out again, working until seven o'clock in the evening. Accompanied by Jacques, whose sledge held a spade, umbrella, easel, and other necessary equipment, he visited the four or five fixed locations discovered during long reconnaissance tours. The canvases were mounted, something that often involved much digging and use of the spade on Jacques' part, due to the continued heavy snowfall. After his stepfather was set up and working, he would set off on a skiing trip by himself, or dig a trench where he could sit, quietly engaging in his Norwegian language studies. Mother Nature, however, frequently had other plans. Monet was used to working outdoors, often in very bad weather conditions. As demonstrated by many of the paintings from before his stay in Norway, he was used to stormy weather, as well as fog and frost. Still, the severe Norwegian winter took him completely by surprise, and his mood shifted from dejection to exultation. "I have tried to work, but so much snow has fallen since last

148. **Claude Monet** (1840–1926): **Norway. The Red Houses at Bjørnegaard,** 1895. Oil on canvas, 65 x 81. Musée Marmottan Monet, Paris, 5170.

night, and we were entirely covered with snow, that I was forced to give it up. I am in complete despair, because it was wonderful to see all the trees, all the spruce covered with snow. But it is impossible even to think of these things, or of finding shelter somewhere in order to be able to paint, and impossible to find a sufficiently large umbrella.[16] A few days later he writes: "I am working incessantly … in spite of the snow … I see only beautiful things, only beautiful visual effects that I was incapable of seeing earlier on … in France one has no idea of such snow effects, it is marvellous."[17]

Claude Monet's mood swings are a typical character trait that emerges during all his expeditions, be it to Rouen, Belle-Île, or London. This tells us a lot about the artist himself, about his state of mind and his relationship with his art. It also underlines the race against time that working in series entailed, and just how vulnerable one is when working outdoors for hours at a time and on many different canvases as did Monet, in order to "freeze" the changing daylight in his paintings. In the end, Monet met the snow in the same way that he had met the cold, wind and stormy

150. **Claude Monet** (1840–1926): **Sandviken, Snow Effect,** 1895.
Oil on canvas, 73 x 92. Næringslivets Hovedorganisasjon, Oslo.

149. **Claude Monet** (1840–1926): **Sandviken, Norway,** 1895. Oil on canvas,
73.4 x 92.5. The Art Institute of Chicago, Gift of Bruce Borland, 1961.790.

weather of Belle-Île. In time it became a source of both inspiration and joy. "The snow … is falling incessantly. You would have laughed if you could have seen me, white from head-to-toe, with the beard full of icicles like stalactites."[18] He also enjoyed traveling in the snow, and wrote rapturously in his letters home about sleigh rides and about falling down and literally blending in with the snow, himself becoming a part of the landscape.[19]

When he had finally adapted to the climate and the snow, however, new problems quickly arose. The month of March held in store not only massive amounts of snow, but also a change in the weather, bringing thaw and melting snow. For Monet this meant a race against the season. Working in series demanded stable weather conditions, yet he was forced to abandon paintings he had begun when it became impossible to reach certain motifs, while other motifs were drastically altered due to sudden changes in the weather. Because of the snow and thaw, it became prohibited to travel on the ice in any kind of vehicle, and so Monet was prevented from doing further paintings of the fjords, giving rise to his complaint about "all the motifs that were being lost."[20] The mild weather and strong sunshine also caused the snow to melt from the rooftops, with the result that he had to abandon the series of red and blue houses he had begun. With irritation and sadness he concludes that he should have arrived earlier and stayed longer.[21]

The resulting restlessness and sense of a lack of time also led Monet to keep apart as far as possible from the social life of Bjørnegaard, and to decline invitations to social gatherings in Christiania and meetings with his colleagues. Once again, these traits are recognizable both from his other expeditions and from his intensely private family life at Giverny. Still, he was unable to avoid all social events at Bjørnegaard. "In the house where I am staying there is always a party going on … It is absolutely impossible to go to bed early and be able to spend some time alone, especially since my room is adjacent to the salon, where people gather from morning till eve. And across the yard-for this is a farm-lives a painter, and in another building a Danish author, and every day one of them has guests over, not to speak of all the painters who are invited here on my account. Last Sunday there were evening guests, a well-known painter and his wife. A toast was proposed in my honor, to the painter Claude Monet, who brings honor to France, glasses clinked, and everyone stood up, men and women, and started singing the Marseillaise. You can picture me there; and the whole thing ended in a deafening 'hip hip hurrah.' Fortunately, I abstain from the many little glasses these people drink, mixed with wine, with milk, with beer—what a strange fare!"[22]

One month later he attended yet another party, but never really got used to the extroverted social life of his Norwegian colleagues. "Once again I managed to avoid giving a speech, by asking the gentleman sitting next to me to give it in my place. Finally, there was a ball and a supper, which lasted from two o'clock in the afternoon until one in the morning. It is now eleven o'clock in the morning and they are dancing again. The Norwegians are crazy about the waltz."[23]

There are numerous stories, myths, and news accounts by his contemporaries about Monet's visit to Norway. Next to his own letters, however, an article written by the Danish author Herman Bang, who stayed at Bjørnegaard at the same time as the artist, stands out as a real jewel in the Monet literature. The article gives a good account of Monet's stay in Norway. The author's deep insights into Claude Monet's personality and his relationship with his art are also of interest here.

"His life is what he paints, and what he paints is his life. He is young on those days that his work is going well, he is an old man when it goes badly. You can immediately hear it in the sound of his voice, you can see it in the wrinkles on his forehead, if: ça va—le travail. His whole being is a mirror of his work's progress, and a cloud shadowing his genius is a cloud shadowing his face. He experiences pleasure and suffering only through and in his work. He is not one-sided—is there such a thing as a one-sided genius?—yet he has one wish only: to express himself through colour.

… And one evening when he returned home exhausted after spending ten hours outdoors in the Norwegian cold, after he—a man almost sixty years of age—had been lying in wait for the sun and the colours in order to capture them on a piece of mounted canvas, he said:

– No, it is too great a passion … And what, then, is it that I want to accomplish?

– I'm chasing a dream, I want what is impossible …

– Yes, if only I could be satisfied by what is possible …

Is not the artist's whole life embodied in these few words? The true artist, who is haunted by the impossible dream that is the same for all artists: to capture the beauty of things, the beauty his eye has beheld and his soul worshipped …

Claude Monet devotes himself entirely to this.

He loves the beauty of Nature, which he perceives, and he is tormented by it: for this beauty must be captured.

The varied, ever-changing beauty of Nature. This is the heart of the matter: Nature is endlessly changing—in the light, minute-by-minute changeable and altered, the skies and the beauty are transformed … But how capture, how represent, how hold what we can only observe as it vanishes? What we can only admire as it ceases to be? What we can comprehend only when it has already disappeared."[24]

On the 26th of March, after barely five weeks of work, Claude Monet left the Bjørnegaard Pension and moved to Christiania, where he would remain until his departure. In the evening of the 1st of April, after exactly two months in Norway, he travelled by train to Paris via Copenhagen. After a working period of merely five weeks, and under the sometimes very difficult circumstances described here, it is impressive that Monet was able to bring back to France as many as twenty-eight paintings and a sketchbook containing some thirty drawings.

The motifs chosen by Monet can be divided into six groups, four of which belong to his so-called "series," in which the same motif is depicted under different light conditions and at different times of the day. That the choice of motifs was partly determined by practical circumstances, since the locations had to be somewhat easily accessible, did not prevent the artist from making bold choices. For example, he had himself carried by horse and sleigh across the ice outside Sandviken as far as the open waters of Oslofjorden, where he painted a series of five works. To his great chagrin he could not do more, as the mild weather had caused the ice to become thin and weak and it became prohibited to travel freely.

The Sandviken with the Løkke Bridge motif had been represented earlier in

146. **Claude Monet** (1840–1926): **The Kolsås Mountain,** 1895.
Oil on canvas, 65 x 100. Private collection, 1408.

147. **Claude Monet** (1840–1926): **The Kolsås Mountain, Sunshine,** 1895.
Oil on canvas, 65 x 100. Private collection, 1409.

Norwegian painting (by Johannes Flintoe in 1836, and Frederik Collet in 1889), and was familiar because of the beautiful cast-iron bridge (the oldest in Norway, from 1829–30) and the picturesque houses with a view of Løkkåsen in the background. Monet painted four versions[25] of this motif, which he compared to a Japanese village, a comparison that he frequently made when painting the Norwegian winter landscape. In her 1995 article, Sylvie Patin goes into greater detail about Monet's fascination with Japanese art and the parallels with his Norwegian work. She emphasizes the fact that Monet's paintings of Christianiafjorden have a compositional structure inspired by Japanese woodcuts, and that the paintings of Sandvika and Kolsåstoppen are also reminiscent of the Japanese art of "ukio-e," in which the same subject is repeated at different times of day and in different seasons. It was through these graphic works that Monet became acquainted with Japan, and his large collection of woodcuts at Giverny included, for example, nine woodcuts from Hokusaï's well-known series of Thirty-six studies of Mount Fuji, in which the subject is represented under different light conditions.

Norway reminded him of this country which he had never visited "… I found a delightful subject in the small islands that barely rise above the surface of the sea, completely covered with snow, and in the background there is a mountain. One might imagine oneself in Japan—as, by the way, one often does in this country. I am working on a view of Sandvika, which resembles a Japanese village, and I am also working on a view of a mountain that is everywhere visible in these parts, and which makes me think of Fujiyama."[26]

Monet did as many as thirteen paintings of Kolsåstoppen, a mountain situated not far from Bjørnegaard where he was staying. At 380 meters above sea-level, it is not a particularly high mountain, but it dominates the Bærum landscape with its strange silhouette that catches all the fascinating light effects typical of the region, and it formed the background for the so-called Fleskum-painters, active there in the summers of 1886–87. It was the majestic snow-clad mountain Monet chose to immortalize, and this series was the most important of those he brought back home. In a newspaper interview with Christian Krohg seven years later, Herman Bang described these paintings almost as if they were works of literature. "I don't know what it is called, it was a mountain, but this mountain resembled a human being. He painted the mountain in different scenes as it were: in one scene it was as if it had thrown a snow mantle over its shoulders, like a mantle of ermine. Like this! Bang had stood up and placed a napkin over his right shoulder and down across his chest. He resembled the mountain of Kolsaas exactly. It was impressive! An indignant Queen stood before us! Or Tragedy, who had arisen, lifting her head high! The waiter approached, filled with respect, offering Kolsaas desert. Monet did more paintings: the same mountain … a weather-beaten old hag, the same mountain … a young bride dressed in white."[27]

When six of the Norwegian works were exhibited for the first time at Durand-Ruel's gallery in Paris in May of 1895, a critic noted that "Monet has really managed to reconcile me with Ibsen through his Norwegian landscapes."[28]

In other words, Monet exhibited several of his Norwegian paintings soon after his return to France, and in doing so he broke with his previous habit of reworking his paintings in the studio after returning from similar excursions. This, however, was one of the reasons why the Norwegian paintings were later considered sketchy and unfinished. Later statements by Monet to the effect that none of these paintings were finished, that they should simply be regarded as sketches, experimental works, or preparatory studies, long gave support to this notion, but careful art historical research now offers a more balanced view and arrives at a different conclusion. Sylvie Patin, for example, notes that Monet frequently made statements of this kind about his paintings, especially when he felt depressed. "Monet rarely considered a work 'finished,' as he reminded Geoffroy in 1893 in a letter from Rouen: '... whoever claims that he has finished a painting is being terribly arrogant. Since finished means complete, perfect ...' The artist did not regard his compositions as final and, consequently, he often did not finish them until the very last moment, filling in the empty areas left around the edges of his canvas, and signing and dating his work with a view to a future sale or exhibition. Only half of the Norwegian paintings carry Monet's signature."[29]

Patin concludes her article by observing that Monet felt satisfied also in the sense that the snow motif continued to interest him, and in photographs of the studio-salon at Giverny taken during Monet's lifetime, we can see that he liked to surround himself with the paintings from Norway. One or more of these was always on display. The fact that, at the 1899 sale of paintings to benefit Alfred Sisley's children, he gave away "the best thing we own," the painting with motifs from Sandviken (now in the Art Institute of Chicago, ill. p. 253, cat.no. 149), points in the same direction. The donation of this painting, which Monet valued especially highly, was a gesture honouring Sisley, who had specialized in paintings of snow landscapes.

Monet's Norwegian paintings belong to his important "series" of the 1890s, while also representing a continuation of the artist's earliest snow landscapes. Even if these twenty-eight paintings are no more than a parenthesis in Monet's total production of two thousand works, they form an interesting group, and Monet's fascination with this exotic country never ceased.

But what about Monet's stay in Norway in terms of its importance for, and influence on, the Norwegian artistic milieu? Despite Andreas Aubert's comments at the time of the artist's arrival, that it would be a true feast for our national art and that the encounter would invigorate our artistic life, the result was altogether different.[30]

Monet's visit does not seem to have had a deeper impact on Norwegian painting than what had already been accomplished by Parisian Impressionism, and it is barely mentioned in writings about Norwegian art. Many remained unsympathetic towards his art, and even Frits Thaulow said, when he later came across some of the Norwegian paintings in a Parisian art exhibit: "Monet's Norway is complete rubbish, on that we all agree down here."[31]

Impressionism was perceived by many in Scandinavia as a continuation of Naturalism and, consequently, as its confirmation. The formally transgressive element was practically overlooked, and achieved its breakthrough only with Post-Impressionism. This subject is thoroughly illuminated by the present exhibition and in other catalogue essays. In this context, Monet's visit becomes a mere interlude, but an exciting one.

Following pages: 197. **Paul Signac** (1863–1935): **Seine, Grenelle,** 1899 (detail). Oil on canvas, 62 x 78.5. Amos Andersons konstmuseum, Helsingfors, Sigurd Frosterus samling, 56/SF.

Under the Sign of the Rainbow Colours. Impressionism and Finland

Bengt von Bonsdorff

SUNLIGHT AND SHADOW and *Triumph of the Rainbow Colours* were the titles of two collections of essays on art theory published by the Finnish architect, author, and art theorist Sigurd Frosterus in 1917. They preceded his doctoral thesis on *The Problem of Colour in Art* of 1920. The *Triumph of the Rainbow Colours* contained lectures and essays in which Frosterus described the Neo-Impressionist technique and discussed the background of the Finnish group of painters known as Septem, founded in 1912. We will return to Frosterus later on.

The Elite in Paris in the 1880s

The Finnish artists in Paris in the 1870s and '80s were not easily influenced by modern art, that is to say, by Impressionism, in the 1880s. Naturalism and Realism were embraced by nearly everyone, principally by Albert Edelfelt, Axel Gallén and Eero Järnefelt, and even Finnish women painters, such as Helene Schjerfbeck, Maria Wiik, Amélie Lundahl, Helena Westermarck, and Elin Danielson, were receptive to the new currents, caused a stir, and were even considered radical. Only a handful of painters were influenced to a greater extent by Impressionism and the Impressionists' methods of representing light by means of colour. Among the first who, in the 1880s, attempted to apply the teachings of French Impressionism, without loosing their clients at home, were Albert Edelfelt, Axel Gallén, Torsten Wasastjerna, and Victor Westerholm. The Finns were more receptive to the Symbolism and Synthetism of the early 1890s. Magnus Enckell, for example, who would become a leader of the Septem group about 1910, developed from Symbolism, which he had come into contact with in Paris as early as 1891, to Neo-Impressionism in the early 1900s.

The Birth of an Art Museum

The Museum of Fine Arts housed in the Ateneum in Helsinki is the youngest of the Scandinavian national galleries. Its collections, which long comprised principally art works purchased after 1846 by the Finnish Fine Arts Association, founded in that year, opened to the public in temporary quarters in late 1863. It may be noted, however, that the Russian Imperial Court had strongly favoured the founding of an art museum in Helsinki, the capital of the Grand Duchy. The nation's university (The Imperial University of Alexander) had been transferred here, and around it the architect Carl Ludvig Engel's other stately buildings in Neo-Classical style rose in the first half of the 19th century. Protector of the Fine Arts Association at the time of its foundation in 1846 was the one-year old Grand Duke Alexander Alexandrovich, later the Emperor Alexander III, son of Alexander II and married to the Danish Princess Dagmar. The museum, which opened its doors to the public in November of 1887, was housed in the new Ateneum building, close to the main railway station, designed by the architect Carl Theodor Höijer. The initiator, and an active promoter, of the project was the historian of literature and art and founder of the *Finsk Tidskrift*, Carl Gustaf Estlander, the first chairman of the Antell delegation from 1894 to 1905. The museum was enlarged and modernized in 1900–01, and its collections were reorganized under the direction of Johan Jakob Tikkanen, Professor Extraordinary of Art History at the University 1897–1920 and subsequently its first permanent Professor until 1926. Tikkanen was acting Curator at the Ateneum 1913–14, and Secretary of the Finnish Fine Arts Association during the long period 1892–1920, when so much was happening in the nation, both politically and culturally.

Thus, the Ateneum opened its doors at a time when Scandinavian artists were winning laurels in Paris, and Finnish artists were also awarded prizes at the Salons. Among the first purchases of the Finnish Fine Arts Association for the collections of the recently inaugurated museum was Helene Schjerfbeck's *The Convalescent* of 1888, one of her best known works. Chief Curator of the Finnish Fine Arts Association's collections housed in the new building was Thorsten Waenerberg, painter and former teacher at the Turku (swe: Åbo) Drawing School. He was Curator at the Museum of Fine Arts in the Ateneum or, as it was known before 1911, the Collections of the Finnish Fine Arts Association, until 1913. Towards the end of his career, however, the knowledgeable Curator represented too much of a traditionalist view of art and had little understanding for contemporary artistic currents. More far-sighted was, without a doubt, Waenerberg's colleague Victor Westerholm in Turku, his junior by fourteen years. He was Director of the Drawing School and was, simultaneously, appointed as the first Director of the Museum of Fine Arts in Turku in 1904, an institution which also housed the Drawing School. Thus, the nation's principal art museums were at that time run by artists.

The Antell Collections and Other Donations
The Finnish Fine Arts Association and the new art museum in the Ateneum received many important donations in the second half of the 19th century. Among the first was the Russian Prince Alexander's donation of, principally, older European art from the collection of Baron Klinckowström, which the Prince had acquired. The Fine Arts Association itself had, already in 1849, begun to establish the collection that was later (1939) incorporated with the other collections of the Ateneum.[1] Among the most important donations was the 1893 bequest of the medical doctor,

Dr. Herman Frithiof Antell, "to the Finnish people." The donation comprised an important art collection, as well as funds for future acquisitions. Antell, who had visited Paris for the first time in 1874–75 and resided there permanently from 1877 until his death, also donated what would become the nucleus of the Finnish Nationalmuseum, the central archeological, ethnographic, and historical museum that opened to the public in 1916. It housed, among other things, Antell's valuable numismatic collections, principally Swedish coins and medals.

Of special interest is the fact that Antell's art collection, in addition to Finnish art—such as Gallén's *Demasquée*, bold for its time, painted on commission for Antell in 1888—also included works by Swedish and French artists. The Swedish works included, in addition to 17th- and 18th-century portraits, paintings by Zorn, among others. The French works included four by Charles-François Daubigny, for example, his *Moonlit Seascape (Marine au clair de lune)*, supplementing the museum's collection of works by painters of the Barbizon school. The latter already comprised paintings by Camille Corot, donated by, among others, the Viborg businessman and patron of the arts, Victor Hoving. Hoving's nephew, the author and businessman Victor Harald Hoving who, for many years, was active in Stockholm and had close ties to Swedish literary and artistic circles, also bequeathed artworks and funds to the Ateneum. Through Antell's donation the Finnish general public, and the younger generation of sculptors, also had the opportunity to become acquainted with three sculptures by Rodin—whom Antell knew personally, and from whom he had purchased the sculptures—as well as works by the Paris-based sculptor Ville Vallgren.[2] One the Rodin sculptures, *I am Beautiful (Je suis belle)*, also known as *Beauty (La Beauté)*, is depicted in the Swedish painter Allan Österlind's watercolour *Rodin in His Studio*. Next to Zorn, Österlind was one of Antell's favourite artists. Works by Per Ekström, such as the *Summer Landscape* of 1879, were also included in the art collection donated by Antell.[3] Although Impressionist tendencies may already be detected in the French paintings that ended up at the Ateneum, usually as donations, there was, for the time being, no sign of the truly great French Impressionists. A series of etchings by Édouard Manet was only purchased in 1932.

Exhibitions Are Organized

That a more dynamic period was approaching for Finnish art in the late 1890s is indicated by an increasing number of exhibitions focused on domestic and other Scandinavian art, but also, as we will see, a few exhibitions of more contemporary European art never before seen in Finland. The Swedish Konstnärsförbundet (Artists' Union) was invited to exhibit at the Ateneum in 1899. The members of the jury Richard Bergh, Eugène Jansson, Nils Kreuger, and Karl Nordström, were all represented in the exhibition. Bergh's *The Knight and the Maiden* was the most expensive work (5 500 kr), followed by Carl Larsson's *My Family* (5 000 kr). Also represented were Prince Eugen, Per Ekström, Ernst Josephson (with works such as *The Neck*, lent by Georg Pauli, and the portrait of the Chief of Police, Rubenson, lent by Mrs. Jeanette Rubenson), Anders Zorn (two portraits), and as many as twelve canvases by Nils Kreuger. Since a work by the Swedish painter Gustave Albert (now in the Museum of Fine Arts, Eskilstuna) has been included in the

present exhibition, it may be interesting to note that he was invited by the Konstnärsförbundet, as the only foreign artist, to exhibit his *Winter Morning, Gouvieux (Oise)* at the 1899 exhibition in Helsinki. The painting was offered for sale at 1 000 kronor, but probably did not find a buyer in Finland.[4] The Swedish exhibition was followed by an exhibition of Danish, Dutch, and French art in 1901, paving the way for a lively exchange of exhibitions amongst the Nordic countries. In 1906–07 there were exhibitions of Anders Zorn (in the University's drawing studio) and J.F. Willumsen, and works by Zorn (*The Door to the Attic* of 1905), among others, were purchased. Works by Ernst Josephson, Carl Wilhelmsson, and Carl Larsson were also added to the collections of the Ateneum. Josephson's portrait of his friend Ville Vallgren was acquired in 1911. Carl Larsson's 1898 portrait of Jac. Ahrenberg had been purchased the year before.[5]

Another sign of change was the emergence of an opposition movement among the young artists of Helsinki in the 1890s. The artists were dissatisfied with the Finnish Fine Arts Association's exhibition policy and principles of selection, and in 1891 they began organizing an annual Finnish Artists' Autumn Exhibition. Founding members were the painters Gunnar Berndtson, Albert Edelfelt, Axel Gallén (known as Akseli Gallen-Kallela after 1907), Eero Järnefelt, and Victor Westerholm, and the leading young sculptors Robert Stigell, Ville Vallgren, and Emil Wikström. Another policy that the artists were protesting against involved the copyright of artworks, which the Fine Arts Association wished to take over at the time of purchase.[6] Copyright issues and exhibition fees have remained divisive issues within the art world.

Turbulent Times at the Turn of the Century
The Finnish Artists' exhibitions made it possible for the Finnish general public to become acquainted with more contemporary currents within domestic art. Thus, Väinö Blomstedt's first purely Symbolist painting, showing a nearly abstract landscape, *The Cemetery at Bourg-la-Reine* of 1894, was, for example, exhibited at the Finnish Artists' Autumn Exhibition the year it was executed. His most important Synthetist works were created during the period 1894–97. Though perhaps not intended by the artists, political and nationalist tendencies in symbolic guise, oppos-

194. **Helene Schjerfbeck** (1862–1946): **The Old Manor (Sjundby Gård)**, 1901. Oil on canvas, 65 x 85. Turku Art Museum, 74.

ing the politics of Russianization culminating in the so-called February Manifesto of 1899, could be detected in Finnish art of the 1890s, in painting as well as in sculpture. In 1894 Edelfelt painted *Särkkä (swe: Långörn)*, representing, in symbolic form, an ominous premonition of what lay in wait beyond the horizon in the east. Eero Järnefelt's *Autumn Landscape from Pielisjärvi*, painted in the year of the February Manifesto—the year Jean Sibelius composed his *Finlandia*—was immediately interpreted as a national, patriotic, and political manifestation. Helene Schjerfbeck's best known landscape painting, *The Old Manor House (Sjundby gård)* of 1901, now in the collections of the Museum of Fine Arts in Turku, is also counted among the Finnish landscape paintings with political associations. The painting reveals distinct Art Nouveau influence and Synthetist tendencies.[7] Axel Gallén studied fresco painting in Italy in 1897 and began applying what he had learnt around the turn of the century. Best known are his ceiling decoration with motifs from the Kalevala in the Finnish pavilion at the World Fair of 1900, the large canvas *Kullervo Goes Off to Battle* of 1902 in the Old Student's House in Helsinki, and the frescoes in the Juselius Mausoleum of 1901–03 at Pori (swe: Björneborg). Gallén's paintings from this time could also be seen as contributions to the National

54. **Akseli Gallen-Kallela** (1865–1931): **Autumn,** 1902. Tempera and oil on canvas, 143 x 77. Sigrid Jusélius Foundation, Helsinki.

200. **Beda Stjernschantz** (1867–1910): **Everywhere a Voice is Sounding,** 1895. Oil on canvas, 85.5 x 129.5. Ateneum Art Museum, Helsinki, Collection Antell, A III 1851.

Romantic and patriotic art typical of this period. The six frescoes in the Juselius Mausoleum, perhaps the most important being the almost abstractly simplified *Autumn*, occupy an important role in Gallén's oeuvre. The original cartoons executed in tempera and oil are in the collections of the Ateneum.[8]

International Exhibitions in 1901 and 1904
The first exhibition of French Impressionists and Neo-Impressionists in Finland was held at the Ateneum in 1901. By this time Impressionism was no longer a novelty in Finland and some of the exhibited works were as much as twenty years old, but for the general public the style still seemed foreign and the exhibition was not a public success. The cover of the exhibition catalogue showed a small bronze by Rodin, the *Portrait of Balzac* (in a drawing by Edelfelt), which was included in the exhibition and purchased for the collections of the Ateneum for 800 francs. The same exhibition included works by, among others, Monet, Pissarro, Renoir, and Sisely, with price tags ranging from 10 000–15 000 francs, or the equivalent in Finnish marks.[9]
All exhibitions of foreign art held at the recently inaugurated museum were run at a loss, something that is not unfamiliar to today's exhibition organizers. Despite the setback in 1901, another exhibition of French and Belgian art was already being organized at the Ateneum in 1904. For the artists this was an important event, though public interest remained slight. Edelfelt's and Tikkanen's reviews in the *Hufvudstadsbladet* (01/30–31, 02/14, 02/23 1904) were positive, while Jac. Ahren-

48. **Alfred William Finch** (1854–1930): **Race Track, Wellington, Ostende**, 1888. Oil on canvas, 49.5 x 59. Ateneum Art Museum, Helsinki, Collection Ahlström, A III 2233.

84. **Paul Gauguin** (1848–1903): **Landscape, La Dominique (Hiva Oa),** 1903. Oil on
canvas, 75 x 67. Ateneum Art Museum, Helsinki, Collection Antell, A II 854.

berg adopted a more reserved attitude in his review for the *Finsk Tidskrift*. The Antell delegation purchased Pierre Puvis de Chavannes' pastel, *Étude de femme (Study of a Woman)*, from the exhibition for 12 000 francs, and also Meunier's bronze *Wood Cutter* and his pastel *Founder*.[10] For the price of the Puvis de Chavannes pastel one would have been able to acquire one of the exhibited pastels by Degas, while another of these cost as much as a Monet. The most expensive work (20 000 francs) was Renoir's *Woman Bathing* of 1888. Paintings by Pissarro, Sisley, and Van Rysselberghe were less expensive, as were some small-size pastels by Degas and watercolours by Signac. A.W. Finch's *Racetrack* of 1888, probably identical with *The Wellington Racetrack (Ostende)* from the same year, cost 400 francs at the exhibition.[11] Puvis de Chavannes was admired by several Finnish artists, among others, Helene Schjerfbeck, Maria Wiik, Pekka Halonen, and Eero Järnefelt. Beda Stjernschantz, who had studied at the Académie Colarossi in 1891–92, became one of the foremost Finnish Symbolists. Her best known painting, painted in 1895 on the Estonian island of Vormsö, *Everywhere a Voice Invites Us*—after a quote from Emil von Qvanten's *Song of Suomi*—recalls Puvis de Chavannes' *Le Pauvre Pecheur (The Poor Fisherman)*, as well as Gauguin's and Émile Bernard's images of the life of Breton people.

The Purchasing of Foreign Art Begins in Earnest
In this period Finnish museums concentrated mostly on domestic art, but other Scandinavian art was also given priority over international art. The Antell delegation's 1908 acquisition of Gauguin's *Landscape, La Dominique. Hiva Oa* (1903) for the collections of the Ateneum may be seen as the expression of a new attitude towards contemporary art. Suggestions for potential purchases often came from Paris-based artists, in this case from Eero Järnefelt and Magnus Enckell, who had "discovered" Gauguin's painting at the Parisian art dealer Ambroise Vollard's. For the purchase to go through, it was necessary to get the go-ahead of the Antell delegation and its members Eliel Aspelin-Haapkyläs and Yrjö Hirn, extended at their own risk, sight unseen. The same year, Félix Vallotton's *Portrait of the Artist F. Jasinsky* was acquired for the Ateneum in connection with the Secessionist Exhibition in Munich, at the suggestion of the architect Armas Lindgren.[12]

Early Finnish Artists in Paris
One of the first Finnish artists to take note of Impressionism was Fanny Churberg, who also adopted a Realist style before anyone else in Finland. At the same time, her painting of the 1870s was early on associated with Expressionism. In 1876 Churberg studied with the Swedish artist Wilhelm von Gegerfelt in Paris. Although her intense paintings, mostly landscapes and still-lifes, were considered raw by her contemporaries, her originality was noted. In 1877 C.G. Estlander wrote in the *Finsk Tidskrift:* "rarely was a woman artist endowed with such spirit." After painting her celebrated winter landscapes, of which the *Winter Landscape* of c. 1880 from the Sourander collections in the Ateneum is one of the last, she suddenly abandoned painting to found the Association of Friends of Finnish Handicraft, an initiative for which she has become known.[13]

Victor Westerholm
Paris 1889

To the right: 214. **Victor Westerholm** (1860–1919): **Seine outside Paris,** 1888. Oil on canvas, 60.5 x 81.5. Turku Art Museum, 417.

Below: 33. **Fanny Churberg** (1845–1892): **Winter Landscape,** 1880 ca. Oil on canvas, 38 x 56. Ateneum Art Museum, Helsinki, Collection Sourander, A III 2367.

Opposite page: 215. **Victor Westerholm** (1860–1919): **From Paris,** 1889. Oil on cardboard, 41 x 32.5. Turku Art Museum, 355.

Albert Edelfelt. Photograph from
1907. Central Art Archives,
Helsinki.

Aimo Reitala devoted a chapter of his doctoral dissertation on Victor Westerholm
to Impressionism and Finland, and Bertel Hintze naturally discussed the subject
of Edelfelt and Impressionism in his important monograph on Albert Edelfelt.
Westerholm studied for several years in Düsseldorf in the 1870s and '80s, but after a
short visit to Paris in 1882—where he saw, among other things, an exhibition of
Courbet—he decided to return there. The recipient of a grant from the Hoving
fund, he was active there in the years 1888–89. As Torsten Gunnarsson points out in
his essay about Impressionism and the North, Westerholm was one of the few
Finnish painters receptive to Impressionism. Among Westerholm's best known
Impressionist works from the late '80s are *The Seine near Paris* of 1888, and *From
Paris* and *Suresnes*, both from 1889, all shown in the present exhibition.

Edelfelt is the foremost Paris-based Finnish painter of all times. He began his
studies there in 1874, coming into contact with Jules Bastien-Lepage. Edelfelt quickly assimilated *plein-air* painting and Realism. He received his breakthrough with
The Funeral of a Child of 1879 (Ateneum), which also marks the breakthrough of
plein-air painting in Finnish art. Edelfelt's most Parisian work, showing realistically

painted figures in the foreground and an impressionistic background, is undoubtedly *In the Luxembourg Gardens in Paris* of 1887, purchased for the Antell collections in the Ateneum in 1908—at a price ten times higher than that of the Van Gogh in 1903![14] The painting was completed in time for the 1887 exhibition at the Gallery Georges Petit, where it was praised to the skies. In the *Finsk Tidskrift* of 1884 Edelfelt adopted a more positive attitude towards Impressionism than previously when, in the same publication, he had viewed the Impressionists as affected reformers who scorned the art of drawing and, generally, anything pertaining to reason. Still, he had mixed feelings about seeing his own work displayed amidst those of modern masters such as Monet, Renoir, Morisot, and Pissarro—too many Impressionists, as he expressed it himself.[15]

The Pioneering Contribution of Berndt Lindholm

As discussed in greater detail by Gunnarsson, Berndt Lindholm was the only Finnish painter who, already in the early 1870s, aspired to a more immediate representation of reality, with an emphasis on light. Lindholm studied at Düsseldorf in 1863–66 and in 1867 he visited Paris for the first time, proclaiming Daubigny to be the greatest living French landscape painter. Lindholm studied with Léon Bonnat and Louis Cabat in Paris in 1867–70 and 1873–75. In a letter to the *Helsingfors Dagblad* published in the spring of 1870 (quoted by Gunnarsson p. 19), he mentioned, for the very first time in a Scandinavian newspaper, the names of Manet, Pissarro, and Jonkind. Lindholm usually spent his summers in Gothenburg, where he finally moved to become a Curator at the Gothenburg Museum of Fine Arts in 1878–1900. He had earlier been appointed a member of the St. Petersburg Academy of Fine Arts. In the early 1870s Lindholm and Hjalmar Munsterhjelm competed for the title of foremost Finnish landscape painter. Lindholm later became known for his Realist coastal landscapes from the west coast of Sweden. The art collector Antell purchased Lindholm's *Harvest Motif* of 1878 from the west coast which revealed, among other things, Lindholm's admiration for Daubigny.[16]

Helene Schjerfbeck Circa 1890

It may be said that Helene Schjerfbeck, like Anders Zorn, did not paint any open landscapes in the early 1890s. Yet, as Lena Holger has suggested, some of her most beautiful depictions of the Nordic summer night were painted in Finland in the years 1890–92. To these may be added a large-size painting from 1890 showing a young girl in a birch forest in the springtime. *In the Open, Young Girl in a Birch Forest* was painted in Raseborg on the beautiful Nyland coast. The painting reveals something of the new developments in the art of the 1890s, embraced by painters such as Zorn. Schjerfbeck's light-filled painting of the early 1890s has not been particularly appreciated in Finland. For example, H. Ahtela wrote about her visit to Finland in the spring of 1890: "Upon her return to Finland she was greeted by the first pungent scent of spring, by the freshness of the North. But when she tried to capture something of the shimmering beauty, it all turned out empty and uninteresting on the canvas."[17] However, the painting *In the Open, Young Girl in a Birch Forest*, which recently returned to Finland, should be seen side-by-side with works

by other Scandinavian women painters, such as Hanna Pauli's *Breakfast-Time* of 1887 and Elin Danielson-Gambogi's *At the Tea Table* from the same year as Schjerfbeck's spring landscape. The works of Pauli and Danielson-Gambogi have been viewed as representing a synthesis of Manet and the loose brushwork of the Impressionists.[18]

Artists' Initial Responses to Impressionism
In his monograph on Westerholm (1967), Aimo Reitala concluded that the Finnish attitude towards Impressionism was predominantly negative. Onni Okkonen, the author of a Finnish art historical survey which, as late as the 1950s, was obligatory reading for all students, called attention to the fact that Impressionism met with resistance and, in his opinion, never had much of an impact on, for example, Norwegian art. Okkonen also referred to a letter written by the 19-year old Gallén to J.J. Tikkanen in late 1884. Gallén had visited an "Impressionist exhibition" in Paris and reported to Tikkanen that it was (my translation) a "horrid collection of the worst paintings ever created." He could not understand how "people can call such things art […] You cannot imagine how poor these Impressionist paintings were. In my opinion, every painting was a piece of crap." Okkonen also considered Edelfelt's article in the *Finsk Tidskrift* of 1877, in which he called the Impressionists' exhibition "an art madhouse," further proof in support of his view. Edelfelt had, it is true, also seen something positive in the exhibition, and considered a seascape by Monet

to be a real jewel. Later statements made by Edelfelt himself, as well as by Tikkanen and Hintze, show, on the contrary, that Edelfelt admired the Impressionists and, as we have seen, was influenced by them. When Edelfelt wrote his article he was still a history painter dreaming of success at the Salons. In his article about Impressionism and Finland, Reitala concluded that it was not Impressionism that caused the strongest resistance in Paris in the second half of the 1880s, but Neo-Impressionism, which was then beginning to crop up at the Independents' exhibitions. What Gallén had seen and become annoyed at was actually an exhibition of this kind, which did not prevent him from adopting Degas' style in his paintings of Parisian motifs. If Degas is considered an Impressionist, then Gallén was one too, according to Reitala, though he did not represent the style in its purest form.[19]

Tikkanen and Strengell on Impressionism

In a speech held on the occasion of the annual meeting of the Finnish Fine Arts Association in 1892, C.G. Estlander had mused about the new artistic styles that continually succeeded each other. The predominant style of the moment "is Impressionism today [...]—tomorrow it is Symbolism ..." Estlander's prognosis proved perfectly accurate.[20]

In February of 1904, during the ongoing Franco-Belgian art exhibition, J.J. Tikkanen published two lengthy articles in the *Hufvudstadsbladet*, "Impressionism In Its Historic Context" (02/14 1904) and "Modern Impressionism" (02/23 1904). Tikkanen noted that Impressionism had undergone major transformations over a period of forty years, but "the Impressionist school [...] is an opposition party, the extreme left wing of contemporary art." [...] "Thus, Impressionism, in my view, represents the struggle for a painterly expression in the broadest sense, and for the necessary visual means. It represents the capture and visual representation of what is perceived and grasped as a rapid sensation, but cannot be held, the momentary, movement, what is rapidly changing, light, air, colours, as opposed to solid form and the local coulors firmly associated with it." The title of the second article was "Modern Impressionism," but the author was not referring to Neo-Impressionism. For example, he wrote "this time, I do not wish to speak of Neo-Impressionism, not to be confused with the older generation," even though the Neo-Impressionists were predominant in the ongoing exhibition (!), but he elucidated further by stating that he did not wish to write a review of the exhibition. Yet, he could not refrain from pointing out that the original Impressionists were all dead or old, and that "its continuation in Belgian Neo-Impressionism is hardly anything but a sequel." Tikkanen reminded his readers that "Impressionism met with strong resistance, which is difficult to comprehend now that Naturalism has accomplished its historic mission and become a part of contemporary artistic consciousness." He wrote, further, that "the movement has had considerable impact on contemporary art, and now seems to ebb and disappear like a river emptying into the sea." The next day, Gustaf Strengell's article about the "Franco-Belgian" art exhibition was published in the *Helsingfors Posten* (02/24 1904). Strengell worries that the public has failed the exhibition "as if it were an event in any world metropolis." Instead of referring to Tikkanen's lengthy commentary on Impressionism in the *Hufvudstadsbladet*, he urges his read-

ers to acquaint themselves with "the essays of the French art philosopher Léon Deshairs in *Euterpe*—an excellent introduction, allowing the reader to penetrate deeper into the history and theory of Impressionism." Finally, Strengell hit the nail on the head when he wrote that Impressionism "perhaps more than any other artistic movement [...] is suited for making life lighter and happier for each and every person."

Contacts with Russia

In addition to Finnish and other Scandinavian art, the Ateneum also acquired Russian art around the turn of the century, perhaps more so than museums in the other Scandinavian countries. As Finland was a part of Russia, this was perfectly natural. Contacts with St. Petersburg were especially frequent in the late 1890s, when Edelfelt, among others, visited the city, painting two portraits of Czar Nicholas II in 1896. During the Russian period, Finnish painters had, however, not frequented the St. Petersburg Academy of Fine Arts as much as one might have expected. Eero Järnefelt studied there in 1883–85, but went to Paris already the following year. Edelfelt had also been active in St. Petersburg in the 1880s and was offered a Professorship at the Academy in the late '90s, which, however, he declined. Finnish artists came into contact with the period's foremost Russian artists and authors. Thus, for example, Isaac Levitan, one of Järnefelt's acquaintances, participated in the Finnish-Russian exhibition organized by Sergei Diaghilev in St. Petersburg in 1898. The following year, many Finnish artists, including Järnefelt, participated in the international *Mir iskusstva's* exhibition, also organized by Diaghilev. Magnus

Enckell also participated in the *Mir iskusstva's* exhibition, making the Diaghilev's acquaintance. At his initiative another Finnish exhibition was planned for St. Petersburg in 1911. It was to include painters of the Septem group, headed by Enckell. The exhibition never came about, nor did the potential encounter between the Finnish and the Russian avant-garde.[21]

Alfred William Finch

Alfred William Finch. Photograph. Central Art Archives, Helsinki.

The Anglo-Belgian, and later naturalized Finnish, artist Alfred William Finch greatly influenced the contacts with contemporary European art, and was the chief promoter of the Neo-Impressionist exhibition held at the Ateneum in 1904. Finch had belonged to the Belgian avant-garde group Les Vingts and was a close personal acquaintance of, among others, Signac, Van Rysselberghe, and Seurat, with whom he had exhibited his work. Finch arrived in Finland in 1897, and together with the Swedish artist Louis Sparre he directed the Iris pottery in Porvoo (swe: Borgå), inspired by the Arts and Craft movement, from 1897 to 1902. From Porvoo Finch moved on to Helsinki, where he became a teacher of ceramics at the Central School of Applied Arts (housed in the building of the Ateneum) and, simultaneously, acquired an important position in the field of contemporary Finnish printmaking, especially etching. Before his death in 1930 Finch re-emerged, following a ten-year hiatus, as a very productive painter.

A.W. Finch is well represented in the present exhibition. In Helsinki, his paintings were exhibited for the first time at the International Impressionist Exhibition held at the Ateneum in 1904, which largely came about due to his efforts, and in a

Above: 204. **Verner Thomé** (1878–1953): **Boys Bathing,** 1910. Oil on canvas, 108.5 x 130. Ateneum Art Museum, Helsinki, Collection Hoving, A II 903.

Opposite page, above: 49. **Alfred William Finch** (1854–1930): **The English Coast at Dover, Cliffs at Southforeland,** 1892. Oil on canvas, 66.5 x 80.5. Ateneum Art Museum, Helsinki, Collection Ahlström, A II 1700.

Opposite page, below: 50. **Alfred William Finch** (1854–1930): **Steamer by the Coast,** 1892. Oil on canvas, 63 x 80. Amos Anderson Art Museum, Helsinki, Collection Sigurd Frosterus, 34/SF.

45. **Magnus Enckell** (1870–1925): **A Theater in Paris**, 1912. Oil on canvas, 100.5 x 66.5. Ateneum Art Museum, Helsinki, A IV 3763.

Magnus Enckell. Photograph from 1905. Central Art Archives, Helsinki.

first solo exhibition in 1906, where his painting revealed a more orthodox Impressionist approach.[22] One of the six works exhibited in 1904 was the above mentioned *Racetrack Wellington (Ostende)* of 1888, acquired by the Ateneum in 1935, which is one of Finch's earliest Neo-Impressionist works. Among the remaining works in the present exhibition may be mentioned *The Coast of Britain at Dover* of 1892. Perhaps Finch's best known work, similarly acquired with funds from the Ahlström bequest in 1928, it was also his last before passing on to the art industry and ceramics and moving to Finland. His *Steamship near the Coast*, one of the principal works in Frosterus' collection, dates from the same period. The steamship outside of Dover is the mail boat travelling between Dover and Ostende, and the painting has a border similar to that of Seurat's canvases from around 1889–90. In 1908 the Antell delegation purchased Finch's *Dull Weather at Hampton Court* of 1907 for the collections of the Ateneum.

Magnus Enckell and the Septem Group

Magnus Enckell is represented in the present exhibition with *Parisian Variety Theatre* painted in 1912, the year of the Septem group's first exhibition. Profiting from his acquaintance with Sergei Diaghilev, Enckell was able to attend performances of the Russian ballet in Paris between 1901 and 1912. Next to his *Parisian Variety Theatre*, the *Bal Tabarin* (in the Hedman collections in the Museum of Pohjanmaa, swe: Österbotten, in Vaasa), painted in the same year, reveals his talent for Impressionism and his ability to capture the special atmosphere of the theatre.[23] Enckell had early on made the acquaintance of Finch's Belgian and French artist friends and been encouraged to try out Pointillism. For seven successive summers, beginning in 1903, he painted together with Verner Thomé at Suursaari (swe: Hogland) in the Gulf of Finland, their light-filled painting culminating, in the summer of 1910, in Enckell's *Young Boys at the Beach* (Frosterus' collection) and Thomé's *Boys Bathing* (the Ateneum). Timo Huusko suggests that Thomé's (and Enckell's) love of Hogland and of the happily sunbathing boys may be connected with Old Norse sun cult, Nietzschean Vitalism, and the physical culture of the German Ernst Haeckel.[24] Up until World War II Suursaari was something of a Skagen for Finnish painters, though with stonier beaches.

Acquisitions of Paintings by Van Gogh and Cézanne

For a long time the Finnish national gallery's collections of foreign art had grown through donations, but gifts of contemporary art could not be counted on. In spite of the politically turbulent years around the turn of the century, the arts and culture flourished. Finland was put on the map, and the expanded art museum in the Ateneum offered space for exhibitions and collections on an international level. The earliest and boldest new acquisition of contemporary art in Finland at the turn of the century (1903) was Vincent Van Gogh's *Street, Auvers-sur-Oise* of 1890, one of the artist's last works. The painting had once belonged to Johanna Van Gogh-Bonger and was subsequently purchased by the French art critic Julien Leclercq, married to the Finnish pianist Fanny Flodin. As a widow Mrs. Leclercq offered to sell the painting to the Ateneum and, not unexpectedly, news of the purchase were

100. **Vincent Van Gogh** (1853–1890): **Street in Auvers-sur-Oise,** 1890. Oil on canvas, 73.5 x 92.5. Ateneum Art Museum, Helsinki, Collection Antell, A I 755.

received with mixed emotions. Members of the Antell delegation disagreed about the purchase and its Chairman, C.G. Estlander, felt the painting "was not suitable for purchase." However, Albert Edelfelt who was then cautious about acquisitions, purchasing many works by, now forgotten, French artists around the turn of the century, was among those in favour of purchasing the painting, which cost only 2 500 mark (about 60 000–70 000 kronor in today's currency). Van Gogh's painting had been exhibited at "The Free Exhibition" in Copenhagen in 1893.[25] The same year Edelfelt was, as the first artist ever, appointed President of the Finnish Fine Arts Association. Van Gogh and Gauguin were not unknown to Finnish artists. Pekka Halonen and Väinö Blomstedt had, for example, both studied with Gauguin in 1893–94.

The Anglo-Finnish art historian Tancred Borenius, since 1909 a permanent resident of London, was consulted on the occasion of important acquisitions for the Ateneum. Among the earliest were Paul Cézanne's *Viaduct at L'Estaque (La maison jaune)* of c. 1883, and Maurice Denis' *Odysseus Visits Calypso (Ulysse chez Calypso)* of 1905, purchased in connection with the 1910 exhibition of Manet and the Post-Impressionists in London. The organizer of the exhibition, the English art histori-

21. **Paul Cézanne** (1839–1906): **The Viaduct at l'Estaque**, 1883 ca. Oil on canvas, 56 x 65.5. Ateneum Art Museum, Helsinki, Collection Antell, A II 906.

an, painter, and art critic Roger Fry, was a close personal acquaintance of Borenius'. Fry's contribution was also decisive when it came to introducing contemporary French art in England. Fry and Borenius encouraged Finnish art collectors to invest in works by artists such as Cézanne and Denis. The Antell delegation surely appreciated the fact that Borenius also managed to have the price of the two paintings reduced by 100 pounds. The board of the delegation was probably aware that Roger Fry's parents had a longstanding association with Finland, which is thought to have promoted the purchase. The total price of the paintings was 800 pounds, or about 20 000 Finnish marks.[26]

Sigurd Frosterus
Sigurd Frosterus was not one to judge the exhibitions at the Ateneum in 1901 and 1904. He received a degree as an architect in 1902, and belonged to the radical Euterpe circle at the Nyland student's corporation, writings about foreign art for its paper of the same title. Together with Gustaf Strengell (1878–1937) the 28-year-old

Frosterus entered an architectural contest for the design of a new railroad station (the existing station had been designed by Albert Edelfelt's father) in Helsinki, and later also for the one in Viipuri. Frosterus and Strengell, who ran their own architectural firm between 1904 and 1906, lost both contests to the architectural group of Saarinen–Gesellius–Lindgren, which had designed the Finnish pavilion in Paris, among other things, and had become very well-known. They proceeded to write the pamphlet *Architecture*, in opposition to their competitors and the National Romantic architecture they espoused. The Stockmann department store, inaugurated in 1930, became Frosterus' best-known architectural work.

A.W. Finch also belonged to Euterpe, contributing an article about Georges Seurat and the Neo-Impressionist technique in 1902. By that time, Frosterus and Finch had become acquainted with each other. The encounter with Finch had a decisive influence on Frosterus, who had artistic ambitions of his own, painting a large number of Impressionist watercolours between 1902 and 1907. Frosterus would later create the theoretic foundations of contemporary Finnish art, and

Above: 197. **Paul Signac** (1863–1935): **Seine, Grenelle,** 1899. Oil on canvas, 62 x 78.5. Amos Anderson Art Museum, Helsinki, Collection Sigurd Frosterus, 56/SF.

Opposite page: 191. **Théo van Rysselberghe** (1862–1926): **Marine,** 1887. Oil on canvas, 66 x 54.5. Amos Anderson Art Museum, Helsinki, Collection Sigurd Frosterus, 51/SF.

become one of the foremost connoisseurs of French and Belgian Impressionism and Pointillism.

In the autumn of 1903 Frosterus went, highly recommended by Finch, to Henry Van de Velde's architectural firm in Weimar, where the latter had moved from Belgium the previous year. Frosterus was influenced by Van de Velde's style of architecture and interior decoration. Soon, he was also able to view Van de Velde's art collection, "glorious landscapes by Seurat, Signac, Rysselberghe, Van Gogh, Cross and Luce," and a Neo-Impressionist exhibition in Weimar, where he was especially impressed by Van Rysselberghe. After his return home in 1904 Frosterus was kept busy with architectural contests. Meanwhile, his interest in contemporary art matured, not least the art he had viewed at Van de Velde's and experienced through Finch. In a very short period, between 1905 and 1915, the barely 40-year-old Frosterus assembled a collection of domestic and foreign art then regarded as the most distinguished private collection of contemporary art in Finland—still preserved nearly intact at the Amos Anderson Art Museum in Helsinki. Nearly all Neo-Impressionists whose works Frosterus helped to acquire for the Ateneum were

already represented in his private art collection before 1915 (when it was first shown to the general public), and he continuously purchased works by Finch and Enckell of a quality acquired by the Ateneum only much later.

Frosterus was also increasingly in demand as a lecturer, giving two lectures at the Finnish Fine Arts Association in 1908. His lecture on colour theory was published in the *Finsk Tidskrift* and later also in the above mentioned collections of essays. The same year—1908—Frosterus wrote in the *Nya Pressen* that Finnish art was being threatened by narrow-mindedness. The main reason being that an exhibition of Finnish art held in connection with the 1908 Autumn Salon in Paris had, for the most part, been poorly received and judged as being fairly traditional next to contemporary French art. Eero Järnefelt who, together with Magnus Enckell, was responsible for the project, responded to Frosterus' criticism with a series of articles published in the daily newspapers in both Finnish and Swedish. Järnefelt's criticism was directed against such things as the Pointillist technique. In her recent book about Järnefelt, Leena Lindqvist maintains that the Finnish exhibition in Paris did not actually receive such bad reviews, and that Järnefelt was accused of conservatism without any cause. Indeed, Järnefelt was one of the organizers of the Neo-Impressionist exhibition at the Ateneum in 1904, had voted in favour of purchasing Munch's *Male Bathers* in 1911 and, with his close friend Frosterus, been consulted on the Antell delegation's purchases of French art for the Ateneum in the late 1910s.[27]

When Frosterus was called on as an expert in connection with acquisitions of contemporary foreign art for the Ateneum after 1908, he noted that works by the Impressionists had already become much too expensive and suggested that one concentrate on the younger generation: Signac, Van Rysselberghe, Cross, Bonnard, Valtat, and Maurice Denis.[28] As early as 1907 he had purchased Signac's *The Seine at Grenelle* of 1899 for his own collection, and Van Rysselberghe's *Seascape* of 1887 had been his first acquisition of foreign art. They are among the principal works in the Frosterus collection. Already in 1909 he acted as an intermediary when a Pointillist painting, Henri-Edmond Cross' *Nude*, was purchased for the Ateneum from the Parisian art dealership of Bernheim, Jeune & Fils. Cross was closely associated with the circle of Seurat and Signac and was one of the founders of the Société des Artistes Indépendants in 1884.[29] The purchase was made during the ongoing Munch exhibition at the Ateneum. Here, too, the Antell delegation made a bold purchase of the *Portrait of Gustaf Schiefler*, supported by a narrow majority of the board. Wentzel Hagelstam's attempt to act as an intermediary in supplying works by Pissarro, Degas, and Durand from Paris was averted due to the high prices. Frosterus was not involved in these transactions—nor in the purchase of works by Munch—and Expressionism never really interested him.

In 1911 Frosterus was appointed to the board of the Finnish Fine Arts Association, which was still very much involved with the Ateneum, and his collaboration with the museum was greatly facilitated by the appointment of his old friend Gustaf Strengell as Curator between 1914–18. In a chapter—titled "The Autonomy of Art"—of his doctoral dissertation on Sigurd Frosterus' modern concepts of architecture and painting and his ideology, as revealed by his numerous publications,

208. **Louis Valtat** (1869–1952): **Marine, Cap Nègre**, 1902. Oil on canvas, 81 x 81.
Amos Anderson Art Museum, Helsinki, Collection Sigurd Frosterus, 60/SF.

203. **Ellen Thesleff** (1869–1954): **Figures in a Landscape.** Oil on canvas, 113 x 113. NORDEA Art Collection in Finland.

Opposite page: 19. **Alvar Cawén** (1867–1949): **St Germain**, 1911. Oil on canvas, 81.5 x 62. Private collection.

Kimmo Sarje has discussed Frosterus' principal theories of contemporary art and, not least, the Neo-Impressionism he so eagerly embraced.[30]

The Expansion of the Collection of International Art
The Nabis and Pierre Bonnard had also become well known, not least to the Finnish artists of the Septem group. A work by Bonnard—probably lent by the Galerie Druet—was shown in the Septem group's second exhibition in 1913. Ker-Xavier Roussel and Charles Guerin had also been invited to participate in the exhibition. Thus, it comes as no surprise that, in 1911, the chief theorist of the Septem group, Sigurd Frosterus, armed with funds made available by the Hoving bequest, went to his main Parisian supplier Bernheim, Jeune & Fils, where Bonnard usually exhibited his work. Here he purchased the artist's *Landscape in the Rain (Paysage pluvieux)* of 1909. It was at this time that the quantitatively largest number of more recent French and Belgian artworks were acquired by the Ateneum. Lucie Cousturier's *Flowers and Fruit (Fleurs et fruits de Provence)* was one of sixteen paintings and four drawings the Antell delegation authorized Frosterus to purchase abroad in 1916. The reason for this generous investment was apparently fear of the inevitable inflation that would follow in the wake of World War I.

In December of 1916 Frosterus wrote to his friends Signac and Van Rysselberghe, urging them to sell their own works and those of others artists. The result was an extensive collection of paintings and drawings by twelve artists: Signac, Van Rysselberghe, Charles Augrand, Lucie Cousturier, Charles Guérin, Maximilien Luce, Henri Charles Manguin, René Piot, Ker-Xavier Roussel, Jeanne Selmersheim-Desgrange, Paul Sérusier, and Louis Valtat. By Signac Frosterus bought the painting *Antibes*, having already acquired the artist's *The Seine at Grenelle* of 1899 for his own private collection more than ten years earlier. With Signac's help Frosterus was able to acquire Maximilien Luce's *Seine, quai de Boulogne* of 1905 and Louis Valtat's *In the Sun (Figures au soleil)*. While Luce had participated regularly in the Neo-Impressionist exhibitions since 1887, Valtat's style heralded Fauvism long before its breakthrough around 1905. With the aid of Van Rysselberghe, Frosterus acquired two works by Charles Guérin from the Galerie Druet: *Head of a Woman (Tête de femme)*, shown at the Septem group's exhibition in 1913, and *Summer Stroll (Promenade d'été)*. Ker-Xavier Roussel's *Landscape* and Paul Sérusier's *In the Light of the Oil Lamp (Sous le lampe)* were purchased from the same gallery.[31] Having been purchased during the war, the artworks only arrived in Finland in 1921. The year before, Finch had been authorized by the Antell delegation to purchase Belgian art, choosing the *Nude Study* by Georges Lemmens, a member of Les Vingts.[32]

The Period 1905–14
Much had happened in Finland since the general strike of 1905 and the dissolution of the February Manifesto. In 1907 the world's first parliamentary elections with universal and equal right to vote were held here. Art no longer had to serve a political purpose, a feeling of general optimism prevailed, and the economy thrived. In his history of the Ateneum, Aune Lindström discusses the dynamic period 1905–14, when the Museum held its most spectacular exhibitions so far. Edelfelt had died in

1905, and C.G. Estlander left his post as Chairman of the Antell delegation the same year. Among other things, Lindström lists the new far-sighted "aesthetes and artists" who contributed to the positive development. In addition to Magnus Enckell, Sigurd Frosterus, and Gustaf Strengell, Lindström also mentions Yrjö Hirn, Torsten Stjernschantz, and Hugo Simberg. As a member of the Antell delegation from 1908 to 1913, Hirn supported the acquisitions of contemporary foreign art. The painter and printmaker Hugo Simberg was appointed to the Finnish Fine Arts Association's purchasing committee in 1907, and that year he exhibited his work together with Enckell at the The House of Nobility in Helsinki. The exhibition was a great success and represented a breakthrough for a new style of painting in the spirit of a "pure palette." In the same period a new generation of Finnish Modernists emerged. One of them was Ellen Thesleff who, next to Helene Schjerfbeck, appears as Finland's foremost woman artist. Like Magnus Enckell, she, too, underwent a sudden metamorphosis in the early 1900s. Traveling to Italy in 1904, Thesleff stayed on in Munich for an extended period of time. Here she came into contact with Modernism and with the Swede Carl Palme, founder of the Phalanx school and conveyor of Kandinsky's teachings. In 1906 Kandinsky quietly contributed twelve works to the Finnish Fine Arts Association's spring exhibition.[33] In the same year, Thesleff painted *Young Girls in the Fields*, regarded as one of the earliest Finnish Expressionist works, and in 1908 the Ateneum purchased her *Tuscan Landscape* of 1906, one of her best known works.[34] New Modernists such as Tyko Sallinen also emerged around 1906. Together with Jalmari Ruokokoski, who was strongly influenced by Munch, Juho Mäkelä and others, he founded the Finnish November-group, which held its first exhibition in 1916. Alvar Cawén who brought Cubism to Finland in 1913–14 and others soon joined the group. Another important event was Gallen-Kallela's participation in the first print exhibition of Die Brücke at Dresden in 1906–07. He was listed as a member in 1909.

The Munch Exhibition of 1909; Felix Nylund's Contacts
The joint exhibition of Gallen-Kallela and Edvard Munch in Berlin in 1895 was an internationally significant event in Nordic art. As a patient at Professor Daniel Jacobsen's nerve clinic in Copenhagen in 1908, Edvard Munch might have come into contact with the Finnish sculptor Felix Nylund, whose Danish wife, Fernanda Jacobsen, was a relative of Professor Jacobsen. Nylund, who had studied at the Copenhagen Academy of Fine Arts in 1899–1901 and was subsequently active in Paris 1901–06, strove to modernize Finnish sculpture. This was easier said than done, since all commissions first went to Emil Wikström and Ville Vallgren. However, Nylund initiated the Munch exhibition in Helsinki in 1909 and surely supported enthusiastically the decision of the Antell delegation to purchase Munch's *Portrait of Gustav Schiefler* of 1908. In a letter from Copenhagen, published in the *Hufvudstadsbladet* (12/16 1908), Nylund described the ongoing Munch exhibition at the Fine Arts Association which would travel to Helsinki in January of 1909. The exhibition "will be an extraordinary event in our artistic life," he wrote, and Helsinki "should congratulate itself on being able to receive such a guest." Nylund was, in the early years of the 20th century, one of the most well-oriented Finnish artists when it

comes to contemporary Scandinavian and French art, both painting and sculpture, keeping the museums back home well informed. While in Copenhagen Nylund had learned nearly all there was to know about Danish art. After his marriage to Fernanda Jacobsen, his circle of Danish and other Scandinavian acquaintances included, among others, J.F. Willumsen—Fernanda Jacobsen had posed for his sculpture *Buxepigen*—the art historian and critic Emil Hannover, and the Norwegian painter Christian Krohg. Nylund was a close friend of Karl Isakson, probably initiating the Antell delegation's purchase of Isakson's *Self-Portrait* in connection with the artist's retrospective at Copenhagen in 1922. Nylund also admired Ernst Josephson, and among the sculptors he was clearly influenced by Carl Milles in Paris, and was a close friend of the Danish sculptor Gerhard Henning. Among the French sculptors Nylund was interested in everyone from Rodin to Meunier, and his interest soon shifted to the modern sculptors Maillol and Bourdelle. Among the painters he took an early interest in Puvis de Chavannes and Gauguin, whose retrospective he had recently viewed in Paris, and he may have been among those who supported the purchase of works by Gauguin for the Ateneum. Nylund had personal contacts within the leading circles associated with the museum. Yrjö Hirn and Hugo Simberg were acquaintances of the Nylund family in Paris, and in Florence he had met Torsten Stjernschantz and Finch in 1908. He also made the acquaintance of Gustaf Strengell, Jac. Ahrenberg, and Wentzel Hagelstam—publisher of the journal *Ateneum* in Paris—and they all praised him. After his return to Finland in 1910 Nylund rented space in one of Sigurd Frosterus' most recent buildings at Töölönkatu 7 in Helsinki, where he established his studio in one of the future shops. Felix Nylund was, without a doubt, the young Finnish sculptor who appealed most to Frosterus, his sculptures being without the usual flourishes and National Romantic attributes. In 1910 Frosterus also designed the base of a fountain planned by Nylund. In the same year, Nylund founded the Finnish Sculptors' Association, further evidence of his tremendous energy and will to improve the conditions of artists, not least, of sculptors.[35]

The Norwegian Exhibition of 1911 and the Acquisition
of Munch's 'Male Bathers'
The Munch exhibition of 1909 soon left its mark on Finnish art, and Wilho Sjöström and others who had seen the exhibition quickly adopted Expressionism. The Antell delegation's decision to purchase Munch's seminal Expressionist work *Male Bathers* at a major exhibition of Norwegian art at the Ateneum in 1911—which included fifteen works by Munch—caused an even greater stir than Munch's solo exhibition and the purchase of his *Portrait of Gustav Schiefler*. Munch's *Male Bathers*, painted at Warnemünde in 1907–08, was intended as the central piece of a triptych illustrating the ages of man. The purchase, for 10 000 Finnish marks, supported by a marginal majority of 3–2, gave rise to vehement polemics. The Antell delegation, and particularly the board members Hirn, Lindgren, and Järnefelt who had voted in favour of the purchase, received threats, and there was an uproar in the press. It was felt that the painting might set a bad example for young Finnish artists.[36] The Norwegian exhibition also included works by, among others, the Matisse pupils Jean Heiberg,

Henrik Sörensen, and Per Deberitz, whose work represented something not previously seen in Finland. Finland, of course, did not have any Matisse pupils, but Enckell knew both him and Maurice Denis, whose students included the Finnish painters Juho Rissanen, Yrjö Ollila, and later also Werner Åström.

In connection with the 1911 exhibition Jens Thiis held two lectures in the ceremonial hall of the University on, among other things, the theme *From Impressionism to Cubism.* The Nordic collaboration functioned very smoothly in other areas as well. Indeed, it was thanks to Thiis that Paul Gauguin's *Landscape from Tahiti. Mahana Maá,* from the private collection of H. Nobel Roede in Oslo, ended up in the collections of the Ateneum in 1911. This time Hoving funds were made available for the acquisition.[37]

Artistic Life and Art Galleries in Helsinki before World War I
Art galleries already existed in Helsinki in the years before World War I. The art dealership of Sven Strindberg Inc., founded as early as 1898, also opened an art gallery in March of 1913. Here one of the most avant-garde exhibitions ever shown in Finland was held already the following year. Strindberg managed to get his hands on a Blaue Reiter exhibition from Berlin, including some of Wassily Kandinsky's earliest abstract paintings. When the art dealer Sven Strindberg offered to sell a work by Kandinsky to the Antell delegation in December of 1916, the offer was turned down. Probably, the work in question was an abstract painting.[38] Gösta Stenman, whose art gallery opened officially in 1914, had a long and distinguished career as a gallery owner in Helsinki and Stockholm. Stenman was regarded as a controversial figure for having, early on, taken care of the younger generation of artists, headed by Tyko Sallinen, Juho Mäkelä, and Jalmari Ruokokoski, among others, organizing an exhibition of their work in 1914.[39] In 1913, before the official opening of his art gallery, Stenman organized an exhibition of contemporary Swedish art in Helsinki, and two of the works by Carl Wilhelmson included in the exhibition—*The Pear* of 1910 and *A Study of Spring* of 1907—were acquired for the Ateneum. Wilhelmson's paintings were closely associated with Neo-Impressionism, and they apparently appealed to those responsible for the purchase.[40] A real hit was the exhibition of 159 works by Helene Schjerfbeck organized by Stenman in the autumn of 1917, a few months before Finland was proclaimed a republic. Similarly, the retrospective organized by Stenman in 1919 of Fanny Churberg, an artist by then largely forgotten, caused a great sensation. After his transfer to Stockholm in the late 1920s, Stenman became known for, among other things, organizing exhibitions of Schjerfbeck in Sweden and for arousing a greater interest in Ernst Josephson's work. Indeed, at the outset Stenman was not a stranger to contemporary foreign art. And the Antell delegation was able to acquire the painting *Terrace in Toulon (Toulon, le terrasse)* of 1918 by Émile Othon Friesz, Impressionist pupil and later admirer of Matisse, in connection with a 1918 exhibition of French art held at Stenman's "palace of art." A few years later, Stenman donated a charcoal drawing by Edgar Degas *The Jockey (La promenade de chevaux)* of c. 1890–92 to the Ateneum. Through an exhibition held at the Galerie Artek in Helsinki thirty years later, the drawing was joined by Degas' sculpture *Woman Taken by Surprise (Femme surprise)* from the late 1890s or early 1900s.[41]

Notes

Impressionism and the North
Torsten Gunnarsson

[1] "Exposition du boulevard des Capucines: Les Impressionistes" in *Le Siècle* 4/29 1874. Reprinted in *The New Painting. Impressionism 1874–1886. Documentation vol. I Reviews*, edited by Ruth Berson (San Francisco 1996), p. 17.
[2] "Från Café de l'Ermitage till Marly-le-Roi," in *Dagens Nyheter* 11/30 and 12/9 1876. Cited after *Samlade skrifter IV, 1912–1920*, pp. 148–49.
[3] Kermit Swiler Champa, *Studies in Early Impressionism* (New Haven & London 1973), pp. 62–63.
[4] Monet's two paintings are in The National Gallery of London and The Metropolitan Museum of Art in New York. Those by Renoir are in the Pushkin Museum, Moscow, the Oscar Reinhart Stiftung, Winterthur, and The Nationalmuseum, Stockholm.
[5] For a discussion of the pictures from La Grenouillère, see the literature cited in Eliza E. Rathbone, "Renoir's Luncheon of the Boating Party. Tradition and the New," in *Impressionists on the Seine. A Celebration of Renoir's Luncheon of the Boating Party* (exh.cat., The Phillips Collection, Washington, 1996–97), pp. 18–24.
[6] This phenomenon was discussed in 1892 by Richard Bergh in his essay "Intensitet och harmoni," reprinted in *Om konst och annat* (2nd ed., Stockholm 1919), pp. 72–75.
[7] Letter published in *Helsingfors Dagblad* on February 18th, 1870.
[8] A selection from *Impressionisten* is reprinted in Anne Siri Bryhni, *Bohem mot Borger* (Oslo 1971). On Krohg's and the other radical painters' relationship to Impressionism, see Magne Malmanger's article "Impressionismen og Impressionisten. Christian Krohg og det moderne gjenembrudd i 1880-årene," in *Christian Krohg* (exh.cat., Nasjonalgalleriet, Oslo 1987), pp. 31–48. See also Nils Messel's article in the present volume.
[9] Richard Bergh, "Karl Nordström och det nordiska stämningslandskapet," 1896, in *Om konst och annat* (2nd ed., Stockholm 1919), p. 123.
[10] Richard Bergh, "Karl Nordström och det nordiska stämningslandskapet," in *Om konst och annat* (2nd ed., Stockholm 1919), p. 131.
[11] Richard Bergh, "Om överdrifternas nödvändighet i konsten" (1886), reprinted in *Om konst och annat* (2nd ed., Stockholm 1919), p. 8.
[12] Richard Bergh, "Karl Nordström och det nordiska stämningslandskapet," in *Om konst och annat* (2nd ed., Stockholm 1919), p. 126.
[13] On this discussion, see Torsten Gunnarsson, *Nordic Landscape Painting in the Nineteenth Century* (New Haven & London, 1998), p. 247, esp. n. 49.
[14] Simon Koch, "Ludvig Find," in *Taarnet* (Oct. 1893), facsimile ed. with an Afterword by F.J. Billeskov-Jansen (Copenhagen 1981), p. 23.
[15] *Taarnet* (Dec. 1893), p. 54.
[16] Julius Lange, "Studiet i Marken. Skilderiet. Erindringens Kunst," in *Bastien Lepage og andre afhandlinger* (Copenhagen 1889).
[17] On the exhibition and its contents, see *Gauguin og van Gogh i København i 1893* (exh.cat., Ordrupgaard, Copenhagen 1983)
[18] Here cited after Nils Gösta Sandblads introduction to Rohde's *Journal fra en Rejse i 1892*, ed. by H.P. Rohde (Copenhagen 1955), p. 42.
[19] Salme Sarajas-Korte, *Vid symbolismens källor. Den tidiga symbolismen i Finland 1890–1895* (Jakobstad 1981), p. 8.
[20] Sarajas-Korte 1981, p. 101.

The Swedish Reception of Late Nineteenth-Century French Avant-Garde Art
Per Hedström

[1] Fredrik Wilhelm Scholander, "Blick på Europas konst 1875," *Ny Illustrerad Tidning* (1876) 112.
[2] Hollis Clayson, "A Failed Attempt," in *The New Painting: Impressionism 1874–1886* (exh.cat., The Fine Arts Museum of San Francisco; The National Gallery of Art, Washington), 1986, p. 145.
[3] Gottfrid Renholm, "Salonen och den franska konsten," *Post- och Inrikes Tidningar* (15 June, 1876).
[4] Geskel Saloman, "Den Mannetska målarskolan," *Ny Illustrerad Tidning* (16 December, 1876).
[5] Degas executed at least four versions of this motif, and it is unclear which one of these was shown in the 1876 exhibition as entry no. 41, *Blanchisseuses*. It is, however, most likely that the exhibited painting was identical with Lemoisne 687.
[6] Göran Söderström, *Strindberg och bildkonsten* (Stockholm 1972), 91–92.
[7] Viggo Loos, *Friluftsmåleriets genombrott i svensk konst 1860–1885* (Stockholm 1945), 235–36.
[8] Among the monographs are works about, for example, Hugo Birger (1947), Carl Fredrik Hill (1951), Victor Forsell (1951), Nils Kreuger (1948), Per Ekström (1947), and Ernst Josephson (1956).
[9] Loos 1945, p. 242.
[10] Ibid., p. 312.
[11] Ibid., p. 82.
[12] Viggo Loos, *Carl Skånberg* (Linköping 1928), 67–68.
[13] Henri Usselmann, *Complexité et importance des contacts des peintres nordiques avec l'impressionisme* (Gothenburg 1979), pp. 94–95.
[14] Adolf Anderberg, *Carl Hill. Hans liv och hans konst* (Malmö 1951).
[15] Loos 1945, pp. 235–36.
[16] Anderberg 1951, p. 212.
[17] Adolf Anderberg associates the change with Impressionism. See Anderberg 1951, p. 211.
[18] Ibid., pp. 148–49.
[19] Loos 1945, p. 220; Anderberg 1951, p. 220; Usselmann 1979, pp. 85–86; Nilsson 1999, pp. 29–34; Gunnarsson 1999, p. 114.
[20] Anderberg 1951, p. 164.
[21] Ibid., p. 214; Gunnarsson 1999, p. 114.
[22] Richard Bergh, "Karl Nordström och det moderna stämningslandskapet," in *Om konst och annat* (Stockholm 1919), pp. 121–22.
[23] Karl Nordström, *Förteckning över tavlor målade av mig 1881–juni 1890*, The Royal Library, Stockholm, Dept. of Mss., L 100:26.
[24] Carl Rupert Nyblom in *Post- och Inrikes Tidningar* (2 May 1885).
[25] Aaron Scharf, *Art and Photography* (London 1968), pp. 158–60.
[26] Gottfrid Renholm wrote that Josephson was really the only Scandinavian painter who "openly confesses that he belongs to Manet's school." He also wrote that Josephson "resembles Manet in his conception of Nature and in his artistic temperament." See Gottfrid Renholm, "Salonen in Paris," *Göteborgs-Posten* (19 May 1883).
[27] Georg Nordensvan, "Impressionism," *Ny Illustrerad Tidning* (19 May 1883).
[28] On Zorn and photography, see: Hans Henrik Brummer, *Anders Zorn. Till ögats fröjd och nationens förgyllning* (Stockholm 1994), pp. 158–59.
[29] Brummer 1994, pp. 156–57.
[30] Ibid., p. 127.
[31] Ibid., pp. 122–24.
[32] Margareta Gynning, *Det ambivalenta perspektivet. Eva Bonnier och Hanna Hirsch-Pauli i 1880-talets konstliv* (Stockholm 1999), p. 45.
[33] Quoted after Maria Görts, *Det sköna i verklighetens värld. Akademisk konstsyn i Sverige under senare delen av 1800-talet* (Stockholm 1999), p. 181. See also Gynning 1999, p. 153.
[34] See Norma Broude, *World Impressionism. The International Movement, 1860–1920* (New York 1990).
[35] Both theories are discussed in Lars Wängdahl, *En natur för män att grubbla i* (Gothenburg 2000), pp. 172–77.
[36] Richard Bergh, "Karl Nordström och det moderna stämningslandskapet," in *Om konst och annat* (Stockholm 1908), p. 121.
[37] Björn Fredlund, "Den inre röstens maning. Richard Bergh om Karl Nordström och stämningslandskapet," i *Det skapande jaget. Konsthistoriska texter tillägnade Maj-Britt Wadell* (Gothenburg 1994), p. 60.
[38] On the relationship between Gauguin's exoticism and the "primitivism" of the Varberg painters, see Nasgaard, *The Mystic North: Symbolist Landscape Painting in Northern Europe and North America, 1890–1940* (Toronto 1984), p. 24.
[39] On this circle, see Thomas Millroth, *Molards salong* (Stockholm 1993).
[40] Quoted after *August Strindberg. "Underlandet"* (exh.cat., Malmö Konsthall 1989–90), p. 57.
[41] The information about Osslund's period as Gauguin's pupil come from Nils-Göran Hökby's still unpublished manuscript for a monograph about Helmer Osslund.
[42] Gösta Lilja, Det moderna måleri-

et i svensk kritik 1905–1914, Malmö 1955, p. 71.

43 Kjell Boström, *Nils Kreuger* (Stockholm 1948), pp. 113–31.

44 The possible significance of these photographs has been discussed in several contexts, most extensively by Håkan Larsson, *Flames from the South. On the Introduction of Vincent Van Gogh to Sweden* (Lund 1996), pp. 30–37.

45 Letter from Prince Eugen to Helena Nyblom on November 19th, 1892 (Archives of Prince Eugen's Waldemarsudde, Stockholm), quoted after Hans Henrik Brummer, *Prins Eugen. Minnet av ett landskap* (Stockholm 1998), p. 97.

46 Brummer 1998, p. 97.

47 Georg Pauli, "Bref om konst. Intryck och reflexioner," *Ord och Bild* (1892): 279.

48 This explanation was commented on by Brummer 1998, p. 79.

49 Sixten Strömbom, *Nationalromantik och radikalism. Konstnärsförbundets historia 1891–1920* (Stockholm 1965), p. 116.

50 Several scholars have earlier tried to identify the exhibited works by Van Gogh, and three of these identifications may be regarded as sure: *The Garden* (now The Art Institute of Chicago, F 468); *Park in Arles* (private collection, F 517); and *Portrait of a Man* (Kröller-Müller Museum, Otterlo). The other two paintings are more difficult to identify with certainty. The *Boulevard St. Rémy, Arles* must, however, be identical with either a painting in The Cleveland Museum of Art (F 657), or a version of the same motif in The Phillips Collection in Washington (F 658). The painting called *River Bank* in the exhibition catalogue is probably identical with one of the two paintings of similar motifs from 1887, now in the Van Gogh Museum in Amsterdam (F 293 or F 299). On these identifications, see Larsson 1996, pp. 115–19; and Carl Nordenfalk, "Van Gogh and Sweden," *Konsthistorisk Tidskrift* (1946): 92–93. The two landscapes from Martinique and Brittany were described so vaguely in the reviews that it is hardly meaningful to attempt and identification. The paintings from Tahiti, on the other hand, received extensive commentary in the press. The painting referred to as *Apparition* (Tahiti 1892) is without a doubt identical with *Manao Tupapau* (W 457), now in the Albright Knox Art Gallery, Buffalo. The painting referred to as *Landscape* (Tahiti 1892) can be identified with the aid of a review signed by the pseudonym Z, Georg Scheutz, published in *Göteborgs-Posten* (March 23rd, 1898). According to Scheutz, a visitor to the exhibition had made fun of the painting's inscription, "Pastorales tahitiennes." The viewer wished, according to Scheutz, to change "tahitiennes" to read "take away again." This painting—*Pastorales tahitiennes* (W 470)—is today owned by the Hermitage in St. Petersburg. The third painting from Tahiti in the exhibition was *The Black Madonna (Te tamai no atua,* W 541, now in the Bayerische Staatsgemäldesammlungen, Neue Pinakothek, Munich).

51 H.A.R. [Herman Anakreon Ring], "Den franska utställningen," *Nya Dagligt Allehanda* (February 22nd, 1898).

52 John Kruse, "Den franska konstutställningen i Konstföreningen", *Nordisk Revy* 1898, pp. 192–198.

53 Görel Cavalli-Björkman has discussed the collectors and collections of impressionist painting in Scandinavia and Finland. Görel Cavalli-Björkman, "The Reception History of Impressionism in Scandinavia and Finland", *Impressionism. Paintings Collected by European Museums* (New York 1999).

54 Ann Dumas, "Introduction," *Impressionism. Paintings Collected by European Museums* (New York 1999), pp. 16–17.

55 Lilja 1955, pp. 150–51.

56 Around this time the Nationalmuseum apparently had yet another opportunity to acquire a painting by Gauguin. Gösta Olson, who was later to found the Swedish-French Art Gallery, supposedly offered the Museum—probably at the beginning of the teens— Gauguin's *Self-Portrait With a Hat* (W 506) of 1893, which then belonged to Ida and William Molard in Paris. On the verso of the canvas, by the way, was Gauguin's portrait of William Molard. Axel Gauffin considered the asking price, according to Olson 10 000 Swedish kronor, too high, and so the painting was returned to the Molards in Paris. See Gösta Olson, *Från Ling till Picasso* (Stockholm 1965), p. 25. The offer was not recorded in the Minutes of the Board of the Nationalmuseum.

57 Lilja 1955, p. 134; Catarina Elsner, *Expressionismens framväxt. August Brunius skriver om konst 1904–1913* (Stockholm 1993), p. 84.

58 Per Hedström & Britta Nilsson, "Genuine and False Van Goghs in the Nationalmuseum", *Art Bulletin of Nationalmuseum* Stockholm, vol. 7 (Stockholm 2000), pp. 98–101.

59 Osterman 1958, pp. 84–85.

60 Osterman 1958, pp. 90–91.

61 Larsson 1996, p. 291.

62 See *Werner Lundqvists samling in Göteborgs Konstmuseum* (exh.cat., Göteborgs Konstmuseum), 1929; Axel L. Romdahl, "Werner Lundqvists samling in Göteborgs museum," *Ord och Bild* (1929): 369–74.

63 Since 1923 the Van Gogh painting owned by Thiel, as well as the Gauguin painting he acquired in Paris in 1908 are in the National Gallery of Prague. See Linde 1969, pp. 93, 99, 105; Larsson 1996, p. 167.

64 Johnny Roosval, "Om herr Klas Fåhræus' konstsamling," *Konst och konstnärer* (1913): 97–108.

65 Oscar Reutersvärd, "Prins Eugen och hans möten med Claude Monet," in *Impressionister och purister* (Stockholm 1976), pp. 72–74.

66 Ragnar Hoppe, *Katalog över Thorsten Laurins samling av måleri och skulptur* (Stockholm 1936).

67 The papers of the Average Adjuster Conrad Pineus, Gothenburg University Library, Mss. Dept., H 63:1.

68 On Gösta Olson's art collecting, see his autobiography *Från Ling till Picasso* (Stockholm 1965).

69 Larsson 1996, p. 187.

70 On the early Swedish reception of Cézanne, see Gösta Lilja, "Cézannes svenska genombrott," in *Vision och gestalt. Studier tillägnade Ragnar Josephson* (Stockholm 1958), pp. 296–311.

71 Lilja 1958, pp. 305–7.

Before and After: Paul Gauguin in Copenhagen 1884–85
Flemming Friborg

1 Merete Bodelsen, *Gauguin og impressionisterne* (Copenhagen 1968); and *Gauguin og van Gogh i København 1893* (exh.cat., The Ordrupgaard Collection) 1984.

2 Anne-Birgitte Fonsmark, *Gauguin i Danmark* (exh.cat., Ny Carlsberg Glyptotek, Copenhagen) 1985.

3 Quoted after Fonsmark 1985, p. 44.

4 Fonsmark 1985, p. 55.

5 Letter from Gauguin to Pissarro, 1881, quoted after Victor Merlhès, ed. *Correspondence de Paul Gauguin: Documents—Témoignages* (Paris 1984), p. 22 (letter 17): "Que diable on ne peut cependant inonder la place des canots canotières et tout les coins des Chatou cela deviendra une estampille exécrable."

6 Letter from Gauguin to Pissarro, 1883 (my italics), after Merlhès, op.cit., p. 48 (letter 36).

7 Fonsmark 1985, p. 48.

8 H. Rostrup in *Gazette des Beaux-Arts* 1958; Bodelsen 1968, pp. 41ff.; and John Rewald, *The History of Impressionism*, 4th ed. (New York 1973), p. 496.

9 Bodelsen 1968, pp. 41–42.

10 Bente Scavenius, *Den frie Udstilling i 100 år* (Copenhagen 1991), pp. 25ff.

11 *Berlingske Tidende* 04/28 1893.

12 *Gauguin och van Gogh i København 1893*, p. 20.

13 *Social-Demokraten* introduced the idea that this type of painting might be as "true" as Naturalism. See *Social-Demokraten*, April 1893, quoted after Scavenius 1991, p. 28.

14 *Politiken* 04/28 1893.

15 Ibid., p. 31.

16 Bodelsen, op.cit., p. 61.

17 *Avisen København*, 04/09 1911.

18 Quoted after *Ekstrabladet*, 04/10 1911.

Painterly Perception and Images of the Soul: Impressionism and Post-Impressionism in Denmark
Peter Nørgaard Larsen

1 The most important publications are: Finn Terman Fredriksen, *Med solen i øjnene. En Theodor Philipsen-studie* (Randers 1992), developed further in "En dansk impressionist," in *Philipsen og impressionismen* (Ordrupgaard 2001) and "Theodor Philipsens indflydelse pa Fynboerne," in *Philipsen og Fynboerne* (exh.cat., Randers Kunstmuseum and Johannes Larsen Museet), 2001. Also, Thomas

Lederballe's articles "Philipsen og impressionismen," in *Philipsen og impressionismen* (Ordrupgaard 2001) and "Philipsens vitalisme. Mellem bondemalere og symbolister 1891–1907," in *Philipsen og Fynboerne* (exh.cat., Randers Kunstmuseum and Johannes Larsen Museet), 2001.

² Karl Madsen, *Maleren Theodor Philipsen* (Copenhagen 1912), p. 32.

³ Terman Fredriksen, "En dansk impressionist," in *Philipsen og impressionismen* (Ordrupgaard 2001), p. 84.

⁴ Johannes V. Jensen, "Foraars-udstillingerne," in *Gads danske Magasin* (May 1912), p. 467.

⁵ Ibid., pp. 470ff. for the above quotation.

⁶ For a discussion of Philipsen's importance for "Fynboerne" see *Philipsen og Fynboerne* (exh.cat., Randers Kunstmuseum and Johannes Larsen Museet), 2001.

⁷ Letter to Viggo Johansen titled 65, Avenue de Wagram, Paris (The Royal Library, Copenhagen), published by Knud Voss, *Breve fra Anna Ancher* (Greve 1984), pp. 50–52.

⁸ Anna Ancher's oil sketches were given a prominent role in the so far most comprehensive retrospective exhibition of her work, *Anna Ancher, 1859–1935. Malerin in Skagen* (exh.cat., Niedersächsisches Landesmuseum, Hannover, Den Hirschsprungske Samling, Copenhagen, and Skagens Museum) 1994–1995. In her essay "Die Malerei Anna Anchers. Einblicke in das Alltägliche," Heide Grape-Albers, the curator of the exhibition, outlines Anna Ancher's choice of motifs and ends with a discussion of the importance of the oil sketch.

⁹ Emil Hannover, *Erindringer fra Barndom og Ungdom*, written in 1914–18, ed. H.P. Rohde (Copenhagen 1966), pp. 144ff.

¹⁰ Ibid., p. 146.

¹¹ Quoted after N.G. Sandblad's introduction to Johan Rohde, *Journal fra en Rejse i 1892*, ed. H.P. Rohde (Copenhagen 1955), pp. 11ff.

¹² Ibid., p. 12.

¹³ For a discussion of Julius Lange and his relationship with contemporary art see Peter Nørgaard Larsen, "Fra Hellas til Hades. Julius Lange og det samtidige danske figurma-

leri," and Jørn Guldberg, "Julius Lange og impressionismen. Noter om Julius Lange og naturstudiets æstetiske og historiografiske status," both in Hanne Kolind Poulsen, Peter Nørgaard Larsen and Hans Dam Christensen, eds., *Viljen til det menneskelige. Tekster omkring Julius Lange* (Copenhagen 1999).

¹⁴ Julius Lange, "Norsk, svensk, dansk Figurmaleri. Indtryk og Overvejelser," in *Tilskueren* (April 1892): 241–72, at pp. 227ff. Lange's view of a study-based art and on the status of the study is representative of the general view on the question in the 1890s. The actual breakthrough of the Impressionist study occurs after 1900. At the initiative of Theodor Philipsen a retrospective exhibition of Danish art was organized in 1901 at the Copenhagen Town Hall, comprising circa 2500 works, of which a great number were painted sketches. The following year Heinrich Hirschsprung transferred ownership of his private collection of Danish art to the State and the city of Copenhagen. The collection, which, in 1902, comprised over 500 paintings, included an important number of studies. In the years after 1900 the first major publications on Danish art history also appeared. And in *Kunstens Historie i Danmark* (1901–07), edited and mainly written by Karl Madsen, as well as in *Danmarks Malerkunst* (1902–03), edited by Ch. A. Been and written by Emil Hannover, the new attitude to study-based art achieves a breakthrough. The Funen Painters represent the most promising contemporary art, and with The Funen painters study-based art has finally freed itself from its servant role and can now be regarded as an independent category.

¹⁵ For the creation of The Free Exhibition and its early history see Leila Krogh, "Den frie Udstillings tilblivelse," in *J.F. Willumsen og Den frie Udstillings første år 1891–1898* (J.F. Willumsen Museum, Frederikssund), 1982, pp. 8–34. For the history of "Den frie Udstilling" see Bente Scavenius, *Den frie Udstilling i 100 år* (Copenhagen 1991).

¹⁶ Quoted after Peter Schindler, *Mogens Francesco Ballin* (Copenhagen 1936), p. 43f.

¹⁷ Simon Koch, "Ludvig Find," in *Taarnet* (October 1893): pp. 22–30, at p. 23. Johannes Jørgensen, "Symbolisme," in *Taarnet* (December 1893): pp. 51–56, at p. 55. For this and the following references to *Taarnet* see the facsimile ed. (Copenhagen 1981).

¹⁸ Johannes Jørgensen, "Symbolisme," at p. 54f.

¹⁹ In her book *Willumsen i halvfemsernes Paris* (Copenhagen 1957), Merete Bodelsen examined Willumsen's relationship with Gauguin and his circle. In the chapter titled "Willumsen and Gauguin," Bodelsen deals with Gauguin's decisive influence on Willumsen's early ceramics and wood carvings, but is forced to conclude that Willumsen hardly learnt more from Gauguin than a few craft techniques: "However, Willumsen has nothing in common with the style Gauguin had developed by the time Willumsen visited him in Brittany in the summer of 1890. [...] There can hardly be any doubt that, in reality, it was more Gauguin's personality and ideas than his art, which captivated Willumsen at their first encounter" (p. 24f.).

²⁰ Johannes Jørgensen, "Foraars-udstillingerne. Symbolismen," in *Politiken* 14 April 1893. Jørgensen was not alone in having this view. The year before, Johan Rohde had asked Gad F. Clement "if Willumsen was like Gauguin in his final years. His answer was a definite no. He explained that he had not encountered anyone like Willumsen among the young French painters," undated letter from Rohde to Emil Hannover in Den Hirschsprungske Samling, quoted after Bodelsen 1957, p. 54 and n. 131.

²¹ Emil Hannover in a review of Clement's debut at The Free Exhibition of 1893, in *Politiken* 26 March 1893.

²² For Ballin's self-portrait see Charlotte Christensen's article "The Noble is Simple," in *Symbolism in Danish and European Painting, 1870–1910* (exh.cat., Statens Museum for Kunst, Copenhagen), 2000, p. 190.

²³ In his travel journal, *Journal fra en Rejse i 1892*, Johan Rohde mentions Bernard as a possible source of inspiration for Clement's "pseudo-decorative compositions," and Cle-

ment himself acquired a painting by Bernard, *Women Picking Fruit* of 1888 (Ny Carlsberg Glyptotek, Copenhagen). The most direct reference, though, is to Maurice Denis' painting *April* of 1892 (Rijksmuseum Kröller-Müller, Otterlo), which seems to have contributed both the landscape and the two young women in the middle ground to Clement's vision. Clement was in Paris at the time that Denis was working on *April*, and in view of the Nabis' close brotherhood-like community, it is quite probable that Clement had an opportunity to study Denis' painting closely.

²⁴ In *Jan Verkade. Hollandse volgeling van Gauguin* (exh.cat., Van Gogh Museum, Amsterdam), 1989, pp. 96ff., Caroline Boyle-Turner discusses the painting's possible attribution to Gauguin, Verkade, and Ballin, as well as its relationship with Gauguin's self-portrait. On the basis of stylistic judgment, and with reference to the painting's provenance—the painting has always been in the possession of the Ballin family, Boyle-Turner is forced to conclude that its author presumably is Mogens Ballin, even though this work and others of the same period also are reminiscent of Verkade. She dismisses as less probable the view that it is a Gauguin self-portrait.

²⁵ Rohde, *Journal fra en Rejse i 1892*, op.cit., p. 51.

²⁶ From a letter from Christensen to Rohde shortly after the painting's arrival in Copenhagen, we know that it was soon shown to, among others, L.A. Ring and Georg Seligmann, *Gauguin og Van Gogh i København 1893*, p. 123f. In 1894 Ludvig Find also describes several visits to Christensen's home, where "the coffee and brandy was served in front of the Van Gogh," see Johan Rohde, *Journal fra en Rejse in 1892*, p. 38.

²⁷ Merete Bodelsen, *Gauguin og Impressionisterne* (Copenhagen 1968). This publication includes the documentation concerning Gauguin's art collection, including the later whereabouts of the paintings, and identifications of the works in Edvard Brandes' large collection.

²⁸ A majority of the paintings belonged to those works left by Gauguin in Copenhagen in 1885, still others, more recent works from

Brittany and Arles had been sent to Copenhagen from Paris, or had been brought there by Mette Gauguin in connection with visits to Paris in 1887 and 1892. In addition, the exhibition included 10 completely new paintings, which Gauguin sent from Tahiti to Copenhagen via Paris.

29 For a facsimile of the catalogue of The Free Exhibition of 1893, listing the names of owners of the paintings, see *Gauguin og van Gogh i København 1893* (Ordrupgaard 1984), pp. 31–42.

30 Philipsen met Gauguin again in 1889 in connection with the World's Fair in Paris, and possibly Gauguin appreciated this opportunity of seeing Philipsen's *A Late Autumn Day in Dyrehaven. Sunshine*, which was a part of the Danish display. Later on, when Gauguin paid a short visit to Copenhagen to take leave of his family prior to his departure for Tahiti on April 4th, 1891, he invited Philipsen for a cup of tea: "My dear Philipsen, do you remember the nice evening that we spent together in Paris? I am here just for a short while and would be very happy to speak to you. If you could come over for tea on Saturday we would have the opportunity to talk. Sincerely yours, Paul Gauguin. 47 Vimmelskaftet." The invitation is preserved at the Royal Library of Copenhagen, and is reprinted in *Gauguin og van Gogh i København 1893* (Ordrupgaard 1984), p. 17.

31 In 1922 the painting was deposited in the Ny Carlsberg Glyptotek, and was reunited with Philipsen's other painting by Gauguin, *The Road to Rouen (II)*, in 1986, when the Ny Carlsberg Foundation purchased it at auction in London and subsequently donated it to the Glyptotek.

32 Rohde's art collection also included one painting and four woodcuts by Maurice Denis, drawings by Jan Verkade and lithographs by, among others, Toulouse-Lautrec and Valloton. In his introduction to Rohde's *Journal fra en Rejse 1892*, Sandblad mentions (p. 40f.) that Richard Bergh, as well as Karl Nordström and Nils Kreuger, on several occasions in 1892–93 visited Copenhagen and Rohde with great benefit, but even Edvard Munch remembered, in Berlin in 1893, his visit to Rohde in the winter of 92/93: "I have often thought about the hours spent in your company in your upstairs room, filled with such a lot of good art."

33 That Ballin in all likelihood purchased his Gauguin painting in Paris in 1891 is also demonstrated by Ballin's painting *Girl from Brittany in front of a Farm*, which in its composition and the girl's placement, as well as in several details, is closely related to Gauguin's *Shepherdess from Brittany*. Ballin's painting was executed after the Gauguin auction, presumably in the summer of 1891, when Ballin was in Brittany together with Verkade and Serusier.

34 Carl Nielsen has described the visit in his diary, published in 1983 by Torben Schousboe: "In the afternoon at the art dealer [...] together with Clement, Ballin, Bendix and wife. Saw for the first time paintings by Vincent (van Gocken) which made the strongest impression on me. Bendix bought one for 300 Frk. Dinner at Bendix, whereupon the whole company went to the Moulin Rouge, where we indulged our appetites."

35 The collection would have been even more superb, had Ballin not previously divested himself of Maurice Denis' *Madonna with the Apple* and Van Gogh's *Portrait of Doctor Gachet* (1890). Both were purchased in 1897 by Mrs. Alice Faber from Ambroise Vollard in Paris. A few years later they were transferred to Mogens Ballin under unknown circumstances, and through Ballin they were sold in 1904 at the Galerie Cassirer in Berlin to Count Harry Kessler. One can read about this fascinating, but not yet fully known story in: Cynthia Saltzman, *Das Bildnis des Dr. Gachet: Biographie eines Meisterwerks* (Munich 2000, Eng. Ed. 1998).

36 For an overview of the Danish collectors, which, in addition to rich illustrations, also contains an extensive amount of biographical information, see Knud V. Jensen, *De glade givere* (Copenhagen 1996). This publication also includes an extensive bibliography. As far as the Statens Museum for Kunst and its role in the collecting activities during the decade around 1900, see Villads Villadsen, *Statens Museum for Kunst 1827–1952* (Statens Museum for Kunst 1998). For all other references see the notes below.

37 For Wilhelm Hansen and his collection, see Marianne Wirenfeldt Asmussen, *Wilhelm Hansens oprindelige franske samling pa Ordrupgaard* (Copenhagen 1993) and Mikael Wivel, *Ordrupgaard—Udvalgte værker* (Copenhagen 1993).

38 At his death in 1929 Pellerin owned 92 works by Cézanne, which were spread to every corner of the world by his heirs. Nine works today belong to the Musée d'Orsay in Paris.

39 Of these works should be mentioned Manet's portrait of *Mademoiselle Isabelle Lemonnier*, Renoir's *Young Girls*, two ballet paintings by Degas, *Ballet Exercises in the Foyer* and *Dancer in a Red Skirt*, Cézanne's *Still-Life with a Bowl of Apples* and *Self-Portrait with Bowler Hat*, Van Gogh's *Portrait of Julien Tanguy*, and Toulouse-Lautrec's *Portrait of Monsieur Delaporte in the Jardin de Paris*.

40 Quoted after Jens Peter Munk, *Fransk Impressionisme* (Ny Carlsberg Glyptotek, Copenhagen), 1993, p. 7.

41 Among Helge Jacobsen's own paintings may be mentioned Maurice Denis' *Madonna and Child with the Infant St. John* (bought from Mogens Ballin), Van Gogh's *Light Red Roses* (donated as early as 1923), two paintings by Bonnard, works by Vuillard and Signac, as well as twelve paintings by Gauguin. For these works see *Post-Impressionisme* (Ny Carlsberg Glyptotek, Copenhagen), 1993.

42 The key article about Tetzen-Lund's collection is Lennart Gottlieb's "Tetzen-Lunds samling—om dens historie, indhold og betydning," *Kunst og Museum* 19 (1984): 18–49. Here we find lists of Tetzen-Lund's purchases of painting during the years 1916–20, a primary source for any reconstruction of the collection. For the collection's importance for Scandinavian art see Teddy Brunius, "Christian Tetzen-Lunds samling i Köpenhamn och de nordiska konstnärerna," *Konsthistorisk Tidskrift* 57, 3–4 (1988).

Norwegian Impressions
Nils Messel

1 Andreas Aubert, "Kunstudstillinger i Paris. III. En impressionist." *Aftenposten* 21/12 1883.

2 For a full discussion see Magne Malmanger, "'Impressionismen' og Impressionisten. Christian Krohg og det moderne gjennembrudd i 1880-årene," in *Christian Krohg* (exh.cat., Nasjonalgalleriet, Oslo, 1987), pp. 31–49.

3 Andreas Aubert, "Claude Monet kommer," *Dagbladet*, 31/1 (1895).

4 Andreas Aubert, "Svensk malerkunst paa Verdensudstillingen, sammenstillet med den norske," *Dagbladet* (30 November 1890).

5 Andreas Aubert, "Kunstudstillinger i Paris. III. En impressionist," *Aftenposten* (21 December 1883).

6 Andreas Aubert, "Fra Kunstudstillingen i Rue de Sèze i Paris," *Aftenposten* (21 December 1883).

7 Lorentz Dietrichson, *Adolph Tidemand, hans liv og hans værker*, vol. 2 (Christiania 1879), p. 106, quoted after Nils Messel, "Tyske og franske fronter i norsk maleri. Kunstkritikk som krigskorrespondanse," in *Konsthistorisk Tidskrift*, 63 (1994): 225.

8 Erik Werenskiold, "Impressionisterne," *Nyt Tidsskrift* (1882): 229–34, quoted after the reprint in Erik Werenskiold, *Kunst. Kamp. Kultur* (Christiania 1917), pp. 63–67.

9 Andreas Aubert, "Kunstudstillinger i Paris. III. En impressionist," *Aftenposten*, 21/12 (1883).

10 Andreas Aubert, "Hostudstillingen II. Impressionisme og Farvedekomposition," in *Dagbladet*, 2/10 (1887).

11 Michel Chevreul (1786–1889), French chemist; Hermann Helmholtz (1821–1894), German physicist; Ernst Brücke (1819–1892), German physiologist.

12 Lorentz Dietrichson, "Impressionisme," in *Norsk Maanedsskrift* (1884).

13 The lecture was given at The Independent Student Association in Christiania, here quoted after C. Krohg, *Kampen for Tilværelsen* (Christiania 1920).

14 For a discussion of Zola's idea of Impressionism and its relationship to Norwegian art, see: Nils Messel's Introduction to the Norwegian edition of E. Zola, *Mesterverket* (Oslo 1993), III–VXI.

[15] Andreas Aubert, "Høstudstillingen. II," in *Dagbladet* (2 October 1887).

[16] Andreas Aubert, "Høstudstillingen. II," in *Dagbladet* (2 October 1887).

[17] Compare Andreas Aubert's critical comments about this generation in his *Det nya Norges Malerkunst* (Christiania 1908), pp. 84ff.

[18] Quoted after Arne Eggum, *Edvard Munch. Malerier—skisser og studier* (Oslo 1983), p. 46.

[19] Quoted after Leif Østby, *Fra naturalisme til nyromantik* (Oslo 1934), p. 130.

[20] The subject is treated at length by Magne Malmanger, "Betryggende modernitet," pp. 27–47 in *Tradition og fornyelse* (exh.cat., Nasjonalgalleriet, Oslo), 1994–95.

[21] Quoted after the reprint of the article in *Udvalgte Skrifter af Julius Lange*, vol. 3 (Copenhagen 1903), p. 162.

[22] See Nils Messel, "Fra realistisk virkelighetsskildring til dekorativ form. Lysaker-kretsen og den 'norske' tradisjon," in *Kunst og Kultur*, no. 3 (1983): 152–71, esp. at pp. 154ff.

[23] Ibid., p. 156.

[24] M. Hamel, "La peinture du Nord," Gazette des Beaux-Arts, 1888, här citerat efter Nils Messel, "Andreas Aubert om kunst, natur og nasjonalitet," *Tradisjon og fornyelse*, utst. kat., Nasjonalgalleriet, Oslo 1994–95, p. 63.

[25] Quoted after Leif Østby, *Fra naturalisme til nyromantik* (Oslo 1934): 67.

[26] Kitty Kielland, "Lidt om norsk kunst," in *Samtiden* (1890), here quoted after Magne Malmanger, "Betryggende modernitet," p. 36 in *Tradition og fornyelse* (exh.cat., Nasjonalgalleriet, Oslo), 1994–95.

[27] In this context it is interesting to note that the Impressionistic movement often came to be regarded in later Norwegian art historical accounts as an art independent of nation and class. Leif Østby suggests in his *Norges kunsthistorie* (Oslo 1966, pp. 14ff.) that those who created the earliest Norwegian rune stones should be considered our first Impressionists: "The complete lack of a plan, organization, composition, whereby even the geometric motifs are distributed without care, does it not illustrate the whole social milieu, the loosely arranged, classless flock or tribe without an established social order, without perspective on the future or the past, the children of the present, the first Impressionists? Their art is, first and foremost, of the eye, not thought […]."

[28] Letter from Erik Werenskiold to B. Grønvold (11 January 1908), here quoted after Nils Messel, "Karstens bilder og bildet av Karsten. En monografisk og historiografisk undersøkelse," M.A.Thesis, Uio 1979, p. 61, n. 1.

French Paintings on Norwegian Soil
Nils Messel

[1] Introduction to his *Utstillingen over fransk kunst* (exh.cat., Nasjonalgalleriet, Oslo), 1914.

[2] Both paintings by Gauguin were executed in 1884, and both became part of the collections of the Nasjonalgalleriet in 1907.

[3] Claude Monet, *Les Rochers de Belle-Îsle*, 1886 (cat.no. 87, 1 600 kr) and *Etretat, temps de pluie*, 1886 (cat.no. 88, 1 300 kr); Pissarro, *The Chat* (cat.no. 125, 600 kr); Edgar Degas, *Dancers*, pastel drawing (cat.no. 190, 900 kr). We know that the paintings of Monet were acquired from the Parisian art dealers Boussod and Valadon. The same art dealers had arranged a Pissarro exhibition in the spring of 1890. It is, thus, reasonable to think that also the Pissarro painting came from the same source. Possibly, the painting is identical with *Two Young Peasant Women Chatting Beneath the Trees, Pontoise*, 1881 (Pissarro/Venturi no. 154), which in the 1920s belonged to the Norwegian collector Jørgen Breder Stang.

[4] Carolus-Duran, *Portrait* (cat.no. 38, p.e); G.P. Jeanniot, *Landscape* (cat.no. 81, 1 500 kr) and *Portrait* (cat.no. 82, 750 kr); Besnard, *Raderinger* (cat.no. 255, p.e.); Auguste Rodin, *Man Lifting a Woman* (cat.no. 275—plaster cast, 1 500 kr, bronze 1 850 kr) and *Zephyrus, Held Back By a Woman* (cat.no. 276—plaster cast 1 500 kr, bronze 1 850 kr); A.P. Roll, *Portrait* (cat.no. 309).

[5] Letter from Thorvald Erichsen to Harriet Backer. In the Nasjonalgalleriet, letter archives no. 47/1905.

[6] Cf. n.2 above.

[7] S.Willoch, *Nasjonalgalleriet gjennem hundre år* (Oslo 1937), p. 160.

[8] S.Willoch, *Nasjonalgalleriets Venner. Kunst i femti år* (Oslo 1967), p. 7.

[9] The Copenhagen exhibit was organized by the Danish Museum Association at the Statens Museum for Kunst 5/15—6/30, 1914. The catalogue had 356 entries. The exhibit at the Nasjonalgalleriet comprised 90 works, of which 48 were paintings. Among these were 11 works by Courbet, Manet, Degas, Cézanne, Renoir, and Gauguin, which had previously been shown in Copenhagen, and mainly belonged to the Galeries Levesque and Vollard in Paris. Many of these works were later purchased by Norwegian collectors and by the Nasjonalgalleriet. The rest were works belonging to the Nasjonalgalleriet, supplemented by pictures from Norwegian and Swedish (Ernst Thiel and Carl Laurin) private collectors.

[10] The Den franske utstilling i Kunstnerforbundet, January–February 1918, comprised 142 catalogue entries, of which 106 were paintings, 5 sculptures, and 31 prints, drawings and water colours. As opposed to the 1916 exhibit, the new exhibition also comprised many works by deceased artists, among others, Cézanne, Courbet, Delacroix, Gauguin, Manet, Pissarro, Redon, Toulouse-Lautrec, Seurat, and Sisley. Half of the works came from an exhibition in Holland, which the French state had recently organized and from which Halvorsen had been allowed to choose art works.

Monet and Norway
Karin Hellandsjø

[1] Daniel Wildenstein, *Claude Monet. Biographie et catalogue raisonné*, Paris 1974–81, letter 1280, to Durand-Ruel (9 March 1895).

[2] W., letter 1274, to G. Geffroy (26 February 1895).

[3] W., letter 1291, to Durand-Ruel (7 April 1895).

[4] Baedeker, *Guide touristique; la Suède et la Norvège*, Leipzig/Paris 1892.

[5] S. Patin, "Les effets de neige absolument stupéfiants, mais d'une difficulté inouïe," in *Monet i Norge*, ed. K. Hellandsjø (exh.cat., Stavanger, Rogaland Kunstmuseum, and Paris, Musée Rodin) 1995.

[6] J. Lescoffier, *Bjørnson et la France*, Oslo 1936. Also quoted by H. Herresthal and L. Reznicek, *Rhapsodie Norvégienne*, Oslo 1994.

[7] O. Reutersvärd, "Monet och hans dragning mot Normandie," in *Somrene i Normandie* (exh.cat., Modums Blaafarveværk), 1994.

[8] A. Aubert, "Høstudstillingen II, Aararbejdet," in *Dagbladet*, Christiania 10/26/1890.

[9] G. de Maupassant, "La Vie d'un paysagiste (Etretat, septembre)," *Gil Blas*, 09/28/1886.

[10] Monet left Paris on the 28th of January and took the express train to Kiel via Cologne and Altona. From Kiel he took a Danish boat to Korsør. Due to the snow and the cold this journey lasted nine hours instead of five, and by the time he arrived the connecting train had already left. He finally reached Helsingør twelve hours late, in the afternoon on the 31st of January. He travelled by boat to Helsingborg, arriving at six o'clock in the evening, and checked into the Hotel Continental for a rest. He then continued his journey by night train to Christiania. This lag of the journey lasted 24 hours as planned, and he arrived in Christiania at eleven o'clock in the evening on the 1st of February.

[11] W., letter 1265, to A. Monet (3 February 1895).

[12] W., letter 1266, to A. Monet (9 February 1895).

[13] W., letter 1267, to A. Monet (11 February 1895).

[14] W., letter 1270, to A. Monet (18 February 1895).

[15] Op.cit.

[16] W., letter 1276, to Blanche Hochedé-Monet (1 March 1895).

[17] W., letter 1282, to A. Monet (12 March 1895).

[18] W., letter 1274, op.cit.

[19] W., letter 1276, op.cit.

[20] W., letter 1282, op.cit.

[21] W., letter 1282, op.cit.

[22] W., letter 1272, to A. Monet (24 February 1895). In spite of his indignation, a set of "snaps" glasses were among the things he brought back to France from Norway.

[23] W., letter 1287, to A. Monet (23 March 1895).

[24] H. Bang, "Claude Monet," in *Bergens Tidende*, Christiania (6 April 1895).

[25] There is a fifth version of the subject, *Village de Sandviken* (Wildenstein no. 2035), in the Latvian Museum of Foreign Art at Riga. The authenticity of this painting is, however, questionable, partly because of the presence of a non-existing church in the background. Monet never made such additions.

[26] W., letter 1276, op.cit.

[27] C. Krohg, "Intervju med Herman Bang I Paris," in *Verdens Gang*, Christiania (26 May 1902).

[28] *Le Rappel*, Paris (15 May 1895).

[29] S.Patin, op.cit., pp. 62–63.

[30] A. Aubert, "Claude Monet kommer!," in *Dagbladet*, Christiania (31 January 1895).

[31] E. Østvedt, *Frits Thaulow*, Oslo 1951.

Under the Sign of the Rainbow Colours. Impressionism and Finland
Bengt von Bonsdorff

[1] Pekka Suhonen, *The Road. Shared Beauty—The Finnish Fine Arts Association's 150-years Anniversary Exhibition in Helsinki, St. Petersburg and Stockholm 1996–97*, p. 26.

[2] Tuukka Talvio, *H.F. Antell ja Antellin valtuuskunta* (Helsinki 1993), p. 25.

[3] Soili Sinisalo, *Samlingen lever, leve samlingen. Konstmuseet Ateneum. Ur den internationella samlingen*, ed. Leena Ahtola-Moorhouse (Helsinki 2000), p. 78.

[4] See the Catalogue of the exhibition, containing information about owners and prices, in the Central Art Archives, Helsinki.

[5] Sinisalo 2000, p. 88.

[6] Aune Lindström, *Konstmuseet i Ateneum 1863–1963* (Helsinki 1963), pp. 48–50.

[7] Leena Ahtola-Moorhouse, "L'Ancienne Gentilhommière," in *L'Horizon Inconnu. L'Art en Finlande 1870–1920* (exh.cat., Musées de Strasbourg; Palais des Beaux-Arts de Lille; Ateneum Helsinki 1999–2000), p. 222.

[8] Sixten Ringbom, "Symbolism, Synthetism and the Kalevala", Art in Finland (Helsinki 2000), p. 224.

[9] *Catalogue de l'Exposition Française des Beaux-Arts à Helsingfors 1904* (Helsinki 1904; Talvio 1993), p. 87.

[10] Sinisalo 2000, p. 35; Talvio 1993, p. 87.

[11] *Catalogue de l'exposition d'artistes français et belges* (Helsinki 1904).

[12] Talvio 1993, pp. 89–90.

[13] Bo Lindberg, "Painting from Romanticism to Realism", Art in Finland (Helsinki 2000), pp. 206–207, 213.

[14] Talvio 1993, p. 54.

[15] Sinisalo 2000, pp. 95–97.

[16] Lindberg 2000, pp. 204–06; Aimo Reitala, *Victor Westerholm* (Helsinki 1967), p. 125.

[17] H. Ahtela, *Helena Schjerfbeck* (Helsinki 1954), p. 59, cat. no. 217; Lena Holger, "Till det förlofvade landet," in *De drogo till Paris* (exh.cat., Liljevalchs Konsthall, Stockholm 1988), p. 261; Rudolf Zeitler, "Svenskt landskap i måleri och diktning under 1800-talet," in *Historiens vingslag. Festskrift till Allan Ellenius 60-årsdag* (Stockholm 1987), pp. 179–80.

[18] Salme Sarajas-Korte, "Maalaustaide 1880-luvulla—ulkoilmarealismi," *Ars* 4 (1989): 241; *1880-tal i nordiskt måleri* (exh.cat., Nasjonalgalleriet, Oslo; Nationalmuseum, Stockholm; Amos Andersons Konstmuseum, Helsinki; Statens Museum for Kunst, Copenhagen 1985–86), pp. 212–13.

[19] Reitala 1967, pp. 123–28.

[20] Ringbom, p. 216.

[21] Leena Lindqvist, *Taiteilijan tiellä—Eero Järnefelt* (Keuruu 2000), pp. 110–111, 223, 227; Olli Valkonen, "Maalaustaide vuosisadan vaihteesta itsenäisyyden aikaan," in *Ars—Suomen taide 5* (Keuruu 2002): 189.

[22] Valkonen 1990, p. 184.

[23] Ibid., p. 189.

[24] See *L'Horizon inconnu—l'art en Finlande 1870–1920*, p. 265.

[25] Marja Supinen, "Vincent Van Gogh, Street in Auvers-sur-Oise. An Acquisition for the Antell Collection 1903," *Ateneum. Statens konstmuseums årsskrift* (1994): 32; Talvio 1993, pp. 47–48, 89.

[26] Sinisalo 2000, p. 4, 20; Talvio 1993, pp. 93–94.

[27] Lindqvist, pp. 140–42.

[28] Lindström 1963, p. 64.

[29] Talvio 1993, pp. 91–92.

[30] Kimmo Sarje, *Sigurd Frosteruksen modernin käsite. Maailmankatsomus ja arkkitehtuuri* (Helsinki 2000); Bengt von Bonsdorff, "Sigurd Frosterus—arkitekten, skriftställaren och konstteoretikern"; Liisa Kasvio, "Sigurd Frosterus samling. Den unge samlarens stämningar—värderingar utformas, samlingen blir till," *Amos Andersons konstmuseums publikation* n.s. 8 (Helsinki 1992).

[31] Sinisalo 2000, pp. 30–31, 42–43.

[32] Talvio 1993, pp. 111–13.

[33] See *L'Horizon inconnu—L'Art en Finlande 1870–1920*, p. 257.

[34] See *Ars* 5, p. 183.

[35] Bengt von Bonsdorff, *Felix Nylund—liv och verk* (Helsinki 1990); see also the author's articles in the *Svenska Litteratursällskapets Historiska och Litteraturhistoriska studier* nos. 57, 59, 60, 61, and 63.

[36] Sinisalo 2000, p. 126.

[37] Lindström 1963, p. 64; Sinisalo 2000, pp. 28–29.

[38] Talvio 1993, pp. 113–14.

[39] Rolf Nummelin, "New Currents in Painting", Art in Finland (Helsinki 2000), p. 248.

[40] Sinisalo 2000, p. 103.

[41] Sinisalo 2000, pp. 24, 25, 27.

Select Bibliography

This bibliography consists of works which on a general level form the points of departure for the articles in this book. References to written sources such as newspaper reviews will be found in the notes to each article.

1880-tal i nordiskt måleri, utst. kat., Nasjonalgalleriet, Oslo; Nationalmuseum, Stockholm; Amos Andersons Konstmuseum, Helsingfors; Statens Museum for Kunst, København 1985.

Anderberg, Adolf, *Carl Hill. Hans liv och hans konst*, Malmö 1951.

Anna Ancher 1859–1935. Malerin in Skagen, Niedersächsisches Landesmuseum, Hannover 1994, Den Hirschsprungske Samling, København og Skagens Museum 1995.

Aubert, Andreas, *Det nya Norges Malerkunst*, Kristiania 1908.

Bergh, Richard, *Om konst och annat*, Stockholm 1908.

Bjurström, Per, *Nationalmuseum 1792–1992*, Stockholm 1992.

Bodelsen, Merete, *Willumsen i halvfemsernes Paris*, København 1957.

Bodelsen, Merete, *Gauguin og Impressionisterne*, København 1968.

Bonsdorff, Bengt von, "Sigurd Frosterus – arkitekten, skriftställaren och konstteoretikern", *Amos Andersons konstmuseums publikation*, Ny följd nr 8, Helsingfors 1992.

Bonsdorff, Bengt von, *Felix Nylund – liv och verk*, Helsingfors 1990

Boström, Kjell, *Nils Kreuger*, Stockholm 1948.

Brettell, Richard R., *Impression. Painting Quickly in France, 1860–1890*, New Haven and London 2000.

Broude, Norma, *World Impressionism. The International Movement, 1860–1920*, New York 1990.

Brummer, Hans Henrik, *Anders Zorn. Till ögats fröjd och nationens förgyllning*, Stockholm 1994.

Brummer, Hans Henrik, *Prins Eugen. Minnet av ett landskap*, Stockholm 1998.

Brunius, Teddy, "Christian Tetzen-Lunds samling i Köpenhamn och de nordiska konstnärerna", *Konsthistorisk Tidskrift* 1988:3/4.

Bryhni, Anne Siri, *Bohem mod Borger*, Oslo 1971.

Cavalli-Björkman, Görel, "Cézanne i Sverige", *Cézanne i blickpunkten*, utst. kat., Nationalmuseum 1997.

Cavalli-Björkman, Görel, "The Reception of Impressionism in Scandinavia and Finland", *Impressionism. Paintings collected by European museums*, exh.cat., High Museum of Art, Atlanta, 1999.

Christian Krohg, utst. kat., Nasjonalgalleriet, Oslo 1987.

Clark, T. J., *The Painting of Modern Life. Paris in the Art of Manet and his Followers*, London and New York 1985.

Correspondance de Paul Gauguin, Documents – Témoignages, ed. Victor Merlhès, Paris 1984.

De drogo till Paris. Nordiska konstnärinnor på 1880-talet, utst. kat., Liljevalchs Konsthall, Stockholm, 1988.

"Den frie Udstilling": 100 år 1891–1991, København 1991.

Dietrichson, Lorentz, "Impressionisme", *Norsk Maanedsskrift* 1884.

Distel, Anne, *Les collectioneurs des impressionistes. Amateurs et marchands*, Düdingen/Guin 1989.

Dreams of a Summer Night. Scandinavian Painting at the Turn of the Century, exh.cat., Hayward Gallery, London 1986.

Eggum, Arne, *Edvard Munch. Malerier – skisser og studier*, Oslo 1983,

Elsner, Catarina, *Expressionismens framväxt. August Brunius skriver om konst 1904–1913*, Stockholm 1993.

Facos, Michelle, *Nationalism and the Nordic imagination. Swedish Art of the 1890s*, Berkeley 1998.

Fonsmark, Anne-Birgitte, *Gauguin og Danmark*, utst. kat., Ny Carlsberg Glyptotek, København 1985.

Friborg, Flemming, *Det Gode Selskab – Kunstforeningens historier 1825–2000*, København 2000.

Fransk Impressionisme, Ny Carlsberg Glyptotek, København 1993.

Frederiksen, Finn Terman, *Med solen i øjnene. En Theodor Philipsen-studie*, Randers 1992.

Fredlund, Björn, "Den inre röstens maning. Richard Bergh om Karl Nordström och stämningslandskapet", *Det skapande jaget. Konsthistoriska texter tillägnade Maj-Brit Wadell*, Göteborg 1994.

Gauffin, Axel, *Ivan Aguéli. Människan – mystikern – målaren*, Stockholm 1940–41.

Gauguin og Van Gogh i København 1893, utst. kat., Ordrupgaard 1984.

Gottlieb, Lennart, "Tetzen-Lunds samling – om dens historie, indhold og betydning", *Kunst og Museum*, 1984.

Guldberg, Jørn, "Julius Lange og impressionismen. Noter om Julius Langes og naturstudiets æstetiske og historiografiske status", *Viljen til det menneskelige. Tekster omkring Julius Lange*, Hanne Kolind Poulsen, Peter Nørgaard Larsen och Hans Dam Christensen (red.), København 1999.

Gunnarsson, Torsten, *Nordic Landscape Painting in the Nineteenth Century*, New Haven and London 1998.

Gynning, Margareta, *Det ambivalenta perspektivet. Eva Bonnier och Hanna Hirsch-Pauli i 1880-talets konstliv*, Stockholm 1999.

Görts, Maria, *Det sköna i verklighetens värld. Akademisk konstsyn i Sverige under senare delen av 1800-talet*, Stockholm 1999.

Hannover, Emil, *Erindringer fra Barndom og Ungdom*, København 1966.

Hedström, Per & Nilsson, Britta, "Genuine and False Van Goghs in the Nationalmuseum", *Art Bulletin of Nationalmuseum Stockholm*, vol. 7, 2000.

Herbert, Robert L., *Impressionism. Art, Leisure, and Parisian Society*, New Haven and London 1988.

Holger, Lena, "Till det förlofvade landet", *De drogo till Paris. Nordiska konstnärinnor på 1880-talet*, utst. kat., Liljevalchs Konsthall, Stockholm, 1988.

Hoppe, Ragnar, *Katalog över Thorsten Laurins samling av måleri och skulptur*, Stockholm 1936.

L'Horizon inconnu. L'art en Finland 1870–1920, exh.cat. Musées de Strasbourg; Palais des Beaux-Arts de Lille; Ateneum Helsingfors, 1999–2000.

Impressionism. Paintings collected by European museums, exh.cat., High Museum of Art, Atlanta, 1999.

Impressionists on the Seine. A Celebration of Renoir's Luncheon of the Boating Party, exh.cat., The Phillips Collection, Washington, 1996–97.

Jensen, Knud V., *De glade givere*, København 1996.

J.F. Willumsen og "Den frie Udstillings" første år 1891–1898, J.F. Willumsens Museum, Frederikssund 1982.

Kasvio, Liisa, "Sigurd Frosterus samling. Den unge samlarens stämningar – värderingar utformas, samlingen blir till", *Amos Andersons konstmuseums publikation*, Ny följd nr 8, Helsingfors 1992.

Krohg, Christian, *Kampen for Tilværelsen*, Kristiania 1920.

Kielland, Kitty, "Lidt om norsk kunst", *Samtiden* 1890.

Landschaft als Kosmos der Seele. Malerei des nordischen Symbolismus bis Munch 1880–1990, exh.cat., Wallraf-Richartz-Museum, Köln, 1998.

Lange, Julius, "Studiet i Marken. Skilderiet. Erindringens Kunst." *Bastien Lepage og andre afhandlinger*, København 1889.

Lange, Julius, "Norsk, svensk, dansk Figurmaleri. Indtryk og Overvejelser", *Tilskueren*, april 1892.

Larsson, Håkan, *Flames from the south. On the introduction of Vincent Van Gogh to Sweden*, Lund 1996.

Lilja, Gösta, *Det moderna måleriet i svensk kritik 1905–1914*, Malmö 1955.

Lilja, Gösta, "Cézannes svenska genombrott", *Vision och gestalt. Studier tillägnade Ragnar Josephson*, Stockholm 1958.

Lilja, Gösta, *Friluftsmålarna och impressionismen*, utst. kat., Skånska konstmuseum, Lund 1957.

Lindberg, Bo, "Painting from Romanticism to Realism", *Art in Finland*, Helsinki 2000.

Lindqvist, Leena, *Taiteilijan tiellä – Eero Järnefelt*, Keuruu 2002.

Linde, Brita, *Ernest Thiel och hans konstgalleri*, Stockholm 1969.

Lindström, Aune, *Konstmuseet i Ateneum 1863–1963*, Helsingfors 1963.

Loos, Viggo, *Friluftsmåleriets genombrott i svensk konst 1860–1885*, Stockholm 1945.

Loos, Viggo, *Carl Skånberg*, Linköping 1928.

Lärkner, Bengt, "Hjalmar Gabrielson – samlare och mecenat", *Konsthistorisk Tidskrift* 1988:3/4.

Madsen, Karl, *Maleren Theodor Philipsen*, København 1912.

Malmanger, Magne, "Impressionismen og Impressionisten. Christian Krohg og det moderne gjennembrudd i 1880-årene", *Christian Krohg*, utst. kat., Nasjonalgalleriet, Oslo, 1987.

Malmanger, Magne, "Betryggende modernitet", *Tradisjon og fornyelse. Norge rundt århundreskiftet*, utst. kat., Nasjonalgalleriet, Oslo 1994-95.

Messel, Nils, "Fra realistisk virkelighetsskildring til dekorativ form. Lysaker-kretsen og den 'norske' tradisjon", *Kunst og Kultur* 1983:3.

Messel, Nils, "Tyske og franske fronter i norsk maleri. Kunstkritikk som krigskorrespondanse", *Konsthistorisk Tidskrift*, 1994:3/4.

Millroth, Thomas, *Molards salong*, Stockholm 1993.

Monet i Norge, utst. kat., Rogaland Kunstmuseum, Stavanger & Musée Rodin, Paris 1995.

Nasgaard, Roald, *The mystic North. Symbolist Landscape Painting in Northern Europe and North America 1890–1940*, Toronto 1984.

The New Painting. Impressionism 1874–1886, exh.cat., The Fine Arts Museum of San Francisco; National Gallery of Art, Washington, 1986.

Nilsson, Sten Åke, "Det gränslösa arbetet. En biografi", *Carl Fredrik Hill*, utst. kat., Nationalmuseum, 1999.

Nordenfalk, Carl, "Van Gogh and Sweden", *Konsthistorisk Tidskrift* 1946.

Nordiskt sekelskifte. The Light of the North, utst. kat., Museo Nacional Centro de Arte Reina Sofia, Madrid; Museu d'art Modern del MNAC, Barcelona; Listafn Islands, Reykavik; Nationalmuseum, Stockholm, 1995–1996.

Northern Light. Realism and Symbolism in Scandinavian Painting 1880–1910, exh.cat., Corcoran Gallery of Art, Washington D.C.; The Brooklyn Museum, New York; The Minneapolis Institute of arts, Minnesota, 1982–83.

Nummelin, Rolf, "New Currents in Painting", *Art in Finland*, Helsinki 2000.

Nørgaard Larsen, Peter, "Fra Hellas til Hades. Julius Lange og det samtidige danske figurmaleri", *Viljen til det menneskelige. Tekster omkring Julius Lange*, Hanne Kolind Poulsen, Peter Nørgaard Larsen og Hans Dam Christensen (red.), København 1999.

Olson, Gösta, *Från Ling till Picasso*, Stockholm 1965.

Osterman, Gunhild, *Richard Bergh och Nationalmuseum. Några dokument*, Stockholm 1958.

Pauli, Georg, "Bref om konst. Intryck och reflexioner", *Ord och Bild* 1892.

Persson, Bengt-Arne, *Varbergsskolan. Richard Bergh, Nils Kreuger, Karl Nordström*, Lund 1993.

Philipsen og Fynboerne, Randers Kunstmuseum og Johannes Larsen Museet, 2001.

Philipsen og impressionismen, utst. kat., Ordrupgaard 2001.

Post-Impressionism. Cross-Currents in European Painting, exh.cat., Royal Academy of Arts, London 1979–80.

Reitala, Aimo, *Victor Westerholm*, Helsinki 1967.

Reutersvärd, Oscar, "Prins Eugen och hans möten med Claude Monet", *Impressionister och purister*, Stockholm 1976.

Reutersvärd, Oscar, "Monet och hans dragning mot Normandie", *Somrene i Normandie*, utst. kat., Modums Blaafarveværk 1994.

Rewald, John, *The History of Impressionism*, 4th revised edition, London and New York 1973.

Ringbom, Sixten, "Symbolism, synthetism and the Kalevala", *Art in Finland*, Helsinki 2000.

Rohde, Johan, *Journal fra en Rejse i 1892*, utgiven av H.P. Rohde, København 1955.

Romdahl, Axel L, "Werner Lundqvists samling i Göteborgs museum", *Ord och Bild* 1921.

Roosval, Johnny, "Om herr Klas Fåhræus' konstsamling", *Konst och konstnärer* 1913.

Sarajas-Korte, Salme, *Vid symbolismens källor. Den tidiga symbolismen i Finland 1890–1895*, Jakobstad 1981.

Sarajas-Korte, Salme, "Maalaustaide 1880-luvulla – ulkoilmarealismi", *Ars Suomen taide* 4, 1989.

Sarje, Kimmo, *Sigurd Frosteruksen modernin käsite. Maailmankatsomus ja arkkitehtuuri*, Helsinki 2000.

Scharf, Aaron, *Art and Photography*, London 1968.

Scavenius, Bente, *Fremsyn – snæversyn. Dansk dagbladskunstkritik 1880–1901*, København 1983.

Schindler, Peter, *Mogens Francesco Ballin*, København 1936.

Sinisalo, Soili, *Samlingen lever, leve samlingen. Konstmuseet Ateneum. Ur den internationella samlingen* (red. Leena Ahtola-Moorhouse), Helsingfors 2000.

Sjælebilleder, Statens Museum for Kunst, København, 2000.

Sprache der Seele. Schwedische Landschaftsmalerei um 1900, exh.cat., Mittelrhein-Museum Koblenz; Kunsthalle zu Kiel, 1995.

Supinen, Marja, "Vincent Van Gogh, Street in Auvers-sur-Oise. An Acquisition for the Antell Collection 1903", *Ateneum. Statens konstmuseums årsskrift* 1994.

Söderström, Göran, *Strindberg och bildkonsten*, Stockholm 1972.

Strömbom, Sixten, *Konstnärsförbundets historia*, Stockholm 1945.

Strömbom, Sixten, *Nationalromantik och radikalism. Konstnärsförbundets historia 1891–1920*, Stockholm 1965

Suhonen, Pekka, *The Road. Shared Beauty—The Finnish Fine Arts Association's 150-years Anniversary Exhibition in Helsinki, St. Petersburg and Stockholm 1996–97*.

Taarnet, utgiven av Johannes Jørgensen 1893–94, fotografsk optryk, med efterskrift og registre ved F.J. Billeskov Jansen, København 1981.

Talvio, Tuukka, *H.F.Antell ja Antellin valtuuskunta*, Helsinki 1993.

Thue, Oscar, *Christian Krohg*, Oslo 1997.

Tradisjon og fornyelse. Norge rundt århundreskiftet, utst. kat., Nasjonalgalleriet, Oslo 1994.

Usselmann, Henri, *Complexité et importance des contacts des peintres nordiques avec l'impressionisme*, Göteborg 1979.

Waern, Lennart, "Pontus Fürstenberg som samlare", *Konsthistorisk Tidskrift* 1988:3/4.

Valkonen, Olli, "Maalaustaide vuosisadan vaihteesta itsenäisyyden aikaan", *Ars. Suomen Taide* 5, Keuruu 1990.

Werenskiold, Erik, "Impressionisterne", *Nyt Tidsskrift* 1882.

Werenskiold, Erik, *Kunst. Kamp. Kultur*, Kristiania 1917.

Werner Lundqvists samling i Göteborgs Konstmuseum, Göteborg 1929.

Wildenstein, Daniel, *Claude Monet. Biographie et catalogue raisonné*, vol. 1–5, Paris 1974–91.

Villadsen, Villads, *Statens Museum for Kunst 1827–1952*, København 1998.

Willoch, Sigurd, *Nasjonalgalleriet gjennem hundre år*, Oslo 1937.

Willoch, Sigurd, *Nasjonalgalleriets Venner. Kunst i femti år*, Oslo 1967.

Wirenfeldt Asmussen, Marianne, *Wilhelm Hansens oprindelige franske samling på Ordrupgaard*, København 1993.

Wivel, Mikael, *Ordrupgaard – Udvalgte værker*, København 1993.

Voss, Knud, *Breve fra Anna Ancher*, Greve 1984.

Wängdahl, Lars, *En natur för män att grubbla i. Individualitet och officialitet i varbergsskolans landskapsmåleri*, Göteborg 2000.

Yta och djup. Den tidiga modernismen i Finland 1890–1920, utst. kat., Konstmuseet Ateneum, Helsingfors 2001.

Zeitler, Rudolf, "Svenskt landskap i måleri och diktning under 1800-talet", *Historiens vingslag. Festskrift till Allan Ellenius 60-årsdag*, Stockholm 1987.

Zeitler, Rudolf, *Skandinavische Kunst um 1900*, Leipzig 1990.

Zola, Émile, *Mesterverket*, med förord av Nils Messel, Oslo 1993.

Østby, Leif, *Fra naturalisme til nyromantik*, Oslo 1934.

Østvedt, Einar, *Frits Thaulow*, Oslo 1951.

Exhibited Objects

Ivan Aguéli (1869–1917)

1. **Egyptian Woman,** early 1890s. Oil on canvas, 41 x 33. Moderna Museet, Stockholm, MOM 839. (Ill. p. 86)

2. **Motif from Stockholm (from the area of the church of St John),** 1891 ca. Oil on canvas, 46 x 55. Moderna Museet, Stockholm, NM 1913. (Ill. p. 39)

3. **Landscape from Gotland,** 1892. Oil on canvas, 55 x 34. Sala konstförening—Aguélimuseet. (Ill. p. 83)

4. **Motif from Visby,** 1892. Oil on canvas, 50 x 90.5. Moderna Museet, Stockholm, NM 2381. (Ill. p. 84–85)

5. **Summer Evening (Landscape),** 1892. Oil on canvas, 45 x 65. Stockholms stad, 103–0834. (Ill. p. 87)

6. **The Plain.** Oil on canvas, 23 x 39.5. Moderna Museet, Stockholm, NM 3280. (Ill. p. 38)

Gustave Albert (1866–1905)

7. **Moret-sur-Loing,** 1893. Oil on canvas, 54.5 x 65.5. Eskilstuna. Konstmuseum, EK 7. (Ill. p. 32)

Anna Ancher (1859–1935)

8. **Sunshine in the Blue Room,** 1891. Oil on canvas, 65.2 x 58.8. Skagens Museum, 222. (Ill. p. 167)

Mogens Ballin (1871–1914)

9. **Landscape. Brittany,** 1891–92. Oil on canvas, 56 x 64. Private collection. (Ill. p. 180)

10. **Landscape. Brittany,** 1891–92. Oil on canvas, 44 x 59. Private collection. (Ill. p. 181)

11. **Landscape. Brittany,** 1892. Tempera on paper, 34 x 53.3. Private collection. (Ill. p. 179)

12. **Still Life with Fruits and Bowl.** Oil on canvas, 39 x 47. Private collection. (Ill. pp. 204–05)

Richard Bergh (1858–1919)

13. **Tank Engine by a Harbour,** 1881. Oil on canvas, 29.5 x 42. Private collection. (Ill. p. 28)

14. **Gerda. Portrait of the Artist's Wife,** 1895. Oil on canvas, 149 x 91.5. Nasjonalgalleriet, Oslo, NG.M.00461. (Ill. p. 76)

Hugo Birger (1854–1887)

15. **Outside a Restaurant in the Bois de Boulogne.** Study. Oil on

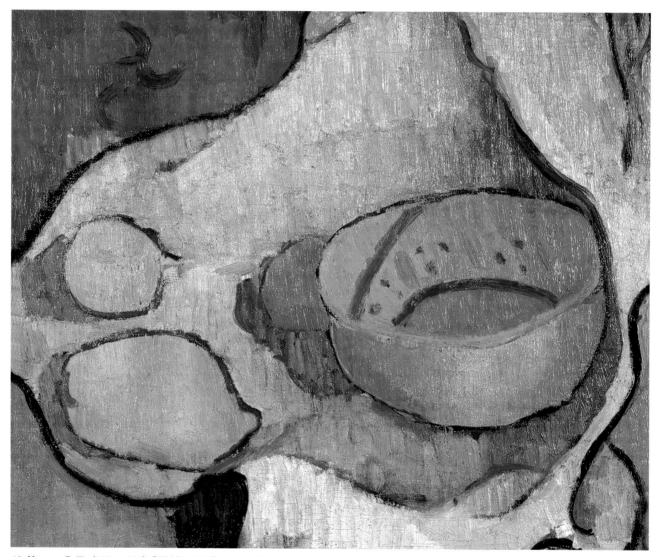

12. **Mogens Ballin** (1871–1914): **Still Life with Fruits and Bowl.** Oil on canvas, 39 x 47. Private collection.

canvas, 33 x 52. Nationalmuseum, NM 4232. (Ill. p. 66)

Väinö Blomstedt (1870–1947)

16. **The Cemetery at Bourg-la-Reine,** 1894. Oil on canvas, 30.5 x 62.5. Turku Art Museum, Collection Nils Dahlström, ND3. (Ill. p. 266)

Pierre Bonnard (1867–1947)

17. **The Hunt,** 1908 ca. Oil on canvas, 110 x 127. Göteborgs konstmuseum, GKM 586. (Ill. p. 110)

18. **Interior with a Woman in a Wicker Chair,** 1920. Oil on canvas, 72 x 51. Nationalmuseum, NM 2733. Gift from the Association for Purchasing Swedish and French Art 1929. (Ill. p. 111)

Alvar Cawén (1867–1949)

19. **St Germain,** 1911. Oil on canvas, 81.5 x 62. Private collection. (Ill. p. 291)

Paul Cézanne (1839–1906)

20. **Midday L'Estaque,** 1879 ca. Oil on paper mounted on canvas, 54.2 x 74.2. National Museums & Galleries of Wales, NMW A 2439. (Ill. p. 144)

21. **The Viaduct at l'Estaque,** 1883 ca. Oil on canvas, 56 x 65.5. Ateneum Art Museum, Helsinki, Collection Antell, A II 906. (Ill. p. 284)

22. **Seated Man,** 1892–95 ca. Oil on canvas, 102.5 x 75.5. Nasjonalgalleriet, Oslo, NG.M. 01287. (Ill. p. 236)

23. **Avenue.** Oil on canvas, 73.5 x 60.5. Göteborgs konstmuseum, GKM 946. (Ill. p. 139)

24. **Bathing Man with Outstretched Arms.** Pencil, 17.6 x 11.8. Nationalmuseum, NMH 303/1919.

25. **Bathing Men (Le Bain).** Pencil, 12.2 x 15.8. Nationalmuseum, NMH 304/1919.

26. **The Bathers, The Small Lithograph.** Colour lithograph, 23 x 29. Nationalmuseum, NMG 136/1921. Gift in accordance to the will of Miss Esther Lindahl 1921.

27. **Bathers, The Large Lithograph.** Lithograph, 40 x 50. Nationalmuseum, NMG 137/1921. Gift in accordance to the will of Miss Esther Lindahl 1921.

28. **The Hanged Man's House.** Oil on canvas, 55 x 66. Musée d'Orsay, Paris; legs du comte Isaac de Camondo, 1911, RF 1970. (Ill. p. 56)

29. **The Cardplayers.** Oil on canvas, 60 x 73. Courtauld Gallery, Courtauld Institute of Art, London, P.1932.SC.57. (Ill. p. 240)

30. **Landscape.** Oil on canvas, 73 x 92. Nationalmuseum, NM 1999. Gift from Nationalmusei Vänner 1916. (Ill. p. 116)

31. **Portrait of the Artist's Wife.** Oil on canvas, 59 x 50. Nationalmuseum, NM 6348. Gift from Grace and Philip Sandblom 1970. (Ill. p. 197)

32. **Still Life with Statuette.** Oil on canvas, 63 x 81. Nationalmuseum, NM 2545. Gift from Nationalmusei Vänner 1926. (Ill. p. 126)

Fanny Churberg (1845–1892)

33. **Winter Landscape,** 1880 ca. Oil on canvas, 38 x 56. Ateneum Art Museum, Helsinki, Collection Sourander, A III 2367. (Ill. p. 273)

Gad F. Clement (1867–1933)

34. **Garden in Brittany,** 1891. Oil on canvas, 93 x 79.8 (with frame). John J.A. Hunov's Collections, Copenhagen. (Ill. p. 183)

35. **Landscape from Brittany with Resting Girl,** 1892 ca. Oil on canvas, 39.4 x 46. Statens Museum for Kunst, Copenhagen, KMS 8240. (Ill. p. 181)

36. **Decorative Painting. The Vision of St Frances.** Pastel on paper mounted on canvas, 161 x 110. John J.A. Hunov's Collections, Copenhagen. (Ill. p. 182)

Edgar Degas (1834–1917)

37. **Woman combing her hair.** Choal, 54.1 x 49. Nationalmuseum, NMH 56/1920.

38. **The Ironer.** Oil on canvas, 92.5 x 74. Bayerische Staatsgemäldesammlungen, München, 14310. (Ill. p. 10)

39. **Lady in Black.** Oil on canvas, 60 x 51. Nationalmuseum, NM 1759. Gift from Nationalmusei Vänner 1913. (Ill. p. 99)

40. **Three Russian Dancers.** Pastel, 62 x 67. Nationalmuseum, NMB 380. (Ill. p. 103)

41. **Two Dancers.** Pastel, 63 x 54. Nationalmuseum, NMB 345. Gift from Nationalmusei Vänner 1913. (Ill. p. 102)

Albert Edelfelt (1854–1905)

42. **The Luxembourg Gardens in Paris,** 1887. Oil on canvas, 144 x 188. Ateneum Art Museum, Helsinki, Collection Antell, AII835. (Ill. p. 274)

Per Ekström (1844–1935)

43. **French Landscape with Water-Lillies.** Oil on canvas, 84 x 38. Private collection. (Ill. p. 31)

44. **Landscape, Carolles.** Oil on canvas, 77 x 46.5. Prins Eugens Waldemarsudde, Stockholm, W140. (Ill. p. 31)

Magnus Enckell (1870–1925)

45. **A Theater in Paris,** 1912. Oil on canvas, 100.5 x 66.5. Ateneum Art Museum, Helsinki, A IV 3763. (Ill. p. 282)

Thorvald Erichsen (1868–1939)

46. **Landscape,** 1894. Oil on canvas, 67 x 98. Lillehammer Kunstmuseum, LKM 44. (Ill. p. 224)

Prins Eugen (1865–1947)

47. **The Temple of Happiness,** 1892. Oil and tempera on canvas, 71 x 72. Prins Eugens Waldemarsudde, Stockholm, WE64. (Ill. p. 93)

Alfred William Finch (1854–1930)

48. **Race Track, Wellington, Ostende,** 1888. Oil on canvas, 49.5 x 59. Ateneum Art Museum, Helsinki, Collection Ahlström, A III 2233. (Ill. p. 269)

49. **The English Coast at Dover, Cliffs at Southforeland,** 1892. Oil on canvas, 66.5 x 80.5. Ateneum Art Museum, Helsinki, Collection Ahlström, A II 1700. (Ill. p. 280)

50. **Steamer by the Coast,** 1892. Oil on canvas, 63 x 80. Amos Anderson Art Museum, Helsinki, Collection Sigurd Frosterus, 34/SF. (Ill. p. 280)

51. **A Night in August,** 1898. Oil on canvas, 35 x 45.5. Ateneum Art Museum, Helsinki, Collection Sourander, A III 2407. (Ill. p. 278)

52. **A Grey Day in Hampton Court (Lanscape from Twickenham),** 1907. Oil on canvas, 63 x 79. Ateneum Art Museum, Helsinki, Collection Antell, A II 837. (Ill. p. 279)

Ludvig Find (1869–1945)

53. **Trees by the Shore,** 1893. Tempera on canvas, 74.5 x 84. Private collection. (Ill. p. 186)

Akseli Gallen-Kallela (1865–1931)

54. **Autumn,** 1902. Tempera and oil on canvas, 143 x 77. Sigrid Jusélius Foundation, Helsinki. (Ill. p. 268)

Paul Gauguin (1848–1903)

55. Portrait of Ingel Fallstedt, 1877. Black chalk, 20 x 25. Göteborgs konstmuseum. (Ill. p. 80)

56. Portrait of Mette Gauguin, 1884. Oil on canvas, 65 x 54. Nasjonalgalleriet, Oslo, NG.M.00771. (Ill. p. 230)

57. Skaters in the Frederiksberg Garden, 1884. Oil on canvas, 65 x 54. Ny Carlsberg Glyptotek, Copenhagen, MIN 3213. (Ill. p. 137)

58. The Queen's Mill, 1885. Oil on canvas, 92.5 x 73.4. Ny Carlsberg Glyptotek, Copenhagen, MIN 1850. (Ill. p. 146)

59. Self-Portrait, 1885. Oil on canvas, 65.2 x 54.3. Kimbell Art Museum, Fort Worth, Texas, AP 1997.03. (Ill. p. 138)

60. The Road to Rouen (II), 1885. Oil on canvas, 57 x 40. Ny Carlsberg Glyptotek, Copenhagen, NCG M.I.N. 3231. (Ill. p. 140)

61. French Landscape, 1885. Gouache on canvas, 27.9 x 55.5. Ny Carlsberg Glyptotek, Copenhagen, MIN 1950. (Ill. p. 145)

62. French Landscape, 1885. Gouache on canvas, 23.6 x 52. Ny Carlsberg Glyptotek, Copenhagen, MIN 1973. (Ill. p. 144)

63. Marine, 1886. Oil on canvas, 71 x 92. Göteborgs konstmuseum, GKM WL19. (Ill. p. 115)

64. Double Vessel with Modelled Breton Girl, 1886–87. Unglazed stoneware, h. 15. Det Danske Kunstindustrimuseum, Copenhagen, 44/1976. (Ill. p. 193)

65. Jug in Unglazed Stoneware with Breton Girl, Geese and Crab on Lid, 1886–87. Unglazed stoneware, h. 24.4. Det Danske Kunstindustrimuseum, Copenhagen, B16/1943. (Ill. p. 193)

66. Jug in Unglazed Stoneware with Bust of Degas-like Woman, 1886–87. Unglazed stoneware, h. 21.6. Det Danske Kunstindustri-museum, Copenhagen, B17/1943. (Ill. p. 193)

67. Jug in Unglazed Stoneware with three Handles and Breton Girl, 1886–87. Unglazed stoneware, h. 13.6. Det Danske Kunstindustrimuseum, Copenhagen, B15/1943. (Ill. p. 193)

68. Jar in Glazed Stoneware Shaped Like a Lumpfish, 1889–90. Glazed stoneware, h. 22. Det Danske Kunstindustrimuseum, Copenhagen, B 3/1931. (Ill. p. 192)

69. Landscape from Arles, 1888. Oil on canvas, 72.5 x 92. Nationalmuseum, NM 1735. (Ill. p. 100)

70. Winter Landscape, 1888. Oil on canvas, 72.5 x 92. Göteborgs konstmuseum, GKM F29. (Ill. p. 120)

71. Landscape from Brittany with Cows, 1889. Oil on canvas, 92 x 74.5. Nasjonalgalleriet, Oslo, NG.M.01006. (Ill. p. 233)

72. Landscape from Brittany, 1889. Oil on canvas, 72.5 x 91. Nationalmuseum, NM 2156. Gift from the Director Hjalmar Granhult 1919. (Ill. p. 78)

73. Letter from Paul Gauguin to J. F. Willumsen, 1890. Ink and wash, 23.2 x 18. J.F. Willumsens Museum, Frederikssund, G.S.585. (Ill. p. 175)

74. Woman from Brittany, 1890. Pencil, pastel and charcoal on paper, 27.4 x 22. J.F. Willumsens Museum, Frederikssund, G.S. 582. (Ill. p. 178)

75. Caricature of J.F. Willumsen and Juliette Willumsen, 1890. Pastel and charcoal, 28.2 x 22.3. J.F. Willumsens Museum, Frederikssund, G.S. 583. (Ill. p. 175)

76. La Luxure, 1890. Wood and metal, 70 x 15 x 7. J.F. Willumsens Museum, Frederikssund, G.S. 14. (Ill. p. 175)

77. Portraits of Roderic O'Connor and Jacob Meyer de Haan, and Self-Portrait, 1890. Pastel, 24 x 44.5. J.F. Willumsens Museum, Frederikssund, G.S. 581. (Ill. p. 178)

78. I raro te Oviri, 1891. Oil on canvas, 67.3 x 95.8. Dallas Museum of Art, Foundation for the Arts Collection, gift of the Adele R. Levy Fund, Inc., 1963.58.FA. (Ill. p. 152)

79. Invitation from Paul Gauguin to J.F. Willumsen, 1891. Ink, 17.2 x 11.3. J.F. Willumsens Museum, Frederikssund. (Ill. p. 175)

80. Stéphane Mallarmé, 1891. Etching and drypoint, 18.2 x 14.3. Nationalmuseum, NMG 107/1934. Gåva 1934 av direktör Thorsten Laurin.

81. Landscape from Tahiti (Mahana Maà), 1892. Oil on canvas, 54.5 x 31. Ateneum Art Museum, Helsinki. Collection Hoving, A II 986. (Ill. p. 205)

82. Parahi te Marae (Sacred Mountain), 1892. Oil on canvas, 66 x 88.8. Philadelphia Museum of Art, Gift of Mr. And Mrs. Rodolope de Schauensee, 1980-001-001. (Ill. p. 149)

83. Composition with Figures and a Horse ("Changement de résidence"), 1902. Oil on canvas, 28 x 45.5. Nationalmuseum, NM 2322. Gift in accordance with to the will of Miss Esther Lindahl 1921. (Ill. p. 149)

84. Landscape, La Dominique (Hiva Oa), 1903. Oil on canvas, 75 x 67. Ateneum Art Museum, Helsinki, Collection Antell, A II 854. (Ill. p. 270)

85. Auti te pape (Play by the Sweet Water). Woodcut, 20.5 x 35.5. Nationalmuseum, NMG 615/1915. Gift from the Director Richard Bergh 1915.

86. L'univers est créé (The Creation of the World). Woodcut, 20.5 x 35.5. Nationalmuseum, NMG 618/1915. Gift from the Director Richard Bergh 1915.

87. Mahna no varua ino (The Day of the Evil Spirit). Woodcut, 20.5 x 35.5. Nationalmuseum, NMG 619/1915. Gift from the Director Richard Bergh 1915.

88. Manao tupapau (The Spirit of the Dead Watching). Woodcut, 20.5 x 35.5. Nationalmuseum, NMG 621/1915. Gift from the Director Richard Bergh 1915.

89. Nave nave fenua (Sweet Land). Woodcut, 35.5 x 20.5. Nationalmuseum, NMG 616/1915. Gift from the Director Richard Bergh 1915.

90. Noa Noa (Fragrance). Woodcut, 35.5 x 20.5. Nationalmuseum, NMG 614/1915. Gift from the Director Richard Bergh 1915. (Ill. p. 109)

91. Te atua (The God). Woodcut, 20.5 x 35.5. Nationalmuseum, NMG 98/1920.

92. Te faruru (To Love). Woodcut, 35.5 x 20.5. Nationalmuseum, NMG 620/1915. Gift from the Director Richard Bergh 1915.

93. Te po (The Night). Woodcut, 20.5 x 35.5. Nationalmuseum, NMG 617/1915. Gift from the Director Richard Bergh 1915.

94. Sketch-Book, 1876–1877 ca. Black chalk, 23.4 x 29.7. Nationalmuseum, NMH 1-36/1936. Purchased from Paul Gauguins' son, the artist Pola Gauguin 1936.

Anton Genberg (1862–1939)

95. Kungsträdgården, 1896. Oil on canvas, 55 x 71. Handelsbanken, Stockholm. (Ill. p. 33)

Vincent Van Gogh (1853–1890)

96. Kitchen Gardens on Montmartre, 1887. Oil on canvas, 96 x 120. Stedelijk Museum, Amsterdam. Gift of Association for the Formation of a Public Collection of Contemporary Art (VVHK), A2234. (Ill. p. 153)

97. Pont de Langlois, 1888. Oil on canvas, 49.5 x 64. Wallraf-Richartz-Museum—Fondation Corboud, Köln, WRM 1197. (Ill. p. 150)

98. Olive Grove, Saint-Rémy, 1889. Oil on canvas, 74 x 93. Göteborgs konstmuseum, GKM 590. (Ill. p. 113)

99. **The Poplars at Saint-Rémy,** 1889. Oil on canvas, 61.6 x 45.7. The Cleveland Museum of Art, Bequest of Leonard C. Hanna, Jr. 1958:32. (Ill. p. 55)

100. **Street in Auvers-sur-Oise,** 1890. Oil on canvas, 73.5 x 92.5. Ateneum Art Museum, Helsinki, Collection Antell, A I 755. (Ill. p. 283)

101. **Poppy Field near Auvers-sur-Oise,** 1890. Oil on canvas, 73 x 91.6. Collection Gemeentemuseum Den Haag, The Hague, long term loan of the ICN, the Netherlands, SCH-1948X0003. (Ill. p. 151)

102. **Banks of the Seine.** Oil on canvas, 32 x 45.5. Van Gogh Museum Amsterdam (Vincent Van Gogh Foundation), S0077V/1963. (Ill. p. 94)

103. **The Road Menders.** Oil on canvas, 73.6 x 92.7. The Phillips Collection, Washington, D.C., O799. (Ill. p. 95)

Albert Gottschalk (1866–1906)

104. **Winter Day at Utterslev,** 1887. Oil on canvas, 33 x 48.5. Statens Museum for Kunst, Copenhagen, KMS 3294. (Ill. p. 168)

105. **From Frederiksberg Bakke, Winter,** 1894. Oil on canvas, 45.8 x 65. Den Hirschsprungske Samling, Copenhagen, 3113. (Ill. p. 169)

Armand Guillaumin (1841–1927)

106. **Garden Behind Old Houses, Damiette,** 1878. Oil on canvas, 58.5 x 72. Ny Carlsberg Glyptotek, Copenhagen, SMK 3569. (Ill. p. 134)

Peter Hansen (1868–1928)

107. **A Field of Waving Rye,** 1894. Oil on canvas, 85 x 115.5. Statens Museum for Kunst, Copenhagen, KMS 3800. (Ill. p. 190)

Carl Fredrik Hill (1849–1911)

108. **Farm Yard, Champagne,** 1876. Oil on canvas, 58 x 69.5. Private collection. (Ill. p. 57)

109. **Apple Tree in Blossom,** 1877. Oil on canvas, 50 x 61. Nationalmuseum, NM 1864. Gift from Friends of Art through the Director Richard Bergh 1915. (Ill. p. 55)

Ernst Josephson (1851–1906)

110. **Miss Louise Breslau, the Artist,** 1883–84. Oil on panel, 54.5 x 44.5. Nationalmuseum, NM 2155. Gift of the Director Hjalmar Granhult 1919 through Nationalmusei Vänner. (Ill. p. 65)

Nils Kreuger (1858–1930)

111. **Landscape from Öland. Riding Gipsy,** 1885. Oil on panel, 31 x 41.5. Malmö Konstmuseum, MM 28.800. (Ill. p. 63)

112. **The Road to Orléans,** 1886. Oil on canvas, 52.5 x 81. Lunds universitets konstsamling, LUK 283. (Ill. p. 62)

113. **After the Hail Storm, Halland,** 1892. Oil on canvas, 48 x 67. Länsmuseet Gävleborg. Gift from Lars Matton, Gävle, 1941, GM 8502 (Ill. p. 89)

114. **Evening before the Storm, September.** Oil on canvas, 62.5 x 93. Per Ekströmmuseet, Mörbylånga. (Ill. p. 89)

115. **Autumn, Varberg,** 1888. Oil on panel, 32 x 41. Nationalmuseum, NM 4120. Gift according to the will of John and Ellen Josephson 1945. (Ill. p. 34)

Christian Krohg (1852–1925)

116. **Look Ahead, Bergen Harbour,** 1884. Oil on canvas, 62.5 x 86. Nasjonalgalleriet, Oslo, NG.M.00967. (Ill. p. 217)

117. **The Painter Gerhard Munthe,** 1885. Oil on canvas, 150 x 115. Nasjonalgalleriet, Oslo, NG.M.01555. (Ill. p. 21)

118. **At the Roof Balcony, Grønnegate,** 1889. Oil on canvas, 62 x 51. Lillehammer Kunstmuseum, LKM 167. (Ill. p. 218)

Carl Larsson (1853–1919)

119. **Woman Reading,** 1888. Pastel, 98.5 x 72.2. Zornsamlingarna, Mora, ZKA92. (Ill. p. 73)

120. **Girl by a Flowering Hawthorn Bush.** Watercolour and gouache, 36 x 45.5. Göteborgs konstmuseum, GKM 1259 (Ill. p. 72)

Justus Lundegård (1860–1924)

121. **Flowering Fruit Tree,** 1892. Oil on canvas, 46 x 65. Malmö Konstmuseum, MM 33.815. (Ill. p. 70)

Édouard Manet (1832–1883)

122. **Portrait of Carolus Duran,** 1876. Oil on canvas, 191.8 x 172.7. The Trustees of the Barber Institute of Fine Arts, the University of Birmingham, 37.12. (Ill. p. 235)

123. **Georges Clemenceau,** 1880. Oil on canvas, 115.9 x 88.2. Kimbell Art Museum, Fort Worth, Texas, AP 1981.01. (Ill. p. 241)

124. **Baudelaire with hat II.** Etching, 11.8 x 8.9. Nationalmuseum, NMG 311/1924.

125. **Dead Bullfighter.** Etching and aquatint, 15.5 x 22.3. Nationalmuseum, NMG 309/1924.

126. **Front Page for Portfolio for Etchings,** 1862. Etching, 32.7 x 24. Nationalmuseum, NMG 320/1924.

127. **Hat and Guitar. Front Page for Portfolio for Etchings.** Etching, 43.8 x 29.4. Nationalmuseum, NMG 303/1924.

128. **Cat and Flowers.** Etching and aquatint, 20 x 15.2. Nationalmuseum, NMG 315/1924.

129. **Cats.** Etching and aquatint, 18 x 22.3. Nationalmuseum, NMG 319/1924.

130. **Marine in Holland.** Oil on canvas, 50.1 x 60.3. Philadelphia Museum of Art, Purchased with the W.P. Wilstach Fund, W'1921-001-004. (Ill. p. 136)

131. **A Parisian Lady.** Oil on canvas, 192 x 125. Nationalmuseum, NM 2068. Gift from a consortium 1917. (Ill. p. 106)

132. **Plainte moresque.** Lithograph, 35.6 x 27.5. Nationalmuseum, NMG 324/1924.

133. **Boy with a Dog.** Etching and aquatint, 20.8 x 14.3. Nationalmuseum, NMG 307/1924.

134. **Boy with a Sword, Turned to the Left.** Etching, 27.5 x 21.7. Nationalmuseum, NMG 322/1924.

135. **Portrait of Manet's Father.** Etching and drypoint, 20.7 x 23.8. Nationalmuseum, NMG 321/1924.

136. **Portrait of Marie Colombier.** Pen and pencil, 19 x 14.5. Nationalmuseum, NMH 528/1938.

137. **Young Boy Peeling a Pear.** Oil on canvas, 85 x 71. Nationalmuseum, NM 1498. Gift from the artist Anders Zorn 1896. (Ill. p. 69)

138. **Victorine Meurend Dressed as a Bullfighter.** Etching and aquatint, 33.5 x 27.8. Nationalmuseum, NMG 306/1924.

Claude Monet (1840–1926)

139. **La Grenouillère,** 1869. Oil on canvas, 74.6 x 99.7. The Metropolitan Museum of Art, New York, H.O. Havemeyer Collection, Bequest of Mrs. H.O. Havemeyer, 1929, 29.100.112. (Ill. p. 16)

140. **Les Bains de la Grenouillère,** 1869. Oil on canvas, 73 x 92. The National Gallery, London, NG 6456. (Ill. p. 18)

141. **The Magpie,** 1869. Oil on canvas, 89 x 130. Musée d'Orsay, Paris, RF 1984–164. (Ill. p. 246)

142. **Village Street, Vétheuil,** 1879. Oil on canvas, 52.5 x 71.5. Göteborgs konstmuseum, GKM 736. (Ill. p. 124)

143. **View over the Sea,** 1882. Oil on canvas, 64 x 82. Nationalmuseum, NM 2122. Gift from a consortium 1919. (Ill. p. 117)

144. **Rain, Etretat, 1886.** Oil on canvas, 60.5 x 73.5. Nasjonalgalleriet, Oslo, NG.M.00368. (Ill. p. 214)

145. **Houses in the Snow, Norway,** 1895. Oil on canvas, 64.7 x 91.4. Private collection. (Ill. p. 248)

146. **The Kolsås Mountain,** 1895. Oil on canvas, 65 x 100. Private collection. (Ill. p. 256)

147. **The Kolsås Mountain, Sunshine,** 1895. Oil on canvas, 65 x 100. Private collection, 1409. (Ill. p. 257)

148. **Norway. The Red Houses at Bjørnegaard,** 1895. Oil on canvas, 65 x 81. Musée Marmottan Monet, Paris, 5170. (Ill. p. 251)

149. **Sandviken, Norway,** 1895. Oil on canvas, 73.4 x 92.5. The Art Institute of Chicago, Gift of Bruce Borland, 1961.790. (Ill. p. 253)

150. **Sandviken, Snow Effect,** 1895. Oil on canvas, 73 x 92. Næringslivets Hovedorganisasjon, Oslo. (Ill. p. 252)

151. **From the Mouth of the Schelde.** Oil on canvas, 34 x 74. Nationalmuseum, NM 2513. Gift from Nationalmusei Vänner 1926. (Ill. p. 124)

Berthe Morisot (1841–1895)

152. **In the Bois de Boulogne.** Oil on canvas, 61 x 73.5. Nationalmuseum, NM 5525. Gift from C.B. Nathorst through Nationalmusei Vänner 1960. (Ill. p. 123)

Christian Mourier-Petersen (1858–1945)

153. **Flowering Peach Trees, Arles,** 1888. Oil on canvas, 55.2 x 45. Den Hirschsprungske Samling, Copenhagen, 3062. (Ill. p. 188)

Edvard Munch (1863–1944)

154. **The Olaf Rye Place in Oslo. Afternoon,** 1883. Oil on canvas, 48 x 25.5. Moderna Museet, Stockholm, NM 2400. (Ill. p. 219)

155. **The Seine at St. Cloud,** 1890. Oil on canvas, 46.5 x 38. Munch-museet, Oslo, M1109. (Ill. p. 220)

156. **Spring Day on Karl Johan Street,** 1890. Oil on canvas, 80 x 100. Bergen Art Museum, Bergen Billedgalleri, BB.M531. (Ill. p. 221)

157. **Rue Lafayette,** 1891. Oil on canvas, 92 x 73. Nasjonalgalleriet, Oslo, NG.M.01725. (Ill. p. 22)

158. **The Roulette Table I,** 1892. Oil on canvas, 54 x 65. Munch-museet, Oslo, M266. (Ill. p. 231)

159. **Vampire,** 1895. Lithograph, woodcut, 48,7 x 64.8. Moderna Museet, Stockholm, NMG 425/1917.

160. **The Kiss,** 1897. Woodcut, 62 x 73. Moderna Museet, Stockholm, NMG 5/1926.

161. **Evening (By the Shore. Melancholy),** 1901. Woodcut, 47.8 x 60.2. Moderna Museet, Stockholm, NMG 424/1917.

Karl Nordström (1855–1923)

162. **The Forest Clearing (Scene from Grez),** 1884. Oil on canvas, 114 x 92. Norrköpings Konstmuseum, NKM A 537. (Ill. p. 60)

163. **Oat Field, Grez,** 1885. Oil on canvas, 117 x 147.5. Malmö Konstmuseum, MMK 1131. (Ill. p. 28)

164. **My Wife,** 1885. Pastel, 100 x 73. Göteborgs konstmuseum, GKM F111. (Ill. p. 30)

165. **Oat Field, Lyrön,** 1887. Oil on canvas, 33.5 x 50. Prins Eugens Waldemarsudde, Stockholm, W566. (Ill. p. 29)

166. **View of Stockholm from Skansen,** 1889. Oil on canvas, 62 x 121. Nationalmuseum, NM 1891. Gift from Friends of Art through the Director Richard Bergh 1915. (Ill. p. 25)

167. **The Varberg Fortress,** 1893. Oil on canvas, 62 x 88.5. Prins Eugens Waldemarsudde, Stockholm, W573. (Ill. p. 78)

Helmer Osslund (1866–1938)

168. **Autumn Day, Fränsta,** 1898–99. Oil on canvas, 63 x 82. Private collection. (Ill. p. 82)

169. **The Son Fjeld,** 1904. Oil on canvas, 69 x 107. Göteborgs konstmuseum, GKM 2347. (Ill. p. 82)

Georg Pauli (1855–1935)

170. **Stockholm, Winter Morning,** 1889 ca. Oil on canvas, 39 x 150. Private collection. (Ill. p. 74)

171. **Sunrise, Visby,** 1894. Oil on canvas, 110 x 66. Private collection. (Ill. p. 79)

Hanna Pauli (1864–1940)

172. **Breakfast-Time,** 1887. Oil on canvas, 87 x 91. Nationalmuseum, NM 1705. (Ill. p. 71)

Theodor Philipsen (1840–1920)

173. **A Late Autumn Day in Dyrehaven. Sunshine,** 1886. Oil on canvas, 66.5 x 84.5. Statens Museum for Kunst, Copenhagen, KMS1950. (Ill. p. 164)

174. **Cowshed on the Island of Saltholm,** 1890. Oil on canvas, 56.5 x 82.5. Statens Museum for Kunst, Copenhagen, KMS3333. (Ill. p. 162)

175. **Long Shadows. Cattle at Saltholm,** 1890 ca. Oil on canvas, 61 x 81.5. Statens Museum for Kunst, Copenhagen, KMS3334. (Ill. p. 24)

176. **Cattle seen Against the Sun on the Island of Saltholm. A Sketch,** 1892. Oil on canvas, 63 x 102. Statens Museum for Kunst, Copenhagen, KMS6340. (Ill. p. 162)

Camille Pissarro (1830–1903)

177. **Landscape from Pontoise,** 1874. Oil on canvas, 65 x 51. Nationalmuseum, NM 2086. Gift from a syndicate 1918. (Ill. p. 104)

178. **Orchard with Flowering Trees, Spring, Pontoise,** 1877. Oil on canvas, 65.5 x 81. Musée d'Orsay, Paris, legs Gustave Caillebotte, RF 2733. (Ill. p. 53)

179. **Woodland Scene. Spring** 1878. Oil on canvas, 73 x 54. Ny Carlsberg Glyptotek, Copenhagen, SMK 3574. (Ill. p. 135)

180. **Landscape, Bazincourt,** 1881. Oil on canvas, 65 x 81.5. Göteborgs konstmuseum, GKM WL34. (Ill. p. 112)

181. **Portrait of Paul Gauguin Working with a Wooden Sculpture.** Black chalk, 29.5 x 23.3. Nationalmuseum, NMH 22/1936. Purchased from Paul Gauguins' son, the artist Pola Gauguin 1936.

Jean-François Raffaëlli (1850–1924)

182. **Boulevard in Paris.** Tempera on cardboard, 50.5 x 67. Göteborgs konstmuseum, GKM F130. (Ill. p. 121)

Auguste Renoir (1841–1919)

183. **Mother Anthony's Tavern,** 1866. Oil on canvas, 194 x 131. Nationalmuseum, NM 2544. Gift from Nationalmusei Vänner 1926. (Ill. p. 129)

184. **Garden,** 1877. Oil on canvas, 61.5 x 50.5. Göteborgs konstmuseum, GKM 986.

185. **Girl in a Spanish Jacket,** 1900 ca. Oil on canvas, 56 x 46. Göteborgs konstmuseum, GKM 585. (Ill. p. 107)

186. **Women Bathing.** Oil on canvas, 40.5 x 51. Nationalmuseum, NM 2103. (Ill. p. 127)

187. **Conversation.** Oil on canvas, 45 x 38. Nationalmuseum, NM 2079. Purchased with contribution from the Average Adjuster C. Pineus and the Banker G.A. Kylberger 1918. (Ill. p. 105)

188. **La Grenoullière.** Oil on canvas, 66.5 x 81. Nationalmuseum, NM 2425. Gift from an unknown donor through Nationalmusei Vänner 1924. (Ill. p. 17)

Johan Rohde (1856–1935)

189. **Summer Night at Tønning,** 1893. Oil on canvas, 86 x 111. Nationalmuseum, NM 1514. (Ill. p. 187)

190. **Self-Portrait.** Oil on panel, 43.2 x 32.7. Den Hirschsprungske Samling, Copenhagen, 3156. (Ill. p. 170)

Théo van Rysselberghe (1862–1926)

191. **Marine,** 1887. Oil on canvas, 66 x 54.5. Amos Anderson Art Museum, Helsinki, Collection Sigurd Frosterus, 51/SF. (Ill. p. 287)

Olof Sager-Nelson (1868–1896)

192. **The Anarchist (The Artist Ivan Aguéli),** 1895. Oil on canvas, 38.5 x 61. Värmlands museum, Karlstad, VM.17.928. (Ill. p. 83)

193. **La Porte St. Croix, Bruges.** Oil on panel, 24.5 x 32.5. Göteborgs konstmuseum, GKM 543. (Ill. p. 87)

Helene Schjerfbeck (1862–1946)

194. **The Old Manor (Sjundby Gård),** 1901. Oil on canvas, 65 x 85. Turku Art Museum, 74. (Ill. p. 267)

Anshelm Schultzberg (1862–1945)

195. **White Frost, Grez-sur-Loing,** 1890. Oil on canvas, 71 x 99. Private collection. (Ill. p. 75)

Paul Sérusier (1864–1927)

196. **Landscape, Brittany,** 1891. Gouache, 25.5 x 51. Private collection. (Ill. p. 179)

Paul Signac (1863–1935)

197. **Seine, Grenelle,** 1899. Oil on canvas, 62 x 78.5. Amos Anderson Art Museum, Helsinki, Collection Sigurd Frosterus, 56/SF. (Ill. p. 286)

Alfed Sisley (1839–1899)

198. **The Seine by Saint-Cloud,** 1877. Oil on canvas, 38.5 x 46. Göteborgs konstmuseum, GKM WL35. (Ill. p. 114)

199. **On the Shores of Loing,** 1896. Oil on canvas, 54 x 65. Nationalmuseum, NM 1770. Gift from Nationalmusei Vänner 1913. (Ill. p. 101)

Beda Stjernschantz (1867–1910)

200. **Everywhere a Voice is Sounding,** 1895. Oil on canvas, 85.5 x 129.5. Ateneum Art Museum, Helsinki, Collection Antell, A III 1851. (Ill. p. 268)

Frits Thaulow (1847–1906)

201. **Flooding by the Seine,** 1893. Oil on canvas, 58 x 95. Private collection. (Ill. p. 216)

Robert Thegerström (1857–1919)

202. **On the Outskirts of the City.** Oil on panel, 37 x 46. Nationalmuseum, NM 6969. (Ill. p. 32)

Ellen Thesleff (1869–1954)

203. **Figures in a Landscape.** Oil on canvas, 113 x 113. NORDEA Art Collection in Finland. (Ill. p. 290)

Verner Thomé (1878–1953)

204. **Boys Bathing,** 1910. Oil on canvas, 108.5 x 130. Ateneum Art Museum, Helsinki, Collection Hoving, A II 903. (Ill. p. 281)

Carl Trägårdh (1861–1899)

205. **Countryside near Grez-sur-Loing,** 1889. Oil on canvas mounted on cardboard, 34 x 47. Nationalmuseum, NM 2483. Gift from Svensk-Franska Konstgalleriet through the Director Gösta Olson 1925. (Ill. p. 70)

Axel Törneman (1880–1925)

206. **Self-Portait with Still Life,** 1904. Oil on canvas, 61.5 x 50.5. Moderna Museet, Stockholm, NM 6160. (Ill. p. 91)

207. **The Farmer from Brittany,** 1905. Oil on canvas, 90 x 83. Vår Gård Kursgården AB, Saltsjöbaden. (Ill. p. 90)

Louis Valtat (1869–1952)

208. **Marine, Cap Nègre,** 1902. Oil on canvas, 81 x 81. Amos Anderson Art Museum, Helsinki, Collection Sigurd Frosterus, 60/SF. (Ill. p. 289)

Erik Werenskiold (1855–1938)

209. **Shepherds I,** 1882. Oil on canvas, 40 x 60. Private collection. (Ill. p. 210)

210. **A Ditcher.** Oil on canvas, 111 x 93.8. Statens Museum for Kunst, Copenhagen, KMS 1329. (Ill. p. 211)

Victor Westerholm (1860–1919)

213. **The Birch Grove,** 1888. Oil on canvas, 80 x 145. Turku Art Museum, Collection Niilo Wilhelm Jokipohja, 4263. (Ill. p. 35)

214. **Seine outside Paris,** 1888. Oil on canvas, 60.5 x 81.5. Turku Art Museum, 417. (Ill. p. 273)

215. **From Paris,** 1889. Oil on cardboard, 41 x 32.5. Turku Art Museum, 355. (Ill. p. 272)

216. **Suresnes,** 1890. Oil on canvas, 31.5 x 45.5. Turku Art Museum, 361. (Ill. p. 36)

J.F. Willumsen (1863–1958)

217. **A Cocotte Hunting in Montagnes Russes,** 1890. Painted and carved wood, 100 x 60.5. J.F. Willumsens Museum, Frederikssund, Acc. 507. (Ill. p. 174)

218. **Breton Woman Walking Towards the Beholder,** 1890. Oil on canvas, 64 x 57.5. J.F. Willumsens Museum, Frederikssund, Acc. 1230. (Ill. p. 176)

219. **Two Breton Women Parting After Having a Chat,** 1890. Oil and tempera on canvas, 100.4 x 93.2. Nordjyllands Kunstmuseum, Aalborg, NK 811. (Ill. p. 177)

Anders Zorn (1860–1920)

220. **The Small Brewery,** 1890. Oil on canvas, 47.5 x 78. Nationalmuseum, NM 6875. Purchased with support from the Pripps Breweries. (Ill. p. 68)

221. **Impressions de Londres,** 1890. Watercolour, 71 x 54. Göteborgs konstmuseum, GKM 2514. (Ill. p. 67)

222. **View From the Skeppsholmen Quay,** 1890. Oil on canvas, 69 x 100. Handelsbanken, Stockholm. (Ill. p. 27)

223. **Omnibus I,** 1895 (92?). Oil on canvas, 99.5 x 66. Nationalmuseum, NM 6810. Purchased with support from the Kjell and Märta Beijer Foundation 1985. (Ill. p. 26)

Photographic Credits

Aalborg, Nordjyllands Kunstmuseum cat. 219.
Photo: Copy Dan

Aarhus, Aarhus Kunstmuseum p. 163. Photo:
Fotografi i 3 generationer Thomas Pedersen,
Poul Pedersen and Ole Hein Pedersen,
Aarhus

Amsterdam, Stedelijk Museum cat. 96

Amsterdam, Van Gogh Museum Enterprises bv
cat. 102

Bergen, Bergen Kunstmuseum (Bergen Billed-
galleri, Rasmus Meyers Samlinger och
Stenersens Samling) © Munch-Museet/
Munch-Ellingsen gruppen cat. 156

Birmingham, The Barber Institute of Fine Arts,
The University of Birmingham cat. 122

Boston, Museum of Fine Arts pp. 238, 239

Buffalo, Albright-Knox Art Gallery p. 96

Cardiff, National Museums & Galleries of Wales
cat. 20

Chicago, The Art Institute of Chicago cat. 149

Cleveland, The Cleveland Museum of Art cat. 99.
Photo: © The Cleveland Museum of Art

Copenhagen, Den Hirschsprungske Samling cat.
105, 153, 190

Copenhagen, Det Danske Kunstindustrimuseum
cat. 64, 65, 66, 67, 68. Photo: Pernille Klemp

Copenhagen, Kunstakademiets Bibliotek p. 43

Copenhagen, Köpenhamns Bymuseum p. 43

Copenhagen, Ny Carlsberg Glyptotek cat. 57,
58, 60, 61, 62, 106, 179, and pp. 142, 203

Copenhagen, Ordrupgaard p. 201. Photo:
Pernille Klemp

Copenhagen, Statens Museum for Kunst cat. 35,
104, 107, 173, 174, 175, 176, 210. Photo:
SMK Photo, Hans Petersen, Dowic Fotografi

Dallas, Dallas Museum of Art cat. 78

Eskilstuna, Eskilstuna Konstmuseum cat. 7

Fort Worth, Kimbell Art Museum cat. 59, 123.
Photo: Michael Bodycomb

Frederikssund, J.F. Willumsens Museum cat. 73,
74, 75, 76, 77, 79, 218, 217. Photo: Bent
Ryberg, Ole Woldbye, Claus Ørsted

Gävle, Länsmuseet Gävleborg cat. 113

Göteborg, Göteborgs konstmuseum cat. 17, 23,
55, 63, 70, 98, 120, 142, 164, 169, 180, 182,
184, 185, 193, 198, 221 and pp. 49, 59, 119.
Photo: Ebbe Carlsson, Lars Noord, Sixten
Sandell

Helsinki, Amos Anderson Art Museum, Collection
Sigurd Frosterus cat. 50, 191, 197, 208

Helsinki, Sigrid Jusélius Stiftelse cat. 54

Helsinki, Ateneum Art Museum, Centralarkivet för
bildkonst cat. 21, 33, 42, 45, 48, 49, 51, 52,
81, 84, 100, 200, 204. Photo: Matti Janas,
Hannu Aaltonen, Jouko Könönen, Janne
Mäkinen

Hoofdorp, Gemeentemuseum Den Haag c/o
Beeldrecht cat. 101

Karlstad, Värmlands museum cat. 192

Köln, Rheinisches Bildarchiv cat. 97

Lillehammer, Lillehammer Kunstmuseum cat. 46,
118

London, Courtauld Institute cat. 29

London, The Bridgeman Art Library 148 and p. 14

London, The National Gallery 140 and p. 12.
Foto: © National Gallery, London

Lund, Lunds universitets konstsamling cat. 112.
Photo: Leopoldo Iorizzo

Lysaker, Lysaker Studio cat. 201

Malmö, Malmö Konstmuseum cat. 111, 121, 163

Maribo, Storstrøms Kunstmuseum p. 160

Middelfart, Studio 64 ApS cat. 11, 12, 53, 196

Mora, Zornsamlingarna cat. 119. Photo: Lars
Berglund

Mörbylånga, Per Ekströmmuseet cat. 114

New York, The Metropolitan Museum of Art cat. 139.
Photo: © The Metropolitan Museum of Art

Nordea-Merita, Nordea Art Collection in Finland
cat. 203. Photo: Seppo Hilpo

Norrköping, Norrköpings Konstmuseum cat. 162

Oslo, © O. Væring Eftf. AS cat. 209

Oslo, Munch-museet, © Munch-Museet/Munch-
Ellingsen Group cat. 155, 158

Oslo, Nasjonalgalleriet cat. 14, 22, 56, 71, 116,
117, 144, 150, 157 and pp. 231, 234. Photo:
J. Lathion © Nasjonalgalleriet; © Munch-
Museet/Munch-Ellingsen Group cat. 157

Otterlo, Kröller Müller Museum p. 189

Paris, Agence photographique de la réunion des
musées nationaux 28, 141, 178 and p. 64.
Photo: © RMH, Hervé Lewandowski

Philadelphia, Philadelphia Museum of Art cat. 82,
130 and p. 125

Prag, Národni galerie p. 122

Sala, Sala konstförening – Aguélimuseet cat. 3.
Photo: Jan Storm

Saltsjöbaden, Vår Gård Kursgården AB cat. 207.
Photo: Peter Fristedt

Skagen, Skagens Museum cat. 8

Stockholm, AB Stockholms Auktionsverk cat. 43

Stockholm, Bukowski Auktioner AB cat. 195

Stockholm, Folkhems Konstsamling p. 64

Stockholm, Moderna Museet cat. 1, 2, 4, 6, 154,
159, 160, 161, 206. Photo: Moderna Museet,
Stockholm

Stockholm, Prins Eugens Waldemarsudde cat.
44, 47, 165, 167, 170. Photo: Lasse
Engelhardt, Per Myrehed

Stockholm, Prisma BildCenter AB cat. 13

Stockholm, Stockholms konstkansli cat. 5

Turku, Turku Art Museum cat. 16, 194, 213, 214,
215, 216. Photo: Kari Lehtinen, P.O. Welin

Washington, D.C., The Phillips Collection cat. 103

Weilheim, Artothek 38 and p. 96

This book is published in connection with the exhibition

Impressionism and the North.
Late 19th Century French Avant-Garde Art and the Art in the Nordic Countries 1870–1920

Nationalmuseum, Stockholm 25 September 2002–19 January 2003
Statens Museum for Kunst, Copenhagen, 21 February–25 May 2003

Exhibition Director: Torsten Gunnarsson
Curator: Per Hedström
Catalogue Editors: Torsten Gunnarsson and Per Hedström
Secretary: Inger Tengqvist
Translation: Carina Fryklund
Architect: Henrik Widenheim
Information: Agneta Karlström and Lena Munther
Marketing: Birgitta Plånborg
Graphic Design: Claes Gustavsson
Photography: The Nationalmuseum Photo Studio and participating
institutions (see Photographic Credits)
Printing: AB C O Ekblad & Co, Västervik
Copyright: The Authors, Nationalmuseum and Bokförlaget Atlantis
Jacket Illustration: Auguste Renoir, La Grenouillère, 1869, oil on canvas, 66.5 x 81, Nationalmuseum, NM 2425, gift from an unknown
donor through Nationalmusei Vänner.

Nationalmuseum, exhibition catalogue no 629
Nationalmuseum ISBN 91-7100-668-0

The Nationalmuseum collaborates with ABB AB, Stora Enso Oyj, SAS
Scandinavian Airlines, Svenska Dagbladet and Grand Hôtel, Stockholm

Dimensions are given in centimetres: height before width
Nationalmuseum is grateful to Letterstedtska Föreningen for financial
support of this publication